BUILDING
LEADERS

Other Books by Aubrey Malphurs

Being Leaders

Developing a Vision for Ministry in the 21st Century, 2nd ed.

Planting Growing Churches for the 21st Century, 2nd ed.

Pouring New Wine into Old Wineskins: How to Change a Church without Destroying It

Vision America: A Strategy for Reaching a Nation

Maximizing Your Effectiveness: How to Discover and Develop Your Divine Design

Biblical Manhood and Womanhood

Strategy 2000: Churches Making Disciples for the Next Millennium

Developing a Dynamic Mission for Your Ministry

The Ministry Nuts and Bolts: What They Don't Teach Pastors in Seminary

Advanced Strategic Planning: A New Model for Church and Ministry Leaders

The Dynamics of Church Leadership

Doing Church: A Biblical Guide for Leading Ministries through Change

BUILDING
LEADERS

BLUEPRINTS FOR DEVELOPING
LEADERSHIP AT EVERY LEVEL
OF YOUR CHURCH

AUBREY MALPHURS

AND

WILL MANCINI

Baker Books
A Division of Baker Book House Co
Grand Rapids, Michigan 49516

Published by Baker Books
a division of Baker Book House Company
P.O. Box 6287, Grand Rapids, MI 49516-6287
www.bakerbooks.com

Printed in the United States of America

Library of Congress Cataloging-in-Publication Data
Malphurs, Aubrey.
    Building leaders : blueprints for developing leadership at every level of your
church / Aubrey Malphurs and William F. Mancini.
        p.   cm.
    Includes bibliographical references and index.
    ISBN 0-8010-9171-3 (pbk.)
    1. Christian leadership. I. Mancini, William F., 1969– II. Title.
BV652. 1. M356 2004
253—dc22   2003025782

Contents

Introduction   7

Part 1 Pouring the Proper Foundation: *Preparation for Developing Leaders*

  1. Leaders, Who Needs Them? *The Importance of Developing Leaders*   19
  2. Some Common Delays: *Problems in Developing Leaders*   31
  3. The Challenge of Empowerment: *The Heart Required for Developing Leaders*   39

Part 2 Following the Blueprints: *Practices for Developing Leaders*

  4. How Jesus Developed Leaders: *What the Savior Teaches Us about Leadership Development, Part 1*   63
  5. How Jesus Used Metaphors to Develop Leaders: *What the Savior Teaches Us about Leadership Development, Part 2*   75
  6. How Early Churches Developed Leaders: *What the Church Teaches Us about Leadership Development*   95

Part 3 Moving from Foundation to Finish: *The Process for Developing Leaders*

  7. Who Will Read the Blueprints? *The Personnel for Developing Leaders*   105
  8. Putting the Process in Motion: *The Procedures for Developing Leaders, Phase 1*   127

9. How to Grow Leaders: *The Procedures for Developing Leaders, Phase 2* 145
10. Designing the Leadership-Development Process: *The Procedures for Developing Leaders, Phase 3* 159
11. The Finishing Touches: *The Procedures for Developing Leaders, Phase 4* 183
12. Home Improvement: *Guidelines for Improving the Process* 189
13. Turning a House into a Home: *Creating a Leadership Culture* 211

Part 4 Looking at Model Homes: *The Product of Developing Leaders*
14. The Story of a Small Church: *Developing Leaders in Small Churches* 239
15. The Story of a Large Church: *Developing Leaders in Large Churches* 249

Appendix A Leadership Development Audit 257
Appendix B Church Leadership Questionnaire 259
Appendix C Sample Leadership Configuration 261
Appendix D Task Skills Inventory 262
Appendix E Relational Skills Inventory 263
Appendix F Training Venues Comparison Chart 265

Notes 267
Index 271

Introduction

Pastor Jeff had just finished having breakfast with Bill Smith at the Pancake House. Walking out the front door, the pastor shook hands with Bill, his church board member. Then he put his hand on Bill's shoulder and wished him and his family God's best as they relocated to another city. Though smiling on the outside, Pastor Jeff was hurting on the inside.

A little more than seven years ago, Bill, his wife, and their two children had moved into the area and begun attending Grace Community Church. Previously Bill had attended an evangelical seminary for one year before deciding that God was leading him to pursue a career in corporate America. He believed that God could use him more effectively working *with* a pastor than *as* a pastor. Bill became an active member of Grace Community Church and was the key person on the pulpit committee that pursued Jeff as the next pastor of the church. Later, when Jeff outlined his Great Commission vision for the church, Bill was most supportive. Jeff was convinced that God had gifted Bill as a significant leader who had an uncanny ability to make wise decisions, especially in difficult situations. *No wonder his company transferred him to a key position in another state on the East Coast*, Jeff mused. *God willing, this man has all the potential to become the company's CEO someday.*

Here's why the parting outside the restaurant was so painful. Jeff knew that Bill was not only the key leader on the board but the only leader. The other four board members meant well but simply weren't strong leaders. Completely unaware of what leadership should entail, they believed their primary purpose was to keep everybody who was a part of Grace Community happy. In their minds, the church was one big family and their mission was to take care of it. That was the board's concept of leadership. During Bill's five-year tenure on the board, God used him to cast a significant vision for making some vital changes at the ninety-year-old church. As a result, ten new families joined the previously struggling, plateaued congregation.

Now Pastor Jeff felt frustrated because he had depended on Bill's leadership on the board to get things done. Bill's departure would create a leadership vacuum that no one was likely to fill. Without strong, capable leadership, Jeff's plans for the church would never come to fruition. He had hoped to see some of the congregation's younger men become passionate, godly leaders, but so far they expressed little to no interest. And Jeff realized that, though trained well at seminary in the areas of biblical languages, theology, Bible, and church history, he had learned little about developing leaders. His seminary viewed the pastor as more of an in-house scholar than a leader, and it didn't take Jeff long to realize that, as they say in the South, "That dog won't hunt!"

Though he had thoroughly enjoyed his time in school and had done well, as a pastor, Jeff quickly discovered that he was only partly prepared for leading a church. True, a pastor must have a good knowledge of the Scriptures and the ability to communicate them to lead a church, but successful pastoring requires more, much more, than that. Jeff had come to realize that he desperately needed to raise up some leaders around him. With no training in leadership development, however, he didn't know where to start. The only book he found with any substance on the topic talked about the importance of training leaders but didn't tell how or relate Scripture to the process. Another used Scripture but focused on developing leaders at the pastoral level, not throughout the church. It seemed that everybody was talking about leadership development, but nobody—at least in his circles—was doing it, not even the megachurches.

The Leadership Challenge

Both inside and outside the church, many people have recognized the need for developing leaders. In a *Fortune* magazine article, Marshall Loeb reports on a gathering of world business leaders, "What worried them the most was not production or profits or competition, but this: Where have all the leaders gone?"[1] "USA Today Snapshots" reports, "Top executives' worries about developing future leaders has become the hottest topic at business meetings." In 2002 the percentage of meetings in which leadership was addressed rose to 62 percent compared to 54 percent in 2001.[2]

Commenting on the shifting role of the CEO, a recent article in *Fast Company* relates, "Perhaps more than anything, the CEO of today is a teacher, working tirelessly to grow the skills and aptitudes of the company's contributors. The job of the CEO is simply to create more CEOs. . . ."[3]

James Bolt, the founder of Executive Development Associates, observes, "The dearth of leadership is apparent throughout society. No matter where we turn, we see the severe lack of faith in the leadership of our schools, religious organizations, and governments."[4] We find it interesting that Bolt, a corporate consultant, has observed the lack of leadership in religious as well as other organizations.

Finally, the need for leadership is evidenced in a powerful way in the church as it struggles to transition into the twenty-first century. George Barna comments on the church's need for leaders:

> I have reached several conclusions regarding the future of the Christian Church in America. The central conclusion is that the American church is dying due to a lack of strong leadership. In this time of unprecedented opportunity and plentiful resources, the church is actually losing influence. The primary reason is the lack of leadership. Nothing is more important than leadership.[5]

Needless to say, Pastor Jeff isn't alone. In the real world he has lots of company. One example is Lewis Cooper, who accepted the call to pastor Faith Temple Baptist Church in Irving, Texas, just outside of Dallas. He discovered that like so many other small churches sprinkled all across North America, Faith Temple's leadership was aging and the church's growth had plateaued. In discussing this situation, Pastor Lewis said he was convinced that the key to revitalizing his church was the development of the church's leadership, both old and new. "We have a critical need for trained leadership," he said. "That will determine whether or not we have a future."

Another example of a church in need of leadership is Lake Pointe Church located in Rockwall, Texas. In contrast to Faith Temple Baptist, Lake Pointe Church is experiencing phenomenal growth under the leadership of its pastor, Steve Stroope. Growing at 20 to 30 percent annually, Lake Pointe averages between five and six thousand people per weekend. So what is Lake Pointe's greatest challenge? "Leadership," answers Pastor Karl Shackleford, one of the assistant pastors whom Pastor Steve has tasked with leadership development. Large churches like this one attract leaders and emerging leaders who need to be developed. Pastor Karl says, "We're convinced that Lake Pointe needs to raise up and train more leaders."

It is noteworthy that both Faith Temple Baptist and Lake Pointe have caught the dream and are implementing the vision. My (Aubrey's) work with these two churches has greatly influenced this book. In the chapters that follow, you will discover some of what they have done to implement their training processes.

A Leadership Development Crisis

Though various books on Christian leadership appeared back in the 1990s, not much has changed in church organizations. Today some experts argue that the problem is a general lack of people with leadership ability—we just don't have as many leaders as we used to. Our experience as church trainers and consultants, as well as Aubrey's involvement in seminary education over the past twenty years, has shown us that we have many potential leaders, but we're not developing them. And it's this failure in development that has precipitated the leadership crisis in our world in general and the church in particular. Our leaders don't know how to train other leaders. Bolt has observed the same in the corporate world: "I contend that this leadership crisis is in reality a *leadership development* crisis. It is this development crisis that leads me to agree that our leaders are 'missing in action.'"[6]

Perhaps the clearest biblical illustration of a leadership-development crisis is found in Exodus 18. Moses is leading the people of Israel, numbering more than one million,[7] out of Egypt toward the Promised Land. As they navigate the treacherous desert wilderness, Moses, the exodus point man, finds himself as the primary "go to" guy for all of the disputes among the massive caravan. The natural result is an unsustainable leadership structure for God's people. From sunrise to sundown men, women, and children end up standing in the blazing desert sun just to get a few minutes with their pastor. Moses himself becomes the bottleneck in the process of fostering a God-honoring community among one million people. During this journey, Jethro, Moses' father-in-law, visits and observes Moses in action. After witnessing this organizational nightmare, Jethro comments, "You and these people who come to you will only wear yourselves out. The work is too heavy for you; you cannot handle it alone" (18:18).

This makes Jethro one of the first church consultants. He advises Moses to find capable men within the community to whom he can delegate responsibility for decision making. Specifically he instructs Moses to divide the group into tens, fifties, hundreds, and thousands. Moses recognizes the wisdom of this and builds a sustainable infrastructure of leaders. Note that, within the great body of the Israelites, God had already provided people capable of leadership. The missing piece was not the people but the process. In fact, in several short verses, Jethro gives Moses a miniblueprint for leadership development, including leadership qualifications (v. 21a), role descriptions (vv. 19b, 22), an organizational chart (v. 21b), and a training strategy (v. 22). Based on the ratios in verse 21, and assuming that there were one million Jews on the journey, God had provided 131,000 potential leaders for Moses to enlist. This translates to one leader for every 7.6 people. Again, this clearly illustrates that the primary leadership issue in an organization may not be the lack of leaders but the lack of a development process to discover and deploy them.

Though many churches have awakened to the need to develop godly, competent leadership and are talking about it, few are doing anything about it. There are several reasons for this. (If your ministry is struggling in the area of leadership development, take the audit in appendix A to discover why.) The primary reason is that many churches don't know how to develop leaders. Few have informal leadership development programs in place. Fewer still have established formal, intentional systems for developing leaders throughout the organization. While many churches want and desperately need such a development process, they don't know how to pull it off.

Leadership training today has yet to become a priority for most Christian organizations, and we're convinced that until all this changes, they as well as the rest of the world will continue to flounder in the sea of change that has ushered in the twenty-first century.

I (Aubrey) have written books on the importance of a church's core values, mission, vision, and strategy, as well as on church planting and revitalization. If a ministry doesn't have strong leaders at every level to implement these vital concepts, however, the church, whether small or large, will not prosper. The statements and strategies are only tools. The key to ministry is and always has been competent, godly leadership.

The solution to the leadership crisis is to do a much better job of leadership development—not the preparation of better senior pastors or church staffs alone but development of committed leaders at every level within the organization. A godly senior pastor and an excellent staff can accomplish only so much. The church's aim should be to train as many leaders as possible and to have competent leadership at every level of ministry. Perhaps the ideal is one leader for every 7.6 people as in Israel's case.

The ultimate test of a leader isn't the magnitude of his or her ministry but whether that leader trains other leaders who can sustain the church or parachurch organization when he or she is no longer present. The true test is the leadership legacy that the pastor leaves behind. You can honor leaders by inscribing their names on plaques on the side of a building, but the greater honor is to see their ministries continue long after the leaders have left them, showing that they've succeeded in developing the next generation of Christ-like leadership throughout the church.

Not many church leaders would disagree with this goal, but few know how to accomplish it, to make it become a living, breathing reality in their ministries. That is what this book is about. Its purpose is to challenge leaders and to guide them in the process of developing other leaders at every level of the ministry. These new leaders will in turn minister to and develop leaders at the same level and beyond.

What the Church Needs

We need a radical change in the typical twenty-first-century pastor's church-leadership paradigm, especially if the pastor attended a classical seminary or is an older person. Pastoral ministry certainly includes the central responsibilities of teaching and preaching the Bible, but far too many pastors stop there. Leading a church in today's and tomorrow's world involves training leaders who will develop other leaders to carry the ministry torch to the third and fourth generations. The danger is that some denominational executives and pastors will continue to believe that a single initiative program, such as preaching the Bible or pastoral care, accomplishes the ministry. Our churches need the mind-set of the military, which has made leadership development a part of their leaders' daily lives and an essential path to success.

We need a leadership-training process that leaders with this new perspective can use to fulfill their dream. This book will present such a leadership development process, providing leaders with a universal format that applies to all churches no matter their size, location, or ethnicity. The goal of this book is to help leaders walk their unique ministry organization through this process to arrive at their unique ministry product or model, ensuring that they touch all the necessary bases. This is important because it's doubtful that one product or final model will be precisely like another, because each church's culture—its leaders, teams, values, mission, ministry location, and the people it seeks to train (its ministry core and context)—is not like any other. Consequently, while leaders may learn from someone else's model, they would be wise not to copy it in its entirety. Instead, they must ask, *What are these models doing that would fit our ministry context and would really help us?* The product must be endemic to the ministry community. In most churches this does not happen.

Developing Training Churches

By introducing a new ministry paradigm, this book instructs pastors in how to intentionally develop leaders at every level, regardless of the church's size. However, it doesn't stop there. It calls for the development of churches that can provide the necessary context in which this training can best take place. This training church model is similar to the medical model of the teaching hospital. While all hospitals do a certain amount of training, some hospitals are designated teaching hospitals. They purpose not only to treat diseases but to train those who treat diseases. Everyone knows this up front, including the medical personnel who train there and those who train them, as well as the patients who come to the training hospital. People who frequent these hospitals are used to seeing medical personnel, such as doctors, nurses, and technicians, walking the halls with a student, intern, or resident in tow. It's a common, everyday occurrence to see certain medical personnel lecturing, modeling, observing, and evaluating those in training. This training model produces excellent, well-trained personnel for the entire medical profession. Obviously, if we stopped training medical personnel and eliminated teaching hospitals, we would jeopardize the health care of our nation. But have we not already jeopardized the spiritual health of our churches by failing to train ministry leaders?

If the medical community works this hard at training leaders who work on people's bodies, shouldn't the church work just as hard at training leaders who care for people's eternal souls? Though not all churches could be training churches, many should aspire to this end whether they are traditional or contemporary, seeker-driven or purpose-driven. These training churches could produce highly qualified leaders, not only for their own churches but also for others that don't have the necessary personnel to be a teaching ministry. Potentially all could benefit.

A Personal Passion for the Church

We have a passion for the church of Jesus Christ and the training of Christ-centered leadership. We, along with many others, believe that Christ's church is the hope of the world and that its leadership is the future of the church. Aubrey has pastored three churches and consulted with and trained people in many others. Thus he realizes the awesome potential of Christ's church. In his last two churches, he made it a practice to invite seminarians to work with him as staff and pastoral apprentices. His purpose was not only to share the ministry load but to use these opportunities as teaching ministries to train and coach future leaders of the church. While he believes that he served these churches well, his greatest contribution was in the training and shaping of the new leaders.

Will has served in various church staff roles and has focused on leadership development. He now works as a coach and consultant to churches in the areas of leadership development, strategy, and communications.

While we believe that Matthew 16:18 assures us that the church will not die off, we bemoan the present state of the church. Consequently it's our dream that early in the twenty-first century we'll see a great number of strong teaching churches, either planted or developed, that train competent, godly leaders for a significant Christ-centered ministry. We suspect that there are others, many others, who share this vision. This book is an attempt to enlist them and others in the cause and accomplish our dream.

Seeing similarities between the process of building a house and building a leadership-development process for the church, we have organized the parts of this book around a building metaphor.

Part 1 covers the preparation needed for developing leaders and explains why a church needs to build its leadership house. The first chapter is foundational and defines and explains the importance of developing leaders. Chapter 2 examines various reasons churches don't develop leaders. Chapter 3 addresses the kind of heart needed for leadership development.

In part 2 we deal with the practices for developing leaders—the biblical-theological principles that are integral to the leadership training process. These are similar to the architectural principles that direct a builder's decisions while building a house. Chapter 4 discusses the leadership lessons we can learn from the Savior in the Gospels, and chapter 5 looks at what we can learn from the metaphors that he used for leadership. Chapter 6 takes the next step and looks at what we can learn from the early church in Acts and the Epistles about developing leaders.

Part 3 explores our process for developing leaders that parallels moving from the builder's blueprints to the actual house. In chapter 7 we discuss the personnel who are needed for the leadership construction team. Then in chapters 8, 9, and 10 we explain the actual leadership-development process. Chapter 11 is a guide for repairing and improving your completed development process, and chapter 12 addresses the creation of a leadership culture in the church.

Part 4 concludes the process by describing some models. And the material in the appendices will help the reader use effectively the information in the chapters.

Leaders can approach this book in several ways.

- If you're a senior pastor or the point person of a parachurch ministry, you would be wise to work your way through this material with your key leaders, such as the staff and the board.
- If you're a consultant or pastor leading a church through revitalization, you should work through it with your leaders.
- If you're a lay leader who wants to influence your church toward leadership development, you should read the book first. Then, as you talk with your pastor or other key leaders, you can address specific ways in which the book may be helpful (as well as buy them a copy!).
- If you're a church planter, you have an easier job, because in most cases there is no one you have to convince of the need for leadership development or this process. You can simply include this process as a part of your church-planting strategy, either in the conception or development stage.
- If you're a leadership or personal development coach, you will want to pay particular attention to the questions in and at the end of the chapters as you work through the book.
- If you're a seminary professor, you may find it most instructive to assign this process as a project for your students. Divide them into teams and ask them to find a church in your area that will serve as a real-life lab for the project. Ask these emerging leaders, "If this were your church, what would a leadership-development process look like and how would you implement it?"
- Finally, this is the second book in a series of three companion books on leadership. The first is *Being Leaders* by Aubrey. In it he lays a foundation for this book. In the third book, *Leading the Leader*, he provides a definition of leadership.

Now, let the adventure begin.

Part 1

Pouring the Proper Foundation

Preparation for Developing Leaders

1

Leaders, Who Needs Them?

The Importance of Developing Leaders

It's possible that our introduction left you with a sense that no one is developing leaders. This isn't the case. Though the majority of churches are not training new leaders, vestiges of leadership development do show up here and there. For example, some churches are recruiting and training leaders for their children's ministries. Others have done the same with their youth ministries and still others with staff leadership development. We believe, however, that few churches are addressing leadership development at every level of the church.

We sense that many pastors across North America and beyond understand the need to develop leaders at all levels of the church. Like construction managers, they want to know how they can build a total leadership-development process. Before we jump to the how of leadership development, we need to lay a foundation by defining our terms and articulating the needs, like wise builders who lay a strong foundation before erecting the superstructure. What are we talking about? What is leadership, and what does it mean to develop leaders? Just as important, why develop leaders?

The Meaning of Leadership

It's rare to attend a church conference in the early twenty-first century and not hear some mention of leadership development. It's become the hot topic at many leadership gatherings. At these events few are surprised when the main speaker or several speakers use in some way the terms *leader, leadership,* and *leadership development.* They've almost become a mantra that turns heads and grabs people's attention.

When we attend such events, however, we find ourselves asking, *What does this speaker mean by these terms?* Are all of the speakers talking about the same thing? If someone asked the various speakers to define these terms, would their definitions agree?

We define a Christian leader as *a servant who uses his or her credibility and capabilities to influence people in a particular context to pursue their God-given direction.* Let's look at this definition. (For an expanded explanation, see Aubrey Malphurs's *Being Leaders,* the first in this three-volume series on leadership.)

Servant

First, a Christian leader is a servant. The message sprinkled throughout the New Testament is that Christian leadership is all about servanthood (Matt. 20:25–28; Mark 10:41–45; John 13:1–17; Phil. 2:5–8). The Savior was very clear about this in Matthew 20:25–28 where he defines servant leadership as the humble service to others based on our love for them. "Jesus called them together and said, 'You know that the rulers of the Gentiles lord it over them, and their high officials exercise authority over them. Not so with you'" (v. 25). Jesus is teaching his disciples that servant leaders lead humbly. The emphasis is on the leader's humility, not his or her ego.

In verses 26–28 Jesus continues his teaching and says, "Instead, whoever wants to become great among you must be your servant, and whoever wants to be first must be your slave—just as the Son of Man did not come to be served, but to serve, and to give his life as a ransom for many." Next, Jesus tells them and us what servants do. The essence of leadership is service, not status. It's the kind of service that involves the giving of self, not taking for oneself. It's selfless, not selfish.

Finally, Jesus states that his purpose in coming was not to be served but to serve others, to give his life for others. Leadership isn't all about us. It's all about other people. We're not to lead for what we can get out of it but for what others, followers, can get out of it that will glorify God.

In John 13:1–17 the Savior adds the basis for our service—our love for the leaders we develop. In verse 1 John says that Jesus showed his disciples "the full extent of his love" and he explains this with the foot-washing account in the following verses.

We know that prior to this event the disciples had continued to argue over who was the greatest (Luke 22:24–30). Though it was the custom of the day to wash people's feet when they entered a home, apparently, on this occasion, no slave was available to perform this duty for Jesus and the disciples, so they reclined around the table with dirty feet. None was willing to wash the others' feet. Perhaps to do so would have lost them the argument and been an admission that one was inferior to another.

So Jesus washed their feet. He did it because of his overwhelming love for them. And the point is that we best develop leaders whom we love. Our love for them helps us, when they disappoint us, to take up the towel rather than throw in the towel, as we might prefer.

Credibility

The key to a leader's ability to influence people is his or her credibility. Leaders can't lead without it. When a leader attempts to influence a person, that potential follower engages in a conscious and unconscious evaluation of the leader's credibility. The degree to which the individual grants the leader credibility is the degree to which that leader can influence him or her.

This raises the question of how one gains credibility. Can you purchase a credibility kit in the local bookstore? There are at least three sources of credibility. One is the leader's character. Godly leaders are people of good character. People follow leaders who are in pursuit of godliness (1 Tim. 4:8) and holiness (Romans 6). First Timothy 3:1–12 and Titus 1:6–9 identify certain required character qualities of pastoral leaders.

Another source of credibility is competence. Competence is the leader's grasp of what he or she is doing and the skills to do it well. Finally, the clarity of the leader's direction contributes to his or her credibility. Leaders don't vaguely affect followers; they infect them with God's direction. This involves a biblical mission and vision. Leaders who know where they're going (mission) and can help their people visualize it (vision) will attract followers.

These three sources of credibility may not be equally weighted in importance, depending on the ministry context. Each is capable of building the leader's credibility and all three together have a huge impact for winning followers for Christ's kingdom and cause.

Credibility Factors

Character

Competence

Clarity of direction

Capabilities

Leaders have special abilities or capabilities for leadership. They may be God-given abilities, such as spiritual gifts (an example is the gift of leadership in Rom. 12:8), a passion for leadership, or a temperament that favors leadership in certain situations. A leader also can develop leadership capabilities. For example, he or she can develop godly character, leadership knowledge, and various skills for leadership. Often both God-given abilities and developed abilities combine to forge exceptional leaders who can make a significant difference for the cause of Christ.

Influence

Leaders exert an influence on people. Leaders are doers, and what they do is influence. The leader's influence is the consistent impact that he or she has on people whom God uses to turn nonfollowers into followers of Christ. This is transformational leadership that the Holy Spirit uses to transform people into fully functioning followers of Christ. This leadership exists in relationships; it is all about people. Without people, there is no leadership.

If you wish to discover your leadership style—how you influence others—take the Leadership Style Inventory, which you will find in the appendices of *Being Leaders,* the companion volume to this book.[1]

Context

Leaders always lead in a particular context. Contrary to what many people believe, there is no superleader who can lead all people in all situations, no matter what the circumstances or the time. God gives leaders certain abilities that fit one particular context but not another. For example, some pastors lead small churches well but not large churches. Others lead large churches better than small churches. Some are church planters while others are church revitalizers. Some lead best in a rural context, and others lead best in an urban or suburban context.

Impact on Followers

Finally, leaders influence their followers to pursue their God-given direction. That direction is twofold, consisting of the followers' mission and vision. The followers' mission also is twofold. It's made up of their personal mission based on their gifts, talents, and temperament, and the mission of the organization they serve. The followers' vision is twofold as well. It's made up of their personal vision and their ministry's vision.[2]

What Is Leadership Development?

What do we mean when we add the term *development* to *leadership?* What is leadership development? We define leadership development as *the intentional process of helping established and emerging leaders at every level of ministry to assess and develop their Christian character and to acquire, reinforce, and refine their ministry knowledge and skills.* We'll expand on this in chapters 8–10.

This definition is based on a major assumption, that people in general and leaders in particular can be developed. A debate exists among some researchers on whether leaders can be developed. Some argue that leaders are born, not made. Others argue that they're developed, and still others believe that both are true.[3]

Based on my (Aubrey's) work with students at Dallas Seminary and pastors outside the seminary, I'm convinced that the last view is correct. Some leaders, such as Martin Luther King Jr., Margaret Thatcher, and Ross Perot, come into this world with natural gifts to lead in certain contexts. We call them born leaders. God also gives certain believers the leadership gift, as we saw in Romans 12:8, when they come to faith. We might call them "born-again leaders." Regardless, as we observed in our definition of a leader, people's character, knowledge, and skills can be developed, some more than others, according to their natural abilities and gifting. Consequently, though we are not born with equal leadership ability or natural leadership gifts, all of us can to some extent develop as leaders (though some are better followers than leaders). Otherwise, implementing a program of leadership development wouldn't make sense.

In 1 Timothy 4:14–15 the words of the apostle Paul to his young protégé Timothy speak well to the reality that leaders can and must *develop:* "Do not neglect the spiritual gift within you. . . . Take pains with these things; be absorbed in them, so that your progress will be evident to all" (NASB). Timothy is exhorted to display personal development with "these things." In the context of verses 6–14, "these things" include character, knowledge, skills, and spiritual gifts, all as facets of leadership.

The Importance of Leadership Development

Few debate the importance of training leaders. There are at least five reasons that this is so.

Jesus Modeled the Priority of Leadership Development: There Is No Plan B!

Leadership development was at the core of Jesus' ministry. If we could catch a glimpse of his ministry priorities, his development of the Twelve would have been at or near the top. Initially, the Savior ministered single-handedly, confining his miracles to a limited area and teaching basic spiritual truths. As the ministry grew over time and his followers multiplied, he selected and began to focus on a few of them—the Twelve. Even while his ministry was attracting large numbers of people, Jesus gave himself to his disciples, not the crowd. Toward the end of his ministry, the Savior poured his life into the Twelve because he knew that they, not the crowd, would make a difference in the first-century world that, in turn, would affect the rest of time. We wouldn't have the privilege of knowing and serving Christ today had it not been for the daring leadership and ministry of his disciples in the first century.

Jesus
↓
disciples
↓
church
↓
world

Although Jesus focused on the Twelve, he spent even more intentional time with three of the disciples—Peter, James, and John.[4] Why did Jesus choose to do this? Perhaps the answer is found in Paul's letter to the Galatians, written years after Jesus' ascension. In Galatians 2:9 Paul explains that these same three men—Peter, James, and John—are "reputed to be pillars" of the church. This further demonstrates that Jesus' intention with the Twelve was to build leadership for the church at large.

Jesus' example serves as a challenge for those of us who desire to take our ministries into the twenty-first century. More megachurches exist today than at any other time in the history of North America, and they draw a crowd. If church pastors aren't careful, they'll become enamored with the crowd. They and their congregations can fall into the subtle trap of measuring their success by the size of the crowd. Jesus' example teaches us, however, that the ministry payoff is not the size of the ministry—the crowd—but the size of the leader's trainees—the core. Success comes in our training a core of competent, godly leaders at every level of the ministry who will take the ministry well into the twenty-first century, long after we've been forgotten.

The Quality of Leadership Affects the Quality of the Ministry: The Speed of the Leader Is the Speed of the Team

The quality of the leadership affects the quality of the ministry. One leader correctly observes that everything rises or falls on leadership. As the ministry's leadership goes, so goes the organization, and the quality of any ministry is in direct proportion to the quality of its leadership. Thus leadership is the key element of ministry, a vital ingredient for success. If a ministry isn't doing well, then much of the time the problem can be traced in some way to leadership or its lack.

This truth surfaces repeatedly throughout the Scriptures. For example, a careful reading of the books of 1 and 2 Kings teaches that the success of Israel's kings and, consequently, the nation depended on the kings' allegiance and obedience to God's law and finally to God himself. God prospered the nation in relation to how its leaders led the people in obedience to the Mosaic law and the teachings of the prophets. When the kings abandoned God's direction, the nation paid a severe price.

Also, the Savior suggests the importance of leaders to a ministry when he alludes to the condition of sheep who are without a shepherd in Matthew 9:35–36. He was traveling through various towns and villages, ministering to the people. In verse 36 Matthew writes, "When he saw the crowds, he had compassion on them, because they were harassed and helpless, like sheep without a shepherd." Jesus' intent here isn't to instruct his disciples on the principles of good leadership in the kingdom. Nevertheless, the sheep-shepherd analogy indirectly demonstrates the importance of the shepherd's leadership to his flock. Without him, the sheep are in dire straits.

Some church ministries are in difficulty because their leaders struggle spiritually, much as in the days of Israel's kings. Most ministries stumble because they have no trained, competent leadership in place. With either scenario, the church loses. Because the church is only as good as its leadership, it becomes imperative that churches in the early twenty-first century raise up and train a new generation of leaders who will make a significant difference in our world for the Savior.

Leaders Expand Ministry by Making More Leaders: The Growth Curve Is the Leadership Curve

It takes leaders to make more leaders. The job of the leader isn't just to enlist more followers but to recruit and equip more and better leaders. It's the leaders' responsibility to develop other leaders. People fall into one of two categories—they're either leaders or followers. Followers don't develop leaders; they follow them. It's leaders who develop other leaders. If they don't do it, it won't get done. God didn't insist that leaders build megachurches. While there is nothing wrong with being a large church, it's God's job to build the church (Matt. 16:18). Building churches is on his job description, not ours. However, it's our job to build leaders—competent, godly leaders. In 2 Timothy 2:2 Paul commands Timothy to train leaders. This is the principle of leadership multiplication: leaders training leaders who, in turn, train other leaders throughout the ministry.

Failure to train emerging leaders puts the future of any ministry in serious jeopardy. Train other leaders, and the ministry sustains itself into the second and third generations. Bill Hybels goes so far as to say, "I think leaders are at their best when they are raising up leaders around them."[5] Based on 2 Timothy 2:2, Paul would agree with Hybels.

Since the job of the leader is to make more leaders, every leader in a ministry must be a leader-maker. This applies especially to those in leadership staff positions. Thus a requisite for hiring staff is their desire to develop leaders as well as accomplish ministry tasks. And if it is a requisite for hiring, then it would be a requisite for evaluation as well. Here's the question: Are you developing leaders? If so, where are they? Show me your leaders in training.

Every leader must ask, *What happens to the work if God should suddenly take me home or direct me elsewhere?* The mark of good leaders is that they continually develop leaders at every level of the ministry who will take the organization well into the future. It is essential to groom more than one or two leaders, because God will direct some of them to other ministries beyond your own. The downside of this is that you'll lose some good leaders. The upside is that you'll have an indirect impact on other ministries, potentially all over the world.

Leadership Development Recognizes the Value of People: All Processes Are Discipleship Processes

Another reason it's imperative that we train leaders is that leadership development recognizes the value of people. Our ministry's leaders are the ministry's most important assets. Not to develop them while involving them in ministry is to use and ultimately to abuse them. This is most often the result of an unbalanced, task-dominated ministry.

There are several potential contributing factors to task-dominated ministry. Each factor can be described more easily with a personification.

- *Pragmatic Paul.* Paul constantly falls to the temptation to value people only for what they can do. When Paul meets a new attendee, he envisions the ministry position that person can fill as he shakes his or her hand. Paul's motives aren't bad; he just has a very complex role as a pastor and there are a lot of things that need to be done. Unfortunately, he values people primarily as cogs in the church machinery.
- *Taskmaster Tom.* Tom is a leadership trainer with a task-oriented temperament. People like Tom with driven personalities can easily run over others who have a much different temperament. While Tom's wiring as a trainer and leader in the church is good, it can easily eclipse the heart and relationship priorities in the ministry.
- *Grow-grow Joe.* Joe has an inordinate desire for explosive growth in his church. While it can be argued that a healthy church should be growing, Joe pursues growth at the risk of the church's spiritual health. The preoccupation with numbers leads Joe to keep his leaders and volunteers running in the red zone because "there are more people to be reached." Any burnout "casualties" along the way are justified by the greater evangelistic cause.

The problem with the task-dominated ministry is that it models a destructive rather than a constructive environment. In doing so, it inhibits an individual's growth and causes a high leadership turnover in the ministry. In short, it fails to value people and burns out the church's valuable assets. People like Paul, Tom, and Joe recruit leaders in every phase of the ministry and turn them loose with little or no preparation. If someone insists on training, they hand him or her a book of instructions or give the person a pep talk under the guise of vision casting. Then they expect the leader to thrive and are perplexed when he or she crashes. This is a frightening formula for disaster that fails to recognize people's assets as leaders.

If we ask our people to lead any ministry of the church, we're responsible to provide them with continual leadership training. If we can't do this, we have no business asking them to serve, doing both them and the ministry an injustice. Without ongoing training, our recruits will struggle and often fail, and the rest of the ministry will experience the effects in the resulting leadership vacuum. People are too important to be treated this way. When a training process is in place, we demonstrate powerfully the value we place on people and combat the "cogs in a machine" mind-set.

Godly Protégés Are the Leader's Ministry Legacy: The Gospel Is Always One Generation from Extinction

Competent, Christ-honoring leaders are the seasoned leader's ministry legacy. Whether leaders want to or not, they leave behind a legacy, and they should pause in their busyness and consider what kind of legacy it will be. At the end of our lives, we'll discover that the best legacy we can leave our family and friends is our passion for the Savior. That's an important part of forming our life's personal mission statement. It affects both our family and ministry.

As far as our ministry is concerned, the challenge is to recruit and develop godly emerging leaders. This is our ministry legacy. When God takes us home, we want people to remember us for the number of godly, competent leaders who are in Christ-honoring ministries around the world because we made leadership development a priority in our busy ministry schedule. Paul's ministry legacy is found in 2 Timothy 2:2: "And the things you have heard me say in the presence of many witnesses entrust to reliable men who will also be qualified to teach others." It consists of Timothy, reliable men, and teachable others. Our burning desire as trainers and consultants is that our leadership legacy be like that of Paul.

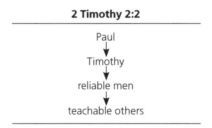

2 Timothy 2:2

Paul
↓
Timothy
↓
reliable men
↓
teachable others

We believe that most pastors as leaders know that they need to develop other leaders. So why are they about so many other things—important things—but not raising up and equipping a new generation of leaders? Regardless of the answer, we pray that articulating in this chapter some of the reasons for pursuing leadership development will fuel a greater passion to be about the business of training up the next generation of leaders.

Questions for Reflection and Discussion

1. What is your definition of a leader?
2. Do you agree with our definition of a leader, given on page 20? If not, where do you differ and why?

3. What are some reasons you are interested in developing leaders in your ministry?
4. How many of the reasons in this chapter are yours? Which ones?
5. Which of your reasons differ from those we gave in this chapter?
6. Our desire is that this chapter add fuel to your passion to train leaders. Was this the case? If not, why not?
7. Do any of your reasons for wanting to equip leaders sound a little selfish and self-serving? If so, which ones?

2

Some Common Delays

Problems in Developing Leaders

One of the problems in building a home is construction delays. It seems as if construction has no sooner begun than it comes to a screeching halt. Bad weather, a shortage of materials, inspection failures, and problem workers can lead to delays that cause the homeowner stress and anguish. When my wife and I (Aubrey) were having a house built, I can remember many days asking my wife why the builders weren't working on our house.

In the process of building your leadership-development process, you should be aware of some of the delays you're likely to encounter. An awareness of these potential hazards can save much time, anguish, and discouragement. We've encountered these while working with churches as they have designed their unique leadership-development models. Following are six common delays.

Existing Leaders' Inability

Leader inability is a primary cause for delays in the leadership-development process. This means that the existing leadership doesn't have the training to equip other leaders. The simple truth is that most churches want to develop leaders but don't know how. As previously mentioned, many seminaries do a tremendous job at equipping pastors to teach Scripture but have not adequately emphasized and taught godly organizational leadership. The purpose of this book is to provide the blueprints, tools, and construction guidelines to increase leaders' ability to develop spiritual leaders at every level of their church.

To clarify this first delay, by way of analogy, imagine that you have been given a new job assignment: One hundred people have been entrusted to your care as a sports league manager. Your job is to assemble, out of the hundred people, a football, basketball, and volleyball team for competitive purposes. It is important to select and train team players as well as team captains and coaches. You are given the freedom to play any role in the development of these teams that you want.

It so happens that you, the league manager, have no strategic or athletic know-how for selecting team coaches and captains. Although you have the best training in understanding the rule book, which is obviously a very valuable skill, it is not enough. You need to be equipped to manage. Your inability becomes a major obstacle to the development of the teams.

Existing Leaders' Need for Ministry Control

The second delay is the problem of *leader unwillingness*. This problem occurs when existing leadership values its control of the ministry over the growth of the ministry. When leaders fear that they will lose power in the ministry and are reluctant to develop new leaders, they must ask if such fear is from God. The cost of such a desire to control is huge both for individuals and the church at large. It costs individuals, because they are being robbed of the opportunity to have their gifts, skills, and abilities nurtured and developed. It costs the church at large, because ministry expansion is limited to the resources of a few, rather than released to the resources of the many. Ultimately this means fewer people coming to Christ and growing in Christ.

Recently I (Will) encountered this attitude while consulting with two different churches. Both churches are trying to develop a greater sense of community in their adult Sunday school. When I introduced the idea of small groups meeting off-campus on a different day of the week, one pastor told me, "I just don't feel comfortable giving away that much control." Then in jest he added, "Not that I have that much control anyway; I'm just not ready to go there." The issue touched him at a deep emotional level, and by his own admission, the issue centered on his desire for control. In the next chapter, on the challenge of empowerment, we will work through this obstacle.

Before moving to the next delay, we want to answer a potential objection. Pastors should view their role of shepherd as one of providing protection for their sheep. The Pastoral Epistles are loaded with concepts and language, such as *entrusted* and *guard,* that relate to the pastoral role of providing protection (1 Tim. 1:2–4; 4:6; 6:20–21; 2 Tim. 1:14; 4:1–4, 15; Titus 1:3, 9; 2:1). These passages teach that the pastor has been given the unique responsibility of guarding and "controlling" the integrity of the gospel message to protect the sheep.

The key point of clarification is that the pastor is entrusted with the *communication of a pure gospel,* not with the *doing of the ministry.* On the one hand, the pastor is called to protect the sheep by guarding the gospel against false teaching and doctrinal impurity. When it comes to the doing of the ministry, on the other hand, the pastor is called not to guard but to give away. Paul highlights this in Ephesians 4:11–13, when he clarifies that pastors are to equip the saints for the works of service.

In the sports league illustration, the problem of leader unwillingness resembles a sad parody. Imagine a community of a hundred people, many of whom have athletic and leadership abilities; some even have significant experience in football, basketball, and volleyball. Yet when it comes time to compete, the league manager takes the role of team captain in each sport. In the football game he takes off his manager's hat and puts on the quarterback's jersey. On the basketball court he plays point guard, and on the volleyball court he steps up as captain. Every once in a while players on the bench wonder if the teams would be stronger if the league manager would give someone else a chance, but the thought quickly vanishes because, after all, he is the league manager. Besides, he knows the rule book better than anyone else.

No Distinction between Leadership and Discipleship

Leader misperception can cause another delay. When leadership does not discern the difference between building leaders and making disciples, it lives with a blind spot. Leader-developers must distinguish between making disciples, developing mature disciples, and making leaders.

Discipleship development is a much broader concept than leadership development, because it targets everyone. Leadership is for a limited number of maturing disciples.

Everyone Should Become Jesus' Disciple

Discipleship targets everyone. The church's mission, according to the Great Commission (Matt. 28:19–20), is to "go and make disciples of all nations." This is evangelism. Jesus isn't instructing the church merely to find believers and mature them. Instead, the goal is to win lost people to Christ—to make disciples. However, the process must not end there. In addition, in verses 19 and 20, Jesus tells the church to baptize and teach these disciples, that is, to lead them to maturity. Therefore, the church's mission or commission is to win lost people (make disciples) and help them become mature disciples (make and mature disciples).

Not all disciples, even mature ones, will become leaders, at least in the narrow sense defined in chapter 1. The problems come when we confuse the two. A good disciple may become but doesn't automatically make a good leader. Some disciples will make good leaders, and some will make even better followers. The church of the twenty-first century desperately needs good followers as well as leaders.

Not Everyone Is a Leader

Leadership is a narrow concept. It targets a limited number of maturing disciples. Early in the process, as disciples grow and mature, experienced leaders should assess them to determine their gifts and abilities. In this way leaders will emerge. They may display natural and spiritual gifts of leadership or they may develop leadership skills. Thus leadership builds on discipleship. It's not only foundational but also imperative that a ministry develop its potential leaders as disciples; otherwise, they will find it most difficult to function well as leaders in the church. Leaders must be growing disciples. However, as disciples are developed, they must receive training in leadership so they can be good leaders.

The sports league illustration shows the problem of leader misperception clearly. Simply stated, the league manager has failed to discern the need for team captains or team coaches as distinct roles from the players themselves. The manager has done a great job of making athletes out of his community. He has even eloquently conveyed the content of the rule book each week. But the teams consistently seem to underperform. The manager puts the best athletes in charge of the teams, but the players never really grow as a team unit. The manager has not discovered that while some are better athletes than others (disciples), there are some who are better team captains (leaders) than others. Within the process of developing athletes, the manager has never devised a separate process for developing team captains.

Inadequate Church Mobilization

Another delay is caused by *church inactivity*. That is, there is a lack of ministry context from which to find leaders and in which to develop leaders. A mobilized congregation is rich soil for the sprouting and nurturing of leaders. Even if you have other essential aspects like seeds, water, and sunlight, without the soil, there will be no plant life. Likewise, a leadership-development process requires the essential elements of ability and willingness, but without the context—clusters of people engaged in ministry—leaders won't grow.

I (Will) see this dynamic played out in two primary ways when I consult with some churches. The first relates to the sheer age of members who have borne the load of ministry over the course of twenty or thirty years. I call this the weary church. If a young leader comes along, they allow him to do as much ministry as he wants, but there is no one for him to lead into ministry.

There are also church structures that inhibit mobilized ministry. I call this the shackled church. For example, a committee selects a young leader as committee chairman. The committee, however, does not function as an actual ministry team. The committee members may make decisions about "ministry," but they are not doing ministry. While committees may be important and necessary, and while leadership is about decision making, a church with too much decision-making structure inhibits leader development because there is more "talk" than "walk." Leaders must be more than talkers. I have seen scores of potential leaders leave both wearied and shackled churches because of the deep-seated, undermobilized church culture.

In the sports league scenario, the problem of mobilization looks like the coach leading all of the teams (football, basketball, and volleyball) with the same fifteen people. The other eighty-five in the community are spectators. They may talk about what plays they like, and they may even cheer for their team, but they are reluctant to get out of the stands and into the game. The coach makes a constant attempt to recruit more players but to no avail. The result is a desertlike environment that limits the opportunity to grow leaders. In chapter 9 the topic of mobilization is considered further as an important component when designing the leadership-development process.

Task-Oriented Church Culture

Another delay is caused by the problem of *church overactivity*—the opposite of the previous delay of inactivity. To some pastors the thought that there are churches in which a majority of the people are struggling with too much activity may be surprising. It can happen in a core group of fifty people who are preparing to launch a church or in an extremely fast-growing congregation of one thousand passionately working to touch its community with the gospel message.

I (Will) served on a staff for which this was a major concern. The seeker service ministry had grown by one thousand people in four years. At the same time more than 85 percent of those committed to church membership were involved in significant ministry. Several other pastors and I agreed that we had pushed our people too hard. Our efforts to offset the tendency toward a task-dominated ministry included the selection of "sanity" as one of our five core values early in the life of the church.

The task-dominated approach, unknowingly, tends to use and ultimately abuse leaders. This is what happens when people spend most of their time leading and ministering without taking time for training and personal development, especially in the area of character. For example, the people in one church that I (Aubrey) worked with told me they weren't interested in becoming or even being called leaders because, in that context, it meant taking on more responsibility when they were already loaded down with work. To be a leader in this church meant being overworked.

One key diagnostic question to ask yourself and your current leaders is *How much time do you spend working* on *the ministry versus working* in *the ministry?* Working *in* the ministry is doing the ministry work. Working *on* the ministry includes anything that improves how the ministry work is done. All uses of time can be placed in one of these two categories.[1]

The difficulty with working *on* the ministry is that it limits the time to work *in* the ministry—a tension that every leader feels. If your leaders are never working *on* the ministry, you are working in a task-dominated church culture. If this is the case, leadership development is a huge challenge because it means working *on* the ministry and not *in* the ministry.

The task-oriented delay can be illustrated by the sports league situation. In the previous scenario the majority of players were sitting in the stands. Now large numbers are overworked on the playing field. The worst part is not that the players get tired—that is natural for any athlete. The challenge is that the teams never get better, and the teams never keep players for the long haul. As crazy as it sounds, the players can never practice or run drills because they have too many games. The coaches never review games on film, spend time with their team captain, or allow players to attend training camps. The teams spend so much time playing *in* the game that they have no time left to work *on* their game.

No Vision for Ministry

The sixth delay is the problem of *church misalignment*. A vision for ministry refers to the stated mission, values, and strategy of the church.

These vision statement components are like the DNA of the church; every leader, ministry, program, and process should begin with a clear understanding of them. The vision serves as a compass, keeping leaders aligned, that is, pointed in the same direction and motivated toward a common picture of what the future looks like. The vision path is critical to the leadership-development process and should be a part of the core content that is repeated and retold so that leaders can share and own the vision. If there is no clear vision path, the misalignment of direction and motivations will make the development of leaders difficult if not impossible. You cannot develop leaders without being crystal clear on the questions Why are we here? and Where are we going?

I (Aubrey) have devoted much of my previous writing to helping pastors and leaders in the areas of ministry vision and strategic planning. If you are ready to pursue further reading on these subjects, start with *Advanced Strategic Planning* (Baker, 1999).

Questions for Reflection and Discussion

1. Does your ministry have a disciple-making (evangelism) and maturing (edification) process? If yes, how would you distinguish it from a potential leadership-training process?
2. What are the top two or three delays in leadership development that you're currently facing? What factors contribute to these delays?
3. Starting with the most problematic delay, list some action steps you could take to overcome it. Who else needs to be aware of the delay? Who else may be a resource to help in developing and implementing the action steps?
4. What church ministries, groups, or committees are structured in a way that inhibits lay mobilization and the doing of ministry?
5. Does your church have a clear statement of mission, vision, values, and strategy that serve to clarify and align the direction and identity of the church? If yes, how can you place this at the center of the leadership-development process? If no, list the action steps to begin developing these statements.

3

The Challenge of Empowerment

The Heart Required for Developing Leaders

Far too many pastors face a common dilemma. They want to develop leaders at every level in their church, but they continue to live with an overloaded ministry schedule that keeps them from training new leaders. Yet the real problem is not busyness; it is what lies behind the busyness. Lurking beneath the long hours and the never-ending task list is a reluctance to empower others.

The typical pastor has too many balls to juggle. His greatest need is not more balls to throw in the air or more time to perform or more juggling tips; his greatest need is more jugglers—individuals who can lead ministry under his guidance. Yet many pastors are reluctant to recognize this need and, if honest, must answer the following question in the negative: As a leadership development process is implemented, will you be able to give ministry away to other leaders? Many are not sure how they will face one of a leader's greatest challenges—the challenge of empowerment.

The juggling metaphor is helpful in introducing the idea of empowerment. Empowerment represents a point in the leadership-development process when a leader stops juggling one of his balls and hands it to someone else, an "emerging juggler," so to speak. This handoff is critical because no amount of classroom training, reading, practicing, or mentoring can produce a juggler without the handoff. Likewise, no amount of leadership development can produce a leader without empowerment.

Therefore, understanding and applying the concept of empowerment are essential to developing leaders.

The purpose of this chapter is to provide a clear definition of empowerment and practical direction on how to empower others. It fits in the preparation section of the book because any effort to develop leaders without a commitment to empowerment is futile. It is also appropriate here because the act of empowerment places unique demands on the leader's heart. As with any heart-level development issue, time for growth is required. Therefore, it is in the leader's best interest to confront these demands early in the process. To help leaders work on the heart level, this chapter provides "heart-building exercises" that will develop courage and conviction for empowering others.

Empowerment Defined

Many authors use the term *empowerment* when writing about leadership, but few pause to define it. For the sake of clarity, let's start with a definition: *Empowerment is the intentional transfer of authority to an emerging leader within specified boundaries from an established leader who maintains responsibility for the ministry.*

Let's explore the components of this definition. First, empowerment involves an *intentional* transfer. *Intentional* means that the transfer is deliberate and thought through ahead of time. Before ministry authority is given away, a degree of assessment and planning is required. The established leader must answer important questions such as:

- What ministry areas require my direct attention and which ones do not?
- What are the most strategic ministry areas at this time (and therefore require emerging leader involvement)?
- Who qualifies as an emerging leader?
- What are the passions and gifts of the emerging leader?
- How will the transfer of authority take place?

If a leader does not think through questions like these, the act of giving away ministry will be hasty or haphazard and can lead to problems down the road. These problems vary, depending on the ministry, but they all flow from the same basic principle. The quality of the emerging leader's ongoing ministry performance is directly related to the quality of his or her initiation as a leader. In the end, the failure to intentionally transfer authority to emerging leaders will inhibit their development and that of their ministries.

There are two general ways for an unintentional transfer to occur. The first relates to the personal limitations of the established leader, limitations such as inexperience or insufficient training. Even for experienced leaders, factors such as stress, lack of time, or apathy contribute to a sloppy handing over of ministry. The second way an unintentional transfer happens is when someone acts like an emerging leader who is not an emerging leader at all. In other words, an individual may assume authority where none is granted. This occurs in some cases by malicious aggression and in others by honest mistake. In either case, when someone seizes authority by his or her own initiative rather than receiving it from an established leader, empowerment is not taking place.

Now to the second component of the definition. Empowerment is about *authority*. Authority is decision-making power. The heart of empowerment is the transfer of decision-making control over an area of ministry. To understand the significance of this transfer, think about teaching someone to drive a car. The student driver must first study the rules of the road, watch more experienced drivers, and learn how to operate the vehicle. But the student cannot actually drive the car until he or she sits in the driver's seat—the place of decision-making power. For the student driver to sit in the driver's seat, the existing driver must take his hands off the wheel and move over. The transfer of authority is clear because only one person at a time can have his hands on the wheel and his foot on the pedal.

Keep in mind that there are many stages of learning for the student leader. If, however, the student leader never sits in the driver's seat of ministry, he or she will never become a leader. In other words, it is just as crazy to try to develop leaders without a commitment to empowerment as it is to operate a driving school without letting students sit behind the wheel of a car.

Empowerment is a transfer of authority *to an emerging leader from an established leader.* The term *emerging leader* implies that the leader is qualified to receive authority in a ministry context. The term is not limited to new leaders. The emerging leader may be starting to lead for the first time or may be emerging from one level of leadership to a higher one.

The idea of an established leader is twofold. The leader is established with respect to God. His position is rooted in true spiritual authority based on character and other spiritual guidelines for the role. The leader is also established with respect to the congregation. The church community recognizes and validates (according to its own theological tradition) the leader's character and competence.

Returning to the definition: Empowerment is the intentional transfer of authority to an emerging leader *within specified boundaries*. The boundaries clarify where and when the leader is empowered to make ministry decisions. One type of boundary is a specific ministry area, such as children's ministry or men's ministry, a specific Sunday school class or small group. Another type of boundary is the kind of decision-making power granted. A lower level of empowerment may limit decision making to tasks, while a higher level may include decisions about finances and people. Also, authority can be categorized into three basic types: inform-act authority, act-inform authority, and act authority. For a brief discussion of these types, refer to pages 104–14 of the companion volume, *Being Leaders*.

The final component of the definition is an important clause that describes the established leader as one *who maintains responsibility for the ministry*. Ultimately the established leader is accountable for the decisions made by those under him or her. By retaining responsibility, the established leader stays conscious of his or her accountability and maintains a vested interest in the ministry outcomes. In essence the established leader holds ownership or final responsibility even though the decision-making power has been transferred. This helps foster a relationship of trust and security with the emerging leader.

Alternatives to Empowerment

To further clarify the definition of empowerment, it helps to explore the different ways an established leader keeps or gives away authority and responsibility. As we have stated, empowerment occurs when a leader gives away authority but keeps responsibility. There are three logical alternatives to empowering: directing, abdicating, and disabling. As you may guess from the terms, the last two, abdicating and disabling, carry a negative connotation because these actions inhibit leadership development. Let's take a look at each of the three.

Directing

Directing occurs when the established leader keeps both authority and responsibility. In some situations directing is a good option, and in others it is not. It is a good option if there is a lack of qualified emerging leaders. For example, a new and inexperienced worship pastor may start off receiving direction from his senior pastor. He is given the program—which songs to sing and the order in which to sing them—from the senior pastor. The senior pastor does not give away authority to make these decisions. He also keeps the responsibility. Whether the response is dynamic or poor, he takes responsibility for the result.

Directing is inappropriate in other situations. If there are qualified emerging leaders and an established leader continues to direct, he or she will hold back the leadership potential in the ministry. Many times the established leader continues to direct because he or she likes being in charge. (We will address this later in the chapter.) Let's return to our new worship pastor as an example. If the worship pastor continues to develop under the directing of the senior pastor, there may come a time when he is ready to receive authority over the music ministry. The senior pastor may resist this change from directing to empowering simply because he likes making all the decisions. In such a case, directing inhibits leader development.

Abdicating

Another alternative to empowering is abdicating. This occurs when the established leader gives away both authority and responsibility. Even though this may appear to be empowering, it is not. Abdicating can actually hinder rather than promote the new leader's development. When the established leader gives away responsibility for the ministry, a vital connection is lost between the established leader and the emerging leader because the established leader no longer feels accountable for ministry outcomes.

To use the student driver illustration, imagine an instructor exiting the vehicle at the moment the student climbs behind the wheel. This shows a blatant disregard for both the driver and the car. In similar fashion an established leader who abdicates leadership is showing a blatant disregard for both the emerging leader and the ministry. This form of disregard may not be conscious on the established leader's part. In our experience, abdicating usually occurs unintentionally through neglect and is perpetuated due to stress and time constraints in the leader's life. Leaders should be careful to evaluate whether ministry they give away is a result of empowering or abdicating.

For the new worship pastor, abdicating would occur if the senior pastor gave away authority over the worship program while disowning the responsibility. To the worship pastor, the senior pastor would seem disengaged. On some Sundays the worship would go really well and on others it wouldn't. In either case the senior pastor would never comment or provide feedback on the program, making his expectations unclear. Training would never be discussed or offered. Even though the worship pastor would love to discuss the upcoming sermon series to plan musical selections better, the senior pastor would never have the time. In this case the senior pastor is not giving away authority *to multiply* the ministry but is giving away authority *to give up* the ministry.

Disabling

Disabling is another alternative to empowering. It refers to the inappropriate act of giving away responsibility but keeping the authority. When this occurs, the established leader holds the emerging leader accountable for ministry outcomes without giving him or her decision-making freedom. In the context of this disempowerment, many negative scenarios result. First, it places a low ceiling on the emerging leader's development potential. Learning is stunted because he or she never gets behind the wheel of ministry. Second, the ministry never multiplies because one person is still making all of the decisions. Third, frustration snowballs because the established leader never considers himself ultimately accountable and can blame others when problems arise.

Leaders who disable will eventually discourage emerging leaders—in many cases to the point of leaving the ministry area. Using the new worship pastor as an example, disabling occurs if the senior pastor gives the worship pastor critical feedback about a poor response from the congregation. Since the worship pastor wasn't given authority to design the program, he should not be held responsible for the outcome of the program (assuming he did what the senior pastor told him to do).

One key to discerning leadership disablement is observing with whom the established leader communicates when problems or critical decisions arise. If a leader bypasses other leaders or emerging leaders in the organization to effect change, disabling occurs. The decision-making power has never really been given away. For example, the senior pastor is guilty of disabling if he goes straight to the pianist to cut a special music piece from the worship program instead of working with the worship pastor.

Alternatives to Empowerment
(from the established leader's perspective)

	Promotes Leader Development		Inhibits Leader Development	
	Empowering	**Directing**	**Abdicating**	**Disabling**
Authority	given away	kept	given away	kept
Responsibility	kept	kept	given away	given away

Let's return to the senior pastor and his new worship pastor to illustrate the positive aspects of empowerment. Six months have passed and the senior pastor decides to empower the worship pastor. The senior pastor still feels responsible for the outcome of the worship event, but now the authority of designing the program rests in the hands of the worship pastor. Imagine the context that develops: The pastor looks for ways to further equip his worship pastor and build his skills. The pastor cares enough to write down his regular feedback with both strengths and weaknesses of the program. The pastor plans time to discuss future sermon series.

On the flip side, the empowered worship pastor appreciates the opportunity to make the programming decisions. (His gifts and training, as opposed to those of the senior pastor, are better suited for the role.) He feels comfortable getting input from his pastor because he knows that the pastor will not simply blame him for negative outcomes but will help him solve problems and make progress. The worship pastor knows that when critical decisions arise, the senior pastor will not go behind his back to give direction to the worship team. Best of all, the pastor openly praises the worship pastor when he does well and personally accepts the responsibility when outcomes don't go well.

Another helpful illustration of empowerment is what Jim Collins calls the pattern of "the window and the mirror."[1] He states that effective leaders always look out the window when things go well (acknowledging someone else's authority and good decision making) but look in the mirror when things go badly (taking responsibility for the situation).

Empowerment Applied

Empowerment is much easier to define than it is to apply. In fact, empowerment places many demands on the heart of the spiritual leader. Any progress in implementing a leadership-development process will necessarily force leaders into a "heart-shaping gymnasium." Let's take a look at four specific challenges of empowerment. For each challenge there is an "empowerment priority" with corresponding exercises needed to build the heart.

Giving Up Control

Challenge 1: *Empowerment increases the scope of unknown ministry outcomes.*
Empowerment priority: *Embrace uncertainty.*

Because empowerment increases the uncertainty of ministry outcomes, the leader's inordinate desire for control will be confronted. By simply involving others in the decision-making process, the potential for new ideas and different decisions multiplies, leading to a greater variety of ministry results. One result could be very positive, such as a lay leader catching a vision for a new service initiative in the community. Another may be very negative, such as a terribly unorganized special event. There is no way around the fact that empowering others requires living with greater uncertainty, and this uncertainty forces a leader to face personal issues of control.

Reggie McNeal explores this connection as he encourages leaders through the heart-shaping process of giving up control: "Some spiritual leaders are reluctant to release the control of ministry. Several factors contribute to this, including fear that the ministry quality might suffer or fear that the leader will lose some leverage in the system."[2] So what happens over time when fear concerning ministry quality and unknown outcomes inhibits empowerment? The leader builds an organization with systems and processes that extend his control. Then a personal problem becomes an institutionalized problem. Stacy Rinehart observes, "In the most extreme form, the need for control will insist on defining ministry in terms of loyalty to a particular group and to programs directly attached to the institution. It simply can't allow freedom and diversity in people or programs."[3] Another Christian leader refers to this problem as the "corruption of political clout" and explains, "Leaders who lead by political control end up cloning subordinates rather than developing new leaders."[4] The bottom line is that trying to empower others while retaining control over ministry is like trying to mix oil and water. Without a commitment to empowerment, it is futile to build a leader-development process.

During my (Will's) college days the foundational scientific model of the atom went through a transition. The old model was represented by a nucleus around which electrons orbited like planets around the sun. In contrast, the new model showed that electrons do not follow predictable orbits at all. Rather, electrons exist as clouds or fields represented by probability patterns. The shift from predictable pathways to probability patterns represents a paradigm shift that is required when embracing empowerment. If leaders want to walk in predictable pathways of doing ministry, kingdom expansion will be difficult if not impossible. If, however, leaders take the risk to release others toward probabilities of success, God can release atomiclike energy through our ministry efforts.

EMBRACING UNCERTAINTY THROUGH INCREASED FAITH

So how should a leader face the uncertainty associated with releasing ministry to others? The answer is faith—trusting that God was, is, and always will be the author and prime mover behind all ministry activity. This includes the ministry we release. Leaders must lead with the perspective of stewardship over ministry rather than ownership of ministry. Stewardship is being responsible for something that belongs to someone else. When leaders insist on control, they are really assuming the role of owner of people and ministry outcomes, promoting themselves to a role that only the sovereign Creator and Manager of the universe can hold.

I (Will) remember the first time this truth made its mark on my life. As a young student on the campus of Penn State, I was an enthusiastic member of Campus Crusade for Christ. By my sophomore year, I was thoroughly trained in evangelism and followed a weekly follow-up routine to share the gospel with other students. With some early success, my evangelistic prowess was affirmed. I remember the satisfaction of recounting how students had given their life to Christ because of my witnessing. Subtly the perspective of my identity began to shift from being a steward of the gospel message to being an "owner"—someone who controlled ministry outcomes.

I can remember the shock of reading Bill Bright's definition of successful evangelism after my pride had fully taken hold of me: "Success in witnessing is simply taking initiative to share Christ in the power of the Holy Spirit, and leaving the results up to God."[5] The idea of leaving the results up to God was radical, because I thought the results were tied to my effective skills in witnessing. The realization that my "success" really flowed from the work of God was a much-needed pin to my inflated head. And it is this same truth that I have needed to refresh over and over again as I have empowered others in ministry. The results are not up to me; they are up to God. God is ultimately in control. Empowerment requires seeing your ministry universe through the eyes of faith and then taking real steps of faith. This kind of faith initiative requires courage and risk taking.

When facing risk, I often remind myself of the words of Helen Keller, "Security is mostly a superstition—it does not exist in nature. Avoiding danger is not safer in the long run than outright exposure. Life is either a daring adventure or it is nothing at all." These words remind me that the control I think I possess is really an illusion. The most absurd truth about control is that we never really have it. It is God's all along. So in the end we can either live with the illusion of control and move toward the illusion of security and predictability, or we can relinquish control to God in a way that frees us to take the risk of empowering others.

Choosing the risk of empowerment requires increased faith and prayerful dependence. It is one of many forms of uncertainty that God uses to build faith into the life of leaders. A passage in Mark 4:35–41 provides a vivid illustration of Jesus' leading his disciples into uncertainty for the purpose of faith building. While crossing the Sea of Galilee, they encounter a sudden, life-threatening squall. Struck with panic, the disciples shake Jesus awake and call to him in fear. After Jesus exhibits his masterful control over wind and sea, he questions his disciples with a mild rebuke, "Do you still have no faith?" It is clear that Jesus is training his disciples about issues of control. He leads them to a situation in which they are out of control so they will embrace a life of prayer and faith to participate in God's control.[6] When it comes to empowerment in the local church, we think that Jesus would ask many church leaders the same question: "Do you still have no faith?" Giving away power and authority will call for leaders to embrace prayer, increase their faith, and participate in God's control.

Heart-Building Exercises: Set One

A key exercise in learning to give up control is to consider the circumstances that bring out our worst tendencies to take charge. In what conditions are we most inflexible and demanding? By reflecting on these areas we can open the door to the Spirit's work in our heart. Consider the following questions to aid the reflection process.[7]

- In what general areas do you gravitate toward control (people, tasks, ideas, processes, environment, and so on)?
- What types of people or roles do you tend to control (leaders, church members, pastoral staff, administrative staff, children, spouse, others)?
- In what kinds of activities do you want control (planning, problem solving, teaching/preaching, facilitating, counseling, studying, socializing)?
- What are your hot buttons (correct appearance, competition, finances, certain personality types, others)?

Everyone deals with tendencies toward control. It is simply a matter of how the tendency manifests itself. For example, I (Will) struggle in the general area of ideas and processes. I find it quite easy to assemble a group of teachers to team teach spiritual formation seminars—as long as I determine the structure and outline of the teaching content. I do not hog the actual teaching event itself, but no one better mess with my outline! An example of one of my hot buttons is church communication materials. I am ashamed to admit how many church flyers, brochures, and signs I have designed myself (late into the night) because I was unwilling to empower another leader to do it.

Each control area we identify opens the door for God to grow our faith and dependence on him. Each area sheds valuable light on personal and organizational development priorities. To the extent we fail to counteract our control issues, we will limit the development of other leaders around us.

Slowing Down

Challenge 2: *Empowerment requires a sacrifice of short-term ministry efficiency.*
Empowerment priority: *Slow down to speed up.*

The slow-down dynamic challenges the leader's inordinate desire for expediency. Ministries carry momentum. When a ministry is going well and a leader is comfortable making the ministry decisions, it can be extremely difficult to hand off decision-making power. There is always a window of transition when the energy required to empower a new leader is greater than the energy required to keep leading oneself. During this window the threat of bogging down the ministry arises, and it is not uncommon for the leader to feel that others are sabotaging his time. We call this the sensation of apparent inefficiency. Indeed, the ministry will slow down—and that feels inefficient—but the purpose of slowing it down is to speed it up faster than it has ever gone before. It is the principle of short-term sacrifice for long-term gain. Empowerment costs something but pays huge dividends.

An illustration of this principle is the story of two lumberjacks who compete in the forest one day. After several hours of working, one lumberjack stops to take a ten-minute break, while the other keeps energetically chopping away. The same thing happens several times throughout the day. At the end of the day, the lumberjack who took the several ten-minute breaks turns out to be the one who chopped the most wood. "I can't understand it," said the other lumberjack. "How did you chop more wood than me?" "Simple," was the reply. "When I stopped chopping, I was sharpening my ax!"

This story illustrates the fact that slowing down can actually speed things up. The lumberjack was willing to feel the sensation of apparent inefficiency for the sake of long-term gain. Leaders must do the same if they are to empower others.

Unfortunately, the attractiveness of short-term effectiveness is too strong for many leaders. To complicate matters, the interest in efficiency is usually accompanied by the pride of competence. Not only can the leader do it faster, he can also do it better. And not only can he do it better, he feels good about the fact he can do it better! Many times this reality eclipses the opportunity for empowerment. All leaders face this defining moment—the choice between performing a function themselves and delegating it to someone with less experience or technical competence. How then should the leader go about choosing the higher road of empowerment when the familiar, expedient pathways of "do it yourself" are so enticing?

SLOWING DOWN THROUGH INCREASED PATIENCE

While empowerment is the higher road, the hard truth is that it is always the slower road, at least in the short run. Therefore, there is no way around the need to cultivate a heart of patience. Patience in these situations is much deeper than simply waiting. It involves a dying to self, which is very painful. In many cases it is allowing someone else to do what you love to do, what you were trained to do, and what you can do better! All the while there are external time pressures—Sunday after Sunday the ministry calendar grinds on.

During the pain of waiting, the leader must foresee the future gain. The pain can take many forms. Maybe for a few months message preparation time is limited. Maybe for the entire year, the quality of the children's ministry suffers. Maybe for eighteen months no new small groups are launched. But eventually the waiting pays off. The right people grow and develop; ideas and resources increase; volunteer time and leadership multiplies; ministry momentum snowballs. The short window of slow-down that lasted for several months is seen from a new perspective. Over the course of years it is evident that the slow-down window was not a cost but an investment in years of increased fruitfulness.

HEART-BUILDING EXERCISES: SET TWO

To walk through these slow-down periods, we must cultivate an attitude of patience. We must stay "legacy minded" rather than "expediency minded." Consider the following action points and corresponding questions designed to expand your perspective on slowing down to speed up.

- Remember and record your own learning curve process. Who had to slow down to get you where you are today? What sacrifices in ministry time or quality did some leader make when you were training? How has his or her investment paid off?
- See the long-term potential in people. How many of your hours is it worth to develop an emerging leader who will serve faithfully for the next twenty years? When you look at an acorn, do you see a mature tree or an entire forest?
- Acknowledge that there is more than one way to accomplish a goal. Ask yourself: *Is my way the only right way when it comes to a particular ministry function? Are there other ways of getting from*

point A to point B? Can I celebrate when another person gets to point B a different way than I would?

- Study the example of Jesus. Did doing ministry while living with twelve men ever slow Jesus down? Did Jesus give up teaching opportunities to train others? Consider, for example, his sending out the seventy-two in Luke 10.
- Focus on the long-term benefits. Ask yourself: *What could the ministry look like if twice as many people were involved? How would this ministry be transformed if the people leading it were more passionate and talented than I am? What would my life be like if I were freed to focus on my top three priorities?*

In his classic work *Spiritual Leadership,* Oswald Sanders counts the cost of the leader's failure to slow down and empower others:

> The man in the place of leadership who fails to delegate is constantly enmeshed in a morass of secondary detail that not only overburdens him but deflects him from his primary responsibilities. He also fails to release the leadership potential under him. To insist on doing things oneself because it will be done better is not only a short-sighted policy but may be evidence of an unwarranted conceit.[8]

But in contrast he adds, "The leader who is meticulous in observing priorities adds immeasurably to his own effectiveness." Slowing down must be a leader's priority if he wants to empower others and add "immeasurably" to the life of the church.

Humility

Challenge 3: *Empowerment requires giving away authority that previously provided the basis of personal ministry success.*
Empowerment priority: *Starve your ego.*

A third dynamic confronts the leader's inordinate desire for power, requiring him to give away authority. Once a pastor has demonstrated his ability to perform ministry tasks, choosing to empower others can easily threaten his sense of security and significance. No pastor is immune to this dynamic as it develops in almost undetectable increments. Over time a sense of personal significance develops out of career achievements rather than through the grace of Jesus Christ. To whatever degree this happens, the leader will have difficulty empowering others, because, in essence, empowering others forces the pastor to starve his own ego.

Stacy Rinehart comments on the abuse of power manifested by some Christian leaders today:

> Abuses of power in our day are often more subtle. The layout of church office space, the titles we assign, the requirements for membership or being a teacher—all indicate underlying beliefs about power. Often such things are meeting the deep needs of the leaders rather than serving the people. Like Linus's security blanket in the *Peanuts* cartoon, such externals become a source of great comfort and meet a need for self-esteem and significance as well.[9]

For some pastors personal ministry success is enhanced by specialized ministry training and finely tuned theological knowledge. The pride of competence kicks in again. Carl George describes this problem well:

> Pastors sometimes fear loss of exclusive authority in matters of guidance and advice. Each of Christendom's traditions contains certain finer points of doctrine that allow for multiple interpretation options. Some pastors have a need to be right and to be in control, lest their competence seem challenged or threatened. This kind of minister will experience difficulty in multiplying teachers, advisors, counselors, and other persons of wisdom, since these lay pastors may come to wield almost as much influence in their small groups as their senior pastor.[10]

How sad to think that the gift of specialized training for ministry could lead to a pride of competence that actually blocks the empowering of others for ministry!

Starving Your Ego through Increased Humility

Every Christian leader struggles to some degree with the "dark side" of the soul that gravitates toward position and power. While it is not our purpose to explore the issue of sanctification, it is worth emphasizing that spiritual leaders need to continually cultivate an attitude of humility. Jesus reveals the importance of this attribute in Matthew 20 when the mother of James and John requests that her sons be promoted to vice presidents in the future kingdom. Jesus replies in verses 24–27: "You know that the rulers of the Gentiles lord it over them, and their high officials exercise authority over them. Not so with you. Instead, whoever wants to become great among you must be your servant, and whoever wants to be first must be your slave." Jesus is teaching that spiritual leaders not only serve by leading, they lead by serving. In a sense leaders are called to *descend into greatness*. It is the character trait of humility, more than any other, that will impact the leader's ability to give away authority and to empower others for servant-led ministry.

Let's explore why the attribute of humility is essential for developing leaders. First, humility implies the ability to see God, self, and others accurately. In Romans 12:6–8 Paul lists several spiritual gifts, including the gift of leadership. In the context immediately preceding this section, Paul writes in verse 3, "I say to everyone among you not to think more highly of himself than he ought to think" (NASB). The leader who thinks too highly of himself will be hard-pressed to give away authority. If for no other reason, this will happen simply because his inflated view of self translates to a deflated view of others. But the more accurately a leader sees himself and those around him, including the diversity of gifts and talents, the more likely he is to release others for ministry.

Second, humility is essential because it gives you the ability to make other people priorities, not merely looking "out for your own personal interests, but also for the interests of others" (Phil. 2:4 NASB). What happens when a pastor takes this seriously in terms of the ministry interests of those in his congregation? What happens when a leader considers the spiritual gifts of others around him as more important than his own? The answer is one word—empowerment. With this Christlike attitude, the leader will not only be open to leadership development, he will intentionally and passionately give away power and authority to others!

Finally, humility fosters gratitude for the opportunity to play a role in God's grand story of redemptive history. This gratitude helps counteract the definition of success in individualized terms. Some athletes measure their success by personal stats and some by team stats. The leader measures only team stats. An attitude of humility keeps the well-being of the church at large as the priority, with organizational success coming before personal ministry success. Otherwise, the preoccupation with self, ego, and career will act as a parasite on the organization. For a pastor's ego to thrive, the empowered church organization must die. For the empowered church organization to thrive, the pastor's ego must die.

THE EXPANDABLE–POWER PIE

As a leader continues to cultivate humility, he is freed to understand and apply the principle of the expandable-power pie.[11] The principle contradicts the traditional and intuitive assumption that there is a fixed amount of power—that if one person has more power, then another person must have less. When leaders operate with this paradigm, they are naturally reluctant to share power.

The expandable-power–pie concept, however, means that when a leader gives away power, the total sum of power expands. It is not true that the leader has no "pie" left as he gives pieces away. On the contrary, the leader who gives away power can actually carry more influence in the organization. In short, the leader gains power by giving away power. After reviewing extensive research on organizational leadership, James Kouzes and Barry Posner observe: "Shared power results in higher job satisfaction and performance throughout the organization . . . the more everyone in the organization feels a sense of power and influence, the greater ownership and investment they feel in the success of the organization." The irony is that power-hungry leaders will never experience the exponential returns of the expandable-power–pie concept and in the end will wield less influence.

HEART-BUILDING EXERCISES: SET THREE

If we accept the concept of the expandable-power pie and the importance of humility, how practically do we go about starving our ego and giving away power and authority? Again, Kouzes and Posner are helpful in outlining four key tasks.[12] We will state these tasks in the form of questions and encourage pastors and staff teams to review them on a weekly basis.

- What important work on critical issues will I give away?
- How will I give people discretion and autonomy over their tasks and resources?
- When will I give visibility to others and provide recognition for their efforts?
- How will I help others build relationships, connecting them with powerful people and finding them sponsors and mentors?

Obviously the cultivation of humility will be accomplished on the heart level only through the leader's spiritual life and walk with God. These questions, however, will provide a clear diagnosis of the "ego factor." After providing a diagnosis, the same questions can be used to push the envelope on the practice of empowerment on a regular basis.

Building Connection

Challenge 4: *Empowerment necessitates close support and authentic community with other leaders.*
Empowerment priority: *Connect with others.*

The fourth dynamic of the challenge of empowerment confronts a leader's inordinate desire for isolation. Let's face it, many ministry leaders are so busy pouring out their lives for others that it can be difficult for them to enjoy true intimacy with others. The tendency (and temptation) to keep people at a safe distance on the journey of ministry can be a significant obstacle to empowerment.

Think back to the definition of empowerment as an intentional transfer of authority. The leader gives something away. When people receive a gift from someone, they ask, whether consciously or subconsciously, *What is meant by this gift? Is the gift a token of genuine kindness or a strategy for manipulation?* The context and closeness of the relationship largely determine the answer. In the same way, the leader who gives away authority must think through the context and atmosphere of the leader-to-leader relationship. If the leader does not cultivate the relationship, the one being empowered may feel used.

One of the most helpful nuggets I (Will) ever received from John Maxwell is the statement, "Touch a heart before you ask for a hand." Over the years this statement has burned into my mind as I seek to empower people for ministry. The more I act on it, the more my energies get multiplied through others. I have learned that life is too short and ministry is too difficult not to enjoy connecting with our fellow servants. Remember that empowerment involves giving away authority but keeping responsibility. The best way to do this is to share life together in the process!

The sheer volume of time that Jesus spent with his disciples is amazing. The record of the Gospels is a snapshot of Jesus and his men, fishing, talking, eating, walking, training, and ministering together. Imagine the connection and intimacy Jesus nurtured when he, as the Master, washed his disciples' feet. Robert Coleman observes: "Amazing as it may seem, all Jesus did to teach these men His way was to draw them close to himself. . . . Knowledge was gained by association before it was understood by explanation."[13] What was Jesus' ultimate objective with this strategy of close association? Great Commission empowerment! At the end of three-plus years of doing life and ministry together, he would release twelve men to spearhead the proclamation of the gospel in the world. Jesus connected with them before he empowered them.

Likewise, I try to develop a life-on-life relationship with any leader under my care. The types of activities we do together range from breakfast to racquetball to mountain biking to family dinners to late nights at the coffee shop. It is important that the leader, who is giving the authority, be the one to initiate times together and to discover points of common interest. Before looking for entirely new things to do together, try to find areas of overlap that exist already.

Years ago, when I first began to develop a relationship with Aubrey, I was impressed by his approachability despite his being a seminary professor and author. I can remember talking about life and ministry in between sets of lifting weights at the Baylor Fitness Center, located near the Dallas Seminary campus. One time I gleaned pointers from his romantic savvy as he showed me a very creative valentine gift package he was preparing for his wife. (I was taking mental notes as fast as I could!) Don't underestimate the importance of connections like these when building a relationship that is conducive to empowerment.

CONNECTING WITH OTHERS THROUGH INCREASED LOVE

A basic question that every Christian leader should ask is *Do I love leading more than I love the people I lead?* or *Do I love serving more than I love the people I serve?* At critical points in my (Will's) development as a leader, God has rebuked me through this question, and I have found the same is true for other leaders. As with the other fruits of the Spirit we have discussed—faith, patience, and humility—increasing love takes much time and reflection, as each leader grows in his or her personal relationship with Christ. The following questions are designed to foster reflection as you walk the journey toward genuine concern and love for those you lead.

- Do you spend time with your ministry leaders outside of ministry?
- How often do you pray with or for your leaders?
- What level of intimacy do you experience within your own family?
- What type of atmosphere do you create when you walk into a room?
- Who will attend your funeral without looking at his or her watch?
- How well do you listen to others day in and day out?

As you seek to design and implement a leader-development process, these kinds of questions will rescue you from a "manufacturing perspective." Leaders are people and they cannot be developed and empowered in an assembly-line fashion. The process is organic and not mechanical—like growing a garden. Strive to cultivate authentic community and genuine concern and you will create rich soil in which leaders can grow and blossom.

HEART-BUILDING EXERCISES: SET FOUR

A practical exercise in building connection with others is to think about how well you know them and then design purposeful interaction to get to know them better. This practice is a very simple way to create bonds with those around you. For example, a new intern came into my (Will's) office last week. She will probably be around for only three months. Despite the short duration of her ministry season with us, my first two agenda items with this intern are relational, not functional. First, I asked a female colleague to arrange a lunch appointment for the three of us so that I can get to know the intern better. Second, I asked the intern to take a temperament indicator so that I can learn a little about how she is wired. I believe that the front-end investment of building the relationship will set the stage for her to grow and be productive under my leadership.

In designing purposeful interaction to connect with others, use the following list of questions as a guide. (Please keep in mind that some of these questions may not be suitable for opposite-sex interaction in a ministry context.)[14]

- What are the key details of my colleague's heritage?
- What communicates importance and concern to him or her?
- What is his or her personality or temperament?
- What are his or her current practices with spiritual disciplines?
- Who has influenced my colleague's life? How?
- What books or literature has impacted his or her life? How?
- What are his or her areas of disappointment?
- What are the areas of joy?
- What does my colleague aspire to become and do?
- What are his or her fears?
- What are his or her primary temptations?
- What is his or her history with the church?

These questions can serve as a guide for getting to know others. For example, fifteen minutes before meeting with an individual, review this list of questions with the person in mind. Then choose a question or two to ask and thus fill in your knowledge gaps and build the relationship.

The leader's world can be very intense, which often defines his or her conversations with others in a way that limits the dialogue and personal connection. The questions above can thwart self-centered tendencies by helping a "world swap" take place in the leader's mind. That is, they help the leader get out of his or her own world and into the world of the other person. My favorite "world swap" activity is a kind of guessing game. Before meeting with a leader, I will guess the two or three most important subjects bouncing around in that leader's mind at that time. My guesses will be the first points of discussion and interaction. For me, this simple practice has helped tremendously in building relationships that lead to empowering others.

Moses Overcomes the Challenge

In the introduction we discussed the leadership advice Moses received from his father-in-law in Exodus 18. As a result, Moses took huge steps to empower others in the community of God's people. You will recall that Moses was the primary decision maker for the entire nation. All of that changed when he selected, developed, and empowered several levels of leadership—leaders of ten, fifty, one hundred, and one thousand people.

Imagine, for just a moment, the challenges Moses must have encountered in setting up the system of leadership. With the innumerable unknown outcomes of involving hundreds of other leaders in the decision-making process, Moses could have let the fear of uncertainty cripple him, but he moved forward with faith. Also, he faced a huge "slowing down" window. It was already taking him all day to serve the needs of his weary people. How in the world could he invest the time in training others to lead? But Moses was patient, and he saw the long-term efficiency that would be gained; he saw a better way to serve, and he chose to slow down to speed up.

Moses could have let his ego get in the way. After all, it must feel pretty important to be *the* decision maker for an entire nation! But Scripture tells us that Moses was a humble man, and we see this humility in action through his willingness to empower others.

Finally, Moses could have been unwilling to face the relational demands of connecting with other leaders. But if his relationship with Joshua is any clue, we know that Moses was able to connect with others. Between Exodus 17 and Joshua 22, Joshua and Moses are mentioned in the same verse twenty-seven times. Many of these illustrate directly or imply a close association. Moses, the man who walked in unique intimacy with God, must have walked in unique intimacy with others as well.

The following chart summarizes the challenges of empowerment.

The Challenges of Empowerment

Empowerment Dynamic	Leader's Inordinate Desire	Empowerment Priority	Area of Heart Building
Empowerment increases the scope of unknown ministry outcomes.	Control	Embrace uncertainty.	Faith
Empowerment requires a sacrifice of short-term ministry efficiency.	Expediency	Slow down to speed up.	Patience
Empowerment requires giving away authority that previously provided the basis of personal ministry success.	Power	Starve your ego.	Humility
Empowerment necessitates close support and authentic community with other leaders.	Isolation	Connect with others.	Love

Questions for Reflection and Discussion

1. In reviewing the definition of empowerment, think through the times you have felt most empowered. Who empowered you and why did you feel empowered?
2. What tendencies do you have when it comes to the alternatives to empowerment—abdicating, directing, and disabling?
3. What specific empowerment dynamic are you facing right now?
4. Review the heart-building exercise for the empowerment dynamic you are currently facing. With whom can you share this material for accountability and continued learning?

Part 2

Following the Blueprints

Practices for Developing Leaders

4

How Jesus Developed Leaders

*What the Savior Teaches Us
about Leadership Development, Part 1*

Scripture is for Christian leaders what a blueprint is for a building contractor. Therefore, when we design and build a leadership-development process, it's imperative that we turn to God's Word for direction. The information in this part of the book is important to any leadership-development process because it provides the critical biblical and theological foundation that should influence our thinking. Thus it serves both to inform and, in some cases, to direct the process. If we profess to be people of the Word, we must not only live but lead by the Word.

What can we learn about training leaders as we study Jesus' ministry to his disciples in the Gospels? The answer forms the content and direction of this chapter. First, we will discover that Jesus' ministry to his disciples consisted of at least three phases. From these we can deduce several leadership-training practices and some principles. We've chosen the term *practices* carefully. In most cases biblical principles are based on biblical prescripts or commands that usually require obedience. However, biblical practices, drawn from descriptive passages, aren't necessarily binding. Jesus' leadership-development principles are binding on us, whereas his practices are not. We're free to follow or not follow them—wisdom should prevail. However, we'll always find them unusually helpful as well as insightful and wise.[1]

We'll begin by briefly examining the three development phases Jesus used to move his disciples from unbelieving seekers to committed leaders. Then we'll distill four instructive leadership-development steps that surface within the three phases. They are the recruitment, selection, training, and deployment of leaders.

The Savior's Leadership-Development Phases

Phase 1: From Seeking to Believing

Phase 1 of Jesus' leadership development takes place at the beginning of his public ministry. It focuses primarily on Jesus' pursuit and conversion of five men who were seekers and, in a sense, followers but not yet believers. This process, during Christ's Judean ministry, is recorded in John 1–4. It raises several questions: Who was involved in this initial recruitment of leaders? What did Jesus want them to do? What was the purpose of this initial recruitment?

In response to John the Baptist's announcement that Jesus was the Lamb of God, Andrew and most likely John began to follow Jesus (John 1:36). They inquired where Jesus lived and began following him when he invited them to come and see (vv. 38–39). After spending a day with the Savior, Andrew went and recruited his brother Simon Peter (vv. 40–42). The next day Christ found Philip and invited him to follow too (v. 43). Then Philip, in turn, found Nathanael and invited him to come and see (vv. 45–46).

We can take Jesus' words (v. 39) and then Philip's words (v. 46), "Come and see," both literally and figuratively. Jesus is in the early stages of inaugurating his ministry and wants them to come and see where he is staying so they can spend some time with him. John follows up on the seeing metaphor and uses the term numerous times in his writing to mean seeing or understanding spiritual truth (1:48, 50, 51; 4:29). This is important because the purpose of John's Gospel and its miraculous signs, according to John 20:30–31, is "that you may believe that Jesus is the Christ, the Son of God, and that by believing you may have life in his name." The disciples were present when Jesus performed his first miracle (2:2–11). Apparently they "saw" and put their faith in him as Messiah and Savior (v. 11).

Jesus' invitation to Philip, "Follow me," most likely was given to all five disciples.[2] In phase 2 of Jesus' work with the disciples, he calls them with a promise: "I will make you fishers of men" (Mark 1:17). But phase 1 is primarily a time for the disciples to come to faith and to spend time with Jesus (John 1:39; 3:22), growing in their faith and knowledge—"seeing" him. Evidently this initial phase didn't require them to leave their professions, because when Jesus calls them at the beginning of phase 2, he finds them fishing. Thus phase 1 was a time of spiritual preparation that led up to phase 2.

Phase 2: From Believing to Following

Jesus' choice of his disciples marks the beginning of phase 2, when he shifted his public ministry to Galilee. In phase 1 the disciples were seekers who became believers. Now as believers they desire to follow him differently—not as seekers but as committed followers.

In this phase, unlike the rabbis who were pursued by their pupils, Jesus took the initiative and pursued the disciples he wanted to follow him. The group included Simon, Andrew, James, John (Matt. 4:18–22), and, later, Matthew (9:9–13). The list is somewhat different from those he called in phase 1. James is here, but Philip and Nathanael are not mentioned. We find Philip included again in phase 3.

How could they know if they were truly his disciples? What was the evidence? According to John, the evidence was threefold. True disciples manifest three characteristics: They abide in his Word (John 8:31–32), they love one another (13:34–35), and they bear fruit (15:8, 16). During this phase his disciples would pass this test.

What is the Savior's plan for them now? In Matthew 4:18–22, Mark 1:16–20, and Luke 5:1–11, Jesus issued a command followed by a promise: "Follow me, and I'll make you fishers of men." He's saying that it's time to "fish or cut bait" (no pun intended). In phase 1 they accepted him as Messiah and came through a recruitment period when they spent some time getting to know him. Now it's time to decide if they will leave behind their current way of life (fishing for fish) and commit to following him (fishing for men) for the rest of their lives.

This would require the disciples to leave their former occupations and work with the Savior full-time, spending most of their waking hours with him. It's important to observe that this phase is descriptive, not prescriptive. It's not teaching that all disciples who are serious about serving the Savior must quit their jobs and pursue ministry full-time to be his leaders. This is a decision that all leaders make privately as God directs them individually. Some will lead and minister full-time, while other, equally committed disciples will lead and minister part-time.

Phase 3: From Following to Leading

Phase 3 begins during Jesus' Galilean ministry and lasts into his Perean ministry. In phase 2 Jesus invited five disciples as new believers to commit to following him. In phase 3 he appoints as apostles and thus leaders certain of his disciples who are committed followers (Matt. 10:2–4; Mark 3:13–19; Luke 6:12–19). This was not a casual event. Before making this selection, Jesus spent the entire night in prayer to the Father (Luke 6:12–13). As we study this phase, we want to know who these men are, what makes them different, and what the Savior's plan is for them as leaders.

Jesus' ministry had attracted many disciples (Mark 2:15). However, in phase 3, he chose to pour his life into a core of twelve (Luke 6:13). Three of the Gospels record their names for us. According to Mark's Gospel, they are Simon Peter, James, John, Andrew, Philip, Bartholomew, Matthew, Thomas, James, Thaddeus, Simon the Zealot, and Judas. Though in phase 2 the text doesn't mention Philip and Nathanael, Philip appears here in the list of the Twelve. Nathanael does not show up in the final cut. Perhaps he opted to go in another direction after experiencing the initial phase.

Of the Twelve, Peter, James, and John, who were with Jesus through phases 1 and 2, stand out (Matt. 17:1; 26:37; Mark 9:2; 14:33; Luke 9:28). Perhaps they were part of an inner circle of his disciples who had more potential as leaders than the others. This would seem to be the case as they ministered later in Acts.

Before a person can be a leader, he or she must be a disciple (believer) and a committed follower. One may be a committed follower but not necessarily a leader, and Jesus didn't invite the disciples to become leaders right away. In phase 1 five seekers believed in and spent some time with Jesus. Eventually they drifted back to their professions. In phase 2 the disciples made a permanent commitment to follow Jesus and they left their professions. In phase 3 Jesus makes a commitment to pour his life into the Twelve, training them to be apostles and leaders.

According to Mark 3:14–15, Jesus appointed the Twelve for two purposes: "that they might be with him and that he might send them out to preach and to have authority to drive out demons." Now they were part of his ministry. We learn from Matthew 10:5 that their association with the Savior implied that he would train and thus develop them. This began immediately as recorded in Matthew 10:5–11:1 where he instructed them on whom to minister to (10:5–6), how to minister (11:7–8), what to take with them (11: 9–10), as well as other matters pertinent to their ministry. He would continue to teach them for much of the rest of his time on earth. For example, in Matthew 16–18 he instructed the Twelve on such topics as discipleship (16:22–28), the kingdom (17:1–8), dependence (17:14–21), humility (18:1–5), and pride (18:6–14). Later he gave them lessons on wealth (Luke 16), forgiveness

(17:1–4), service (17:7–10), thankfulness (17:11–19), prayer (18:1–14), and other vital topics.

Not only did Jesus train his disciples for ministry, he sent them out to do ministry—his ministry. He didn't isolate them in some class-room somewhere, totally separated from actual ministry in the field. Instead, Jesus taught them in the context of ministry. They learned while doing. They would make mistakes, most of which had to do with their lack of faith (Matt. 8:26; 17:19–20; and other passages), but that didn't seem to matter to the Savior as long as they learned from their mistakes.

Several other practices of Jesus' ministry to the disciples are notewor-thy. One is that eventually he sent the disciples out in twos (Mark 6:7; 11:1; 14:13). He did this for two reasons. The first is practical. A team of persons is much more effective than one person. As Ecclesiastes 4:9–10 says: "Two are better than one, because they have a good return for their work: If one falls down, his friend can help him up. But pity the man who falls and has no one to help him up!" The second is legal. The witness of two people was superior to that of one (John 8:17).

Another noteworthy practice of Jesus was his giving his disciples power as leaders in ministry. Not only did Jesus give them power for their ministries (in this case to cast out demons and heal diseases), but he also granted them the authority to exercise that power (Luke 9:1). He understood that there is no power without authority.

We've seen here that Jesus chose to develop his disciples as leaders in three phases. The number of phases probably isn't important. As we develop leaders, we could use two, three, or perhaps four phases. What's instructive is that Jesus intentionally moved a core of his followers from seeking unbelievers to committed leaders.

We know that not all Christians who are committed believers will be leaders in our churches, but many of them will be. Consequently it is wise to have in place a developmental process that articulates and explains all the phases through which people move from seeking un-believers to followers, and some move on to committed leaders. We know of no spiritually healthy churches in North America that haven't developed such a process.

Development Phases of Jesus' Disciples

Phase 1: Seekers to Believers

Phase 2: Believers to Followers

Phase 3: Followers to Leaders

The Savior's Leadership-Development Steps

Today's leaders and those who develop them can learn much from Jesus' ministry with and to his disciples. The three phases of Jesus' ministry reveal how he cultivated his disciples as they moved from unbelieving seekers to committed leaders. Again, we must remember that much of this material is descriptive, not prescriptive. Thus Jesus and the Gospel writers aren't telling us that we have to do it the way the Savior did it. He gives us much freedom in how we develop leaders out of disciples. However, we can learn from what Jesus did.

We have seen that Jesus' leadership development occurred in three phases. It may be even more helpful to note that it consisted of four basic steps: recruitment, selection, training, and deployment of leaders. Just as these steps proved helpful in Jesus' day, they also can be most instructive as we cultivate leaders in the twenty-first century.

Step 1: Recruitment

Jesus recruited the disciples as leaders. Without recruitment, he would have had no disciples to train. In practice he accomplished this in two ways and prescribed a third for his disciples. First, in the first phase of his ministry, some, such as Andrew and probably John, sought him out and asked to be his disciple (John 1:35–40). This practice was typical of the rabbi-disciple relationship of the first century. A pupil who desired to train with a particular rabbi would ask to be allowed to follow him.

Second, unlike the rabbis, Jesus took the initiative and sought his own followers in phases 1 and 2. Thus he found Philip and invited him to follow (John 1:43). He did the same with Andrew, Peter, James, and John (Mark 1:16–19). This is recruitment by invitation.

Finally, in Matthew 9:36–37, shortly before he commenced phase 3, Jesus saw the downcast and distressed multitudes, felt compassion for them, and instructed his disciples: "The harvest is plentiful but the workers are few. Ask the Lord of the harvest, therefore, to send out workers into his harvest field." He instructed his disciples to pray for workers, teaching that prayer is the key to any recruitment effort.

If we are to shape leaders, we have little choice but to involve ourselves in the leadership recruitment business. Many church leaders attempt to recruit workers in general and other leaders in particular by making an announcement from the pulpit or in the church bulletin. When we take this approach, we usually get one of two responses. Either no people respond or the wrong people respond.

Jesus teaches that we should recruit the leaders we want to develop; however, he doesn't prescribe how we're to do this. His example provides two good approaches for recruiting people we believe will be valuable assets to our leadership team. Like Jesus we should recruit those who come to us on their own initiative and express a genuine, God-given interest in our giving them leadership training. The Christian who has little interest in serving Christ won't seek us out for leadership development. However, those who desire to move forward and grow in Christ will often seek our training.

The second approach is to pursue competent, godly people who show great promise of becoming leaders. We would be wise to keep on the lookout for these people and go after them when we find them. They often network with other leaders (John 1:40–45). Thus, where you find one leader, there may be additional potential leaders.

Finally, Jesus' point in Matthew 9:36–37 is that the time to pursue lost people is now. The problem is that not enough people are doing it. Since prayer is foundational to our recruitment process, this approach of praying and asking God to recruit more workers is basic.

Step 2: Selection

In phases 2 and 3 of his ministry to his disciples, Jesus selected the ones he would train to be leaders. In phase 2 the Savior selected five men (Simon, Andrew, James, John, and, later, Matthew) to be his disciples. Matthew 4:18–20 tells the story of how Jesus was walking beside the Sea of Galilee when he saw Simon and Andrew fishing. We might mistakenly assume from the text that Jesus was out taking a casual walk when he just happened to come across these two brothers. Jesus, being the omniscient God-man, was not simply out taking a walk. He knew what he was doing and where these two men would be. This event has intentionality written all over it. Obviously he had selected them to be his disciples and was going there with the intention of inviting them to be "fishers of men."

In phase 3 Jesus selected the Twelve as his apostles and leaders of the future church. Again, Jesus is intentional. He had spent the entire night in prayer (Luke 6:12), and the next day he called his disciples to him and designated them apostles and thus leaders (v. 13). His ministry to the crowd had produced a number of disciples (Mark 2:15; Luke 6:17), but at this point he is focusing on the core, a committed group of people who would serve with him full time.

Most of his prayer vigil must have been concerning these Twelve, whom he selected either prior to or during this prayer event. It is no surprise that before selecting and appointing his disciples as leaders and deploying them in ministry, Jesus prayed for them. What is surprising, however, is that he prayed to the Father all night. The implication from the position of the passage in its context is that he prayed about and for the disciples whom he was about to choose and send out for ministry. Jesus continued to pray for his leaders. A great example is his prayer in John 17:9–19 in which he prayed for their preservation (v. 11), especially from the evil one (v. 15), and for their sanctification (vv. 17, 19).

The principle is that leader-developers are wise to bathe their leadership-selection process in much prayer. Since the passage is descriptive, not prescriptive, we don't have to assume that Jesus is teaching that we must pray all night when selecting new leaders. If Jesus prayed all night, however, it underlines how vital prayer is to the leadership-selection process. In Philippians 4:6 Paul commands, "Do not be anxious about anything, but in everything, by prayer and petition, with thanksgiving, present your requests to God."

In addition, we must not forget to pray for our new leaders once they launch their ministries. Our training of new leaders for ministry obligates us to pray for them while they are leading those ministries. If we model our prayer after that of Jesus in John 17:9–19, we will pray for their preservation and their sanctification.

Each time Jesus selected a disciple, nothing was left to happenstance. He selected disciples with intention, for he had present and future plans for them. What were their qualifications? All except Judas were men of faith. At least six and probably all had been with him as his disciples prior to his prayer in Luke 6:12. We know this was the case with Peter, Andrew, James, John, Philip, and Matthew (Matt. 4:18–22; 9:9–13).

Step 3: Training

Though Jesus ministered to the crowd, he focused on and trained the core. Jesus began his public ministry (phase 1) with a small core of disciples. As his ministry moved into its second and third years, increasingly he turned his attention to these disciples, who were now his leaders. Finally, with his rejection by the Jews, he turned from his public ministry and focused his attention on the core of twelve. This involved preparing these leaders for their ministry following his death and resurrection (Matt. 19–20; Luke 14–19; John 10–11).

What can we learn about training leaders from the way Jesus trained his core of disciples? He believed that leadership training was vital to the success of his ministry during his time on earth and later. Thus it was important that he spend much time in developing leaders for the kingdom. He trained his disciples before sending them out to minister.

Matthew 10:5 says, "These twelve Jesus sent out after instructing them" (NASB). And Jesus continued to instruct them while they ministered. John's Gospel records more of Jesus' instructions to his disciples than any of the other Gospels. In particular, chapters 13–17 concentrate on his training of the Twelve and demonstrate as well his constant ministry to his serving disciples.

It would be wise for today's leaders to focus on and develop the core and not the crowd. Good leaders will always attract crowds. However, those crowds often prove fickle and eventually fall away because so many are following out of their own self-interests. Jesus committed his life to the Twelve because he knew that they, not the crowd, would make a difference that would have eternal consequences. Jesus' example teaches us that the size of our core, not the crowd, is what ultimately counts in ministry and will honor him over the long haul. We can measure our success not by the numbers of people we attract but by our relating to and training a competent, godly core of leaders who will have significant ministries long after we have been forgotten.

It is also wise that today's churches develop their leaders before and after they assume their ministry. While leaders learn much while doing ministry, they, like the disciples, benefit as well from preparation before practice. However, preparation should last only so long before the leaders are immersed in ministry. This is the mistake that seminaries make. Far too many attempt to train leaders in the classroom for three or four years with very little time in ministry. The result is that graduates finish the program with a piece of paper that says they can do ministry, but since they've really never done ministry, no one is sure of their competence.

Good leaders never stop learning. If they do, they cease to lead well. It's imperative that they continue to learn long after they begin their ministries. Therefore, any good leadership program must continue to train its leaders even while they pursue their ministries.

Step 4: Deployment

As we noted above, phase 1 of Jesus' leadership-development process was a kind of discipleship exploratory phase, after which the disciples apparently returned to their occupations, specifically fishing. Consequently Jesus' initial call didn't result in a long-term deployment. However, after phase 2, Jesus indicated that his plan was to deploy the disciples to be full-time fishers of men. Then in phase 3 Matthew's Gospel becomes most specific. First, Jesus appointed the Twelve, and right before deploying them he instructed them as apostles and leaders to go only to Israel (Matt. 10:5–6); he gave them their mandate or precise message and ministry (vv. 7–8), told them what they can and can't take on their journey (vv. 9–10), and added other specifics.

Then Jesus deployed or sent out the Twelve to reach the world. The mandate had changed. In Mark 16:15, well after Israel had rejected him, Jesus instructed his disciples: "Go into all the world and preach the good news to all creation." In Matthew 28:19–20 he instructed them to "make disciples." The Book of Acts records how the Twelve and their disciples accomplished this. One conclusion is that Jesus didn't merely win converts but followed them up with training that eventually led to actual deployment in ministry.

The leaders of today's churches must not only win lost people to Christ but train them as well, especially those with leadership potential, and see that they are deployed in ministry. Far too often we pursue a person only until he or she accepts Christ. It's imperative as well that we pursue and mobilize people to maturity and deployment in ministry. In the Great Commission (Matt. 28:19–20), Jesus' imperative is to "make disciples." This means making and maturing believers. Thus deployment involves our winning lost people to faith in Christ and then moving them to spiritual maturity. God has gifted all to serve him and some specifically to lead for him. Deployment is key to seeing disciples become involved in leading a particular ministry.

Jesus' Leadership Training Steps

Recruitment

Selection

Training

Deployment

Questions for Reflection and Discussion

1. In the past how have you recruited your core leaders for leadership training? Are you satisfied with this approach? If not, how do you plan to alter your recruitment efforts in light of Jesus' approach?
2. Has prayer for your leaders and leader-trainees been an emphasis in your private and personal ministry? If yes, how? If no, why not and will it be in the future?
3. Has the focus of your leadership development been the core or the crowd? (Preachers tend to focus on the crowd, not the core.)

If the crowd, are you willing to focus on the core? Who are the core people in your ministry?

4. Have you attempted to develop your core leaders in the past? If yes, what have you done? What have you learned from the Savior's example that you may do differently in the future?

5. Do your plans for leadership development include the deployment of the new leaders in ministry? How do you plan to accomplish this?

5

How Jesus Used Metaphors to Develop Leaders

What the Savior Teaches Us about Leadership Development, Part 2

While discussing the leadership practices of the early church, we ask what for some will be a provocative question. If leadership development is so critical to Jesus and the early church, why didn't he use terms like *leader* and *leadership*? If Jesus didn't use these terms explicitly, what terms did he use to convey the concept and various nuances of leadership to his disciples?

Aristotle said that the mind thinks in pictures. This very basic yet profound insight is one key in understanding Jesus' strategy in communication. As a teacher, Jesus did more than explain truth; he painted "truth pictures" in the mind's eye of his followers. He created these truth pictures primarily through stories (parables) and metaphorical language. For example, Jesus told common stories about seeds, vines, and soil with characters such as farmers, merchants, and bandits as he described the kingdom of God. He used concrete objects like pearls, coins, and lamps to teach spiritual realities. Jesus referred to his followers as salt and light. The Gospel of John records several of Jesus' "I am" statements including "the light of the world," "the bread of life," "the gate for the sheep," "the good shepherd," and "the way." Warren Wiersbe observes, "It's by using metaphorical language that you turn people's

ears into eyes and help them to see the truth."[1] This was exactly Jesus'
strategy as he instructed people primarily with metaphorical language
and everyday imagery.

Jesus also used this method for developing his disciples as leaders.
He never referenced a "leadership manual" with his disciples, but he
did use fresh imagery from life to convey leadership principles. In the
context of leadership development, the most significant imagery he used
was metaphors that described his followers. David Bennett highlights
this observation in his work *Metaphors for Ministry*:

> Even if we cannot find paragraphs in which Jesus delineates detailed
> job descriptions for future leadership of the disciples in the Jerusalem
> church, we can find passages that describe the impact that he expected
> them to have on the lives of other people. Many of the insights we
> need are embedded in the images which Jesus used to describe his
> followers.[2]

The purpose of this chapter is to review the key metaphors that Jesus
used to paint truth pictures with regard to his followers and to draw
implications for leadership development in the church today.

Before going to the metaphors, it is helpful to note that every metaphor that Jesus used falls into two general categories: metaphors that
emphasize community and those that emphasize cause.[3] While these
categories are somewhat arbitrary, they are helpful "hooks" for beginning to think along this line.

The first category—emphasizing community—includes the metaphors
of brother (and sister), son, child, the Twelve, wedding guest, and sheep.
The second category—emphasizing cause—divides further to include
both "people" metaphors and "thing" metaphors. People metaphors
emphasizing cause include servant, shepherd, harvester, apostle, and
fisherman. Thing metaphors emphasizing cause include soil, branch
(of a vine), wheat, salt, and light.

Jesus' Metaphors for His Followers

Community Oriented	Cause Oriented	
	People	Things
brother (sister)	servant	soil
son/child	shepherd	branch (of a vine)
the Twelve	harvester	wheat
wedding guest	apostle	salt
sheep	fisherman	light

Let's now take a closer look at this list of metaphors. Our purpose is not to provide a detailed description of the terms but rather to scan them in an effort to find common themes that correlate with leadership development in the church.[4]

Community-Oriented Metaphors

We have used the idea of community to categorize the first set of metaphors. The idea of community is very broad and encompasses the concept of intimacy with God and others. The term speaks to the human capacity for relationship on both a horizontal and vertical axis, the horizontal representing fellowship with believers and the vertical representing communion with God.

Jesus uses the closest family relationships to signify the deep bond and love that his followers should have with and for one another. Topping the list is *brother*, which Jesus used frequently (see Matt. 5:21–26, 43–48; 7:1–5; 12:48–50; 18:15–35; 23:8; 28:10). *Sister* is a similar term (see Matt. 12:48–50; Mark 3:33–35). Siblings can do nothing to change their identity as such. They are connected by virtue of their source and the blood running through their veins. My (Will's) brother, although he lives a thousand miles away, is one of the closest relationships in my life. He knows my deepest joys, hurts, and failures. The connection between followers of Christ should be as strong and tight as the connection between blood brothers. Based on this relationship, followers of Christ should always forgive, even in the face of repeated offense (Matt. 18:15–35), and should view themselves as equals and not as superior to one another (23:8).

Another family term is *son* or *child*. Using the metaphor of offspring, Jesus is emphasizing not only a deep bond but also the family resemblance between a parent and child. In Matthew 5:45–48 Jesus instructs his followers to "be perfect . . . as your heavenly Father is perfect," just after referring to them as "sons of your Father in heaven." There are several other passages in which Jesus uses *son* or *child* to describe his followers, including Matthew 5:9; 13:38; Luke 6:35; and 20:36. This image is further reinforced by more than twenty-five stand-alone references to God as Father in the Gospels, including the familiar "Our Father," the introduction to the model prayer in Matthew 6:9.

While the terms for siblings and children describe relationships defined by birth, Jesus also described followers with relationship images defined by personal choice. These terms include *the Twelve* and terms associated with wedding ceremonies. Jesus uses the term *the Twelve* to describe his closest group of disciples in John 6:70. In doing so he emphasizes his own initiative in selecting them while adding symbolic significance to the group, based on the tribal leadership heritage of Israel.

Jesus uses wedding imagery several times to describe his followers. In Matthew 22:1–14 his followers are compared to those who respond willingly to a wedding banquet invitation. They are not invited because of any status they possess. Therefore, they distinguish themselves simply by their desire to be present at the celebration. In Luke 5:34 Jesus compares his disciples to "guests of the bridegroom" at a wedding. This reference highlights close comradeship in a context of a significant life celebration. Both of these images draw on the theme of friendship as they describe voluntary association.

A final relationship-oriented metaphor Jesus uses is that of sheep. This image is one of vulnerability. Sheep need constant protection, care, and guidance (Matt. 10:16; Mark 14:27; Luke 12:32). Jesus, of course, is the good shepherd and provides for his sheep to the extent of "laying down his life" (John 10:11). While this metaphor conveys primarily the dependence of the sheep on the shepherd, it also speaks to the significance of sheep living "in community" as a flock. Together they share a common need for guidance and find the provision through one source—the shepherd. Therefore, the sheep metaphor speaks to both the relationship between Christ and his followers and the relationship of his followers to one another.

Cause-Oriented Metaphors

Cause-oriented metaphors are images that convey the idea of living with purposeful activity. In physics class we learned that speed and direction are two separate characteristics of an object in motion. It is entirely possible to describe the speed of an object even though the direction is unclear. But if an object has both a defined speed and direction, the combination is described as velocity. In a similar way cause-oriented metaphors are "velocity images." They reflect a sense of both purposeful direction and activity.

People Metaphors

The first set of terms that emphasize cause are images of people in various roles: servant, shepherd, harvester, messenger, and fisherman. As we scan these terms, we notice how each role carries implicitly a sense of purposeful action. The servant metaphor, from the Greek word *diakonos*, denotes the role of table waiter. Jesus employs this metaphor to convey the importance of acts of personal service and the attitude of humility (Matt. 18:4; 23:11; Mark 9:35; 10:35–45; Luke 12:37; 17:8; John 12:24–26).

Jesus also uses the image of shepherd. Although he refers to himself as a shepherd, he also refers to his follower Peter as a shepherd in John 21:15–17. Here Jesus emphasizes the care and spiritual provision that Peter is to offer as a leader among God's flock (his fellow believers).

The next metaphor is harvester. Jesus uses the imagery of the harvest in Matthew 9:37–38 (although he uses a general term for worker in this context). In John 4, after the account of the woman at the well, Jesus tells his disciples that the fields are ripe for harvest, adding, "I sent you to reap what you have not worked for" (v. 38). In both texts Jesus uses this metaphor to focus on the size of the task and the sheer amount of the work to be done as it relates to the work of ministry. In verse 35 there is also the sense of anticipation and reward that comes from a bountiful crop.

Another role Jesus describes is that of messenger (Luke 6:13; John 13:16–17). This idea is derived from the term *apostle*, which means "a messenger who is sent." The messenger metaphor has two strong connotations. The first emphasis is on the authority of the one who does the sending. The second emphasis is on the privilege of being authorized to speak as a representative of an important person.

The final metaphor in the list of roles is that of fisherman. Jesus related the act of following him with that of being a "fisher of men" in Matthew 4:19; Mark 1:17; and Luke 5:10. The impact of this metaphor is its focus on reaching people. For Peter (as well as for James and John), as a vocational fisherman, it held special significance because it signaled the break from a previous way of life. He went from catching fish to "catching" men.

Images of Things

The second set of terms that emphasize cause is images of things: soil, branches, salt, light, and wheat. In each case Jesus uses the image to describe how his followers should live. These metaphors reflect cause by virtue of the intentional growth, influence, and dispersion that the object or thing creates.[5] They are missional at their core. Followers are good soil that nourishes plants and produces a harvest thirty, sixty, or one hundred times what was sown (Matt. 13:1–23; Mark 4:1–20). Followers are branches sprouting forth with fruit as they remain in vital union with Jesus, the vine (John 15). In the world, followers are salt, which permeates and influences by preserving and enhancing flavor

(Matt. 5:13; Luke 14:34). Followers are light that invades the darkness, drawing others to glorify the Father (Matt. 5:14–16; Luke 16:8; John 12:36). And finally, followers are wheat seed that grows, lives in proximity to the world (Matt. 13:24–30, 36–43), and is willing to end its life through sacrifice by falling to the ground and dying to produce more life (John 12:24).

Each of these images carries the idea of creating a new reality or disrupting the status quo. In this sense they promote the cause-oriented kingdom movement that Jesus came to establish.

Observations for Leadership Development

When Jesus used these metaphors to describe his followers, he was indirectly providing guidelines for leadership development. We will attempt to draw out these guidelines and suggest specific implications we see for leadership in the church.[6]

Balance of High Expectations

Jesus could have used metaphors that emphasize only the growth of strong relationships among his followers, or he could have used language to reveal only his expectation of radical actions from his followers. The fact is that Jesus used both types of metaphor, and it is his equal emphasis of healthy relationships (community) and productive tasks (cause) in his followers that is worth considering further.

The wide range of relationship images raises the bar of expectation when it comes to developing intimacy with God and others. Believers should live with a deep bond to one another as brothers and sisters under the rule of their Father in heaven. Their close connection as children of God should be seen in their family resemblance to the Father's character. But they are not "stuck" together in family relationship—they are the Twelve, making the intentional choice of being together. They are like groomsmen and bridesmaids at a wedding banquet, sharing the joy of deep mutual affection. They are God's sheep, equally dependent on the good shepherd for their sustenance.

But don't think that Jesus' message was only about "holding hands" and "warm fuzzies." He built his community around a radical cause that is balanced by another set of metaphors. Think of the roles of servant, shepherd, messenger, harvester, and fisherman, each an image of action and hard work. In the term *servant*, we see a table waiter bringing plates of food and filling empty glasses; in *harvester*, we see the glistening brow of a worker in the field; and so on. While each of these terms holds a special significance of its own, the common thread is that they all represent action, a task being accomplished.

Or think of the images of soil, branches, salt, light, and wheat. These metaphors are especially powerful because of the inherent sense of accountability they express. Each can be seen as effective or ineffective. And Jesus paints the contrasting pictures with great artistry—good or bad soil (Matt. 13:1–23), fruitful or unfruitful branches (John 15:1–11), good salt or salt that has lost its saltiness (Matt. 5:13), a glowing lamp on a stand or hidden under a container (vv. 14–16).

When a follower of Christ reflects on these terms, he or she is faced with an immediate context for self-evaluation and asks, *Am I having impact on the world around me the way Christ wants me to have impact?* For example, if Jesus is likening his followers to branches, the metaphor almost forces the listener to assess whether he or she is a fruitful branch. Therefore, the metaphor challenges believers to get connected to God's cause in the world. Jesus chose language intentionally to push people out of their comfort zones.

If Jesus expected his disciples as future leaders of the church to pursue healthy relationships (community) and productive tasks (cause), shouldn't this same expectation be expressed in the design of leadership development in the church? We believe it should, and we also believe the hard part of the work is to create and maintain a healthy balance between the two.

IMPLICATION FOR LEADERSHIP

Because Jesus expects both healthy relationships and productive tasks, the church must maintain a healthy balance of "community" and "cause" in the leadership-development process. Unfortunately, it is not uncommon for a church leadership culture to drift one way or the other on the community-cause balance.

I (Will) recently met with a ten-member executive staff team of a church with more than five thousand people in weekly attendance. This was the first meeting in a six-month consulting process. Usually I begin with a community-building focus to get to know the pastors better. (And the interaction is a significant part of my assessment.) This time the community-building quickly absorbed the first hour of our meeting. I was somewhat surprised by the staff's eagerness to share, and I soon found myself struggling to reel in the group to stay on track. The same day I spent time one-on-one with two of the staff members. They both indicated how refreshing it was to be able to talk freely in the executive staff meeting. As I probed further, I discovered that the team is so task focused that they rarely enjoy time just being together.

In such a church, the leadership culture drifts toward cause and leaves the leaders relationally malnourished. The following diagram illustrates this dynamic. The increased area of the shape representing cause expands as organization develops. Early in the life of the church the balance may have existed, but over time the sense of cause eclipses the sense of community. As a result, the measure of good leadership becomes "making things happen" to the neglect of promoting healthy relationships.

Cause-Dominated Leadership Development

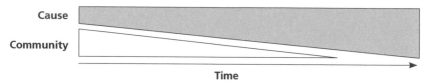

A similar dynamic can occur in the opposite direction, when community becomes emphasized to the neglect of cause. When this happens, "koinonitis" works its way into the leadership-development process. Recently I (Will) worked with a church that demonstrated this dynamic. The church, which is fifteen years old, is currently led by the founding pastor. For the first five years of the church's life, there was a healthy cause-community balance, and the church experienced steady growth. In the last five years, however, the church has plateaued to just over four hundred in weekend attendance.

It is clear to me that the church is now focused inwardly and is unbalanced toward community. The staff, leaders, and members enjoy healthy community, but they have lost their sense of cause. Several years ago additional pastoral staff were added on the basis of personal relationships rather than strategic thinking. As ministries developed, increasing amounts of energy were invested into fellowship and education-oriented ministry to the neglect of evangelism and service to the outside community. They reached a point where staff and church leaders were not held accountable for having salt-and-light impact in the world around them. In short, the church let a good thing—healthy relationships—become the only thing, and the church's "cause quotient" declined.

An extreme example of this focus-on-community dynamic is the monastery, where the development of spiritual leadership is forged within an extreme community inside a relatively contained physical area.

Many pastors are all too familiar with this dynamic inside the church—the "us four and no more" mentality. When people live in the "us four" mind-set, the suggestion of a cause focus ultimately means that a "fifth person" is going to enter the comfortable circle. Of course the fifth person will forever change the fellowship that the four have enjoyed. In such an environment the quality of the fellowship becomes so important that the quantity of fellowship is limited.

The same dynamic can infiltrate the leadership culture. As a leader develops within the organization, the sense of community can drown out the distinct call for cause. At higher levels, elitism can develop that resists adding new leaders so that those already in power remain the "select few." Ultimately in this leadership culture, leaders are held more accountable for maintaining healthy relationships and preserving the status quo than for having Great Commission influence. This dynamic is illustrated by the figure below.

Community-Dominated Leadership Development

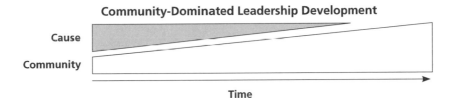

As stated earlier, the proper goal is maintaining a cause-community balance. Over time, in the development of leadership, a church can emphasize both cause and community in the way that Jesus did—with stunning balance. The next diagram illustrates this balance.

Balanced Leadership Development

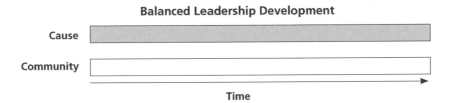

KEEPING THE BALANCE

Having stated the balance in theory, let's explore how a church can move toward keeping this balance day to day in practical ways. Attention to seven basic areas will drive a healthy balance. These are role descriptions, training content, training structure, evaluation, complementary team building, modeling, and biblical and contemporary metaphors. Take a moment as you read about these areas below to reflect on your church situation.

Role descriptions. The leader's role description should adequately convey both community and cause aspects. This foundational piece of communication must come early in the leadership-recruitment process and serves as a map of what spiritual leadership will look like within the church organization. What do your role descriptions currently emphasize?

Training content. When leaders are trained, the teaching content should reflect both cause and community emphases. Review the last training/ teaching sessions with leaders. What did the content emphasize?

Training structure. In many ways the structure of leadership training teaches as much as the actual training content. Structure refers to the way the training takes place. It includes, for example, whether people sit in rows or circles or cluster in groups of four or forty, whether inter-action is encouraged or limited, whether leaders pray together and/or play together, the length of the event—a one-hour meeting or a half-day retreat. Dividing into small groups, having a longer event, and providing many varied opportunities to interact help form relationships and show that this is an important aspect of training. Evaluate the structure of your last training meeting. Did that structure emphasize cause or community?

Evaluation. Closely related to role description is leader evaluation, because the work that is measured is what gets done. A leader should be evaluated as to the kind of brother/sister, son/daughter, and sheep he or she has been (community) and what kind of servant, harvester, and fisherman he or she has been (cause). If you have an evaluation form for leaders, what does it currently emphasize?

Complementary team building. People have God-given temperaments and personalities that orient them toward people or tasks. Many times people of like temperaments are attracted to one another. This can lead to groups, teams, and committees that exhibit a clear cause or com-munity orientation. If the individual temperaments are assessed and considered as teams are being built, the teams will express a better community-cause balance. Reflect on the key leadership teams in your church. Which way does each team tend to lean?

Modeling. If leaders who are developing others are not modeling an emphasis on both cause and community, it is unlikely that a healthy balance will be achieved. A church probably will not develop community beyond the depth of community that the staff team experiences. Cause and community must be lived and not just talked about. You can teach what you know but you can only reproduce what you are.

Biblical and contemporary metaphors. Finally, leaders should know and understand the biblical metaphors in this chapter. Also, the senior pastor or primary teacher must provide compelling new metaphors from everyday life, because contemporary metaphors deliver scriptural truths with cultural relevance. For example, the Internet or a global positioning system (GPS) could be an apt spiritual metaphor today. In chapter 13 we will touch on some closely related ideas in the section on symbols.

Jesus used language that demands an amazing symmetry between healthy relationships and productive tasks. The same equilibrium should be translated into the leadership culture of the local church by intentionally emphasizing both cause and community at all levels of leadership.

Authority

Jesus emphasized that those who exercise authority in the kingdom are also under authority. This observation is supported by the metaphors Jesus crafted when emphasizing tasks. The three primary images are shepherd, harvester, and apostle. With each metaphor there is a dual implication—the person exercises authority but is also under authority. For example, a shepherd is given authority over the sheep, yet he remains under the authority of the sheep's owner. Likewise the harvester is responsible to bring in the crop, but he is also under the authority of the landowner. An apostle, as a sent one, is given authority to deliver a message, but he is also under the authority of the message's author.

The image of the vine and branches in John 15 also relates to this concept. Although the context is not specifically about authority, it does assert the subordinate role of the believer to Christ and the vital connection required to do fruitful work.

The significance of these terms is that Jesus is protecting his disciples from thinking that they can exercise authority completely on their own. Their role as disciples involves responsibility derived from a higher authority—and these images keep this truth in front of them. Thus Jesus strategically selects metaphors that will help protect his disciples as future leaders from their own egos.

The truth found implicit in these metaphors parallels Jesus' explicit teaching. In Luke 22 a dispute arises among the disciples about positions of authority in the future kingdom. In response, Jesus clarifies what it means to have authority in his kingdom:

> Also a dispute arose among them as to which of them was considered to be greatest. Jesus said to them, "The kings of the Gentiles lord it over them; and those who exercise authority over them call themselves Benefactors. But you are not to be like that. Instead, the greatest among you should be like the youngest, and the one who rules like the one who serves. For

who is greater, the one who is at the table or the one who serves? Is it
not the one who is at the table? But I am among you as one who serves.
You are those who have stood by me in my trials. And I confer on you a
kingdom, just as my Father conferred one on me, so that you may eat and
drink at my table in my kingdom and sit on thrones, judging the twelve
tribes of Israel."

Luke 22:24–30

In emphasizing servant-leadership, Jesus draws a contrast between
the way worldly leaders exercise authority and how his disciples should
exercise authority. They are not to "lord it over them" as do the "kings
of the Gentiles." Rather they are to follow the model of Jesus, who exercises his authority as "one who serves." In verse 27 Jesus first appeals
to his own model of leadership for them to follow, consistent with the
metaphor of servant. In verse 29 he reminds them that they are under
his authority as he "confers" on them a kingdom. Both of these verses
highlight the truth set forth in the metaphors previously mentioned—the
disciples are to exercise their own authority as individuals who are also
under the authority of Jesus.

IMPLICATION FOR LEADERSHIP

An implication of this observation concerning authority is that a
primary requirement for a leader in the church is the ability to follow;
that is, following Christ by following other God-given authorities. The
metaphors that Jesus selects indicate that a proper understanding of
being under authority is critical for leadership in the kingdom and
therefore should be important to the church. As the church develops
leaders, it must observe how emerging leaders respond to authority.
The ability to be under authority should drive who emerges as leaders
and when they emerge.

This particular facet of a leader's character is easy to overlook
when he or she is gifted in other areas of leadership. When recruiting
leaders, we often face what we call the "talent trap." The talent trap
is the presence of a very gifted leader in the church whose character
strengths may be questionable. It's a trap because it may be tempting
to recruit or hire such a person based on extreme gifting alone and
without adequate assessment of spiritual qualifications. To discern
through any "gray areas" on the character side, evaluate the individual's
responsiveness to other leaders and God-given authorities as a primary
point of reference.

The assessment of this quality is important for leaders at every
level—from the pastoral search committee looking for a senior pastor
to an associate pastor recruiting a small group leader and so on.

QUESTIONS TO ASK

The following questions will aid the observation process for those who recruit and select leaders. Does the person . . .

- hesitate in following the clear will of God?
- seek God regularly for guidance in life?
- recognize the levels of authority in the local church?
- agree with the mission, vision, and values of the church?
- know how to appeal to authority appropriately?
- question habitually other authorities inside or outside the church?
- demonstrate the ability to follow authority even when there is disagreement?
- view all authority roles as from God?
- recognize and honor governmental authority?
- have a demonstrated track record under authority (in all areas, including the church and workplace and as a citizen)?
- demonstrate submission to God's Word?

Constantly be aware of the presence or lack of this positive quality as you look for emerging leaders. Those with the greatest leadership potential will most likely be the ones who follow well.

A Penetrating Influence

Jesus guided his followers to be a penetrating influence in the world. As mentioned earlier, the images of the productive soil, fruitful branches, salt and light, all have a common thread of an increasing, ever-expanding growth and influence. We must not overlook how these metaphors loaded the disciples' hearts and minds with instructive meaning. These disciples, whose faith would soon be designated "the Way," were not given positions in an organization but were drawn up into a movement. They were participants in a fast-moving stream, continuously forced out of their comfort zone of slow-moving eddies into white-water action.

Jesus' selection of metaphors kept his followers outwardly focused and mission-minded. As light penetrates the darkness, the disciples were commissioned to penetrate the dark world with the purpose of making other disciples. When the shepherd leaves the ninety-nine sheep in search of the one, he displays a radical commitment to enter the world.

IMPLICATION FOR LEADERSHIP

An implication of this observation of disciples being a penetrating influence is that the church should work to help leaders maintain an outer rather than an inner focus. Vision always leaks and mission always drifts. Something about the human heart leaves us susceptible to enjoying fellowship to the neglect of expanding the fellowship. If we are to take Jesus' images of productive and penetrating influence seriously, the church must move in centrifugal motion, sending out leaders who will courageously engage the world rather than take refuge from it. The church must stay missional.

Keep in mind that the pharisaical attitudes represented the exact opposite of what Jesus was trying to produce in his followers. The Pharisees were proud and elitist and worked to distance themselves from the world. When they saw Jesus welcome sinners, they swelled with indignant self-righteousness rather than celebrate his redemptive movement. While no church would intentionally adopt a "pharisaical strategy," it is unfortunate that many churches slip into the mode of retreating from the world rather than engaging it.

MAINTAINING AN OUTWARD FOCUS

What are some practical ways that the church can keep leaders focused outwardly? The beginning point is to remember the evangelism principle of disproportionate energy: If the church is going to have balanced output in its primary purposes, it must put a disproportionately larger amount of energy into the purpose of evangelism.[7] We can think of the evangelism purpose as a bigger boulder than the others—it takes more energy to get it rolling and to keep it rolling. We have found this guiding principle to be self-evident to many church leaders and helpful in our own ministries.

When I (Will) work with church leaders, I ask them, "Who is the most important person to the Coca-Cola company?" No one has ever answered correctly. The answer is the person who drinks Pepsi. Imagine a church that pours the same intentional energy and resources into winning the lost to Christ as Coca-Cola does trying to convince Pepsi drinkers that they should drink Coke.

Once a church makes the commitment to a missional, outward focus, there are many specific ways to incorporate this focus into the leadership culture. Although we will address the leadership culture in chapter 13, it is worth touching on a few of these ways now.

Missional Catalyst 1: Clear Focus

Keep the missional focus clear in the mission and values statements of the church. When I (Will) help churches craft mission statements, I encourage them to explicitly identify the individuals they are attempting to reach. Since the mission statement serves as a compass, this keeps the evangelistic purpose in focus. The following mission statements are good examples.

Grace Point Church, San Antonio, Texas:
To lead unsaved people into a relationship
of full devotion to Jesus Christ.

Clear Creek Community Church, Houston, Texas:
To establish a community of believers
with the priority of leading unchurched people
to become fully devoted followers of Christ.

Morgan Hill Bible Church, San Jose, California:
To connect the disconnected
into a vital relationship with Jesus Christ.

Notice that each statement identifies the lost person with the terms *unsaved, unchurched,* and *disconnected.* When the evangelistic purpose is made this clear, it aligns the leaders to an outward focus. As Grace Point Church was developing its statement, at one point it read, "To lead people into a relationship of full devotion to Jesus Christ." When the term *people* instead of *unsaved people* was used, it *could* identify the activity that takes place inside the church only. It did not make evangelism explicit. When they added the phrase *to lead unsaved people* to the front end of the statement, the missional intensity was obvious.

The same is true for the values statement of the church. Many times a church will forge a values statement with a specific reference to lost people and the purpose of evangelism. Several churches have used or adapted a sentence written by Willow Creek Community Church to express the value of evangelism: *Lost people matter to God; therefore they matter to us.*

Missional Catalyst 2: A Model for Intentional Evangelism

As we have worked with churches, we have been astounded by the fact that most have no clear process or strategy for evangelism. That means there is no clear plan to engage, prepare, and remind believers how to win others to the Lord. As a result, evangelism is a very ambiguous concept to many evangelical believers.

The church needs to provide a plan for evangelism that church members can understand and embrace. The first step is to identify the ways evangelism may already be taking place in the church. Usually there is a predominant evangelistic tool or strength in the church. Thom Rainer has noted that evangelistically effective churches usually have one of three general strengths: evangelistic preaching, evangelistic prayer ministry, or evangelistic Sunday school/small groups.[8] Two other evangelistic strengths are evangelistic service projects and evangelistic special events.

Study the way God has used your church. What ministries have yielded the most fruit? If your church does not have a clear evangelistic strength, select a direction in which to lead the church in intentional evangelism that best fits your people and the context of your community.

The second step in developing the church's evangelism plan is to think through the major components of a personal evangelism strategy. There are at least four that are important: initiation, prayer, invitation, and sharing. *Initiation* is the process of engaging and building a relationship with lost people. *Prayer* is asking God to bring about the ultimate life change of repentance and salvation in lost people. *Invitation* is asking lost people to attend church events or venues designed for them—the evangelistic events of your church. *Sharing* is telling a personal testimony and explaining the gospel message to lost people.

Any good evangelism model has these four basic components. The following questions will help you think through how your church encourages its members to practice these components of personal evangelism.

1. How do we talk about the component as it relates to evangelism?
2. How do we train to the component?
3. How do we provide tools and support for the component?
4. How do we encourage people to have a heartfelt commitment to continually apply the component?

When you can answer the questions, you are moving toward a clear model for intentional evangelism. While the purpose of this chapter is not to help you design your evangelism strategy, we do want to encourage you to think through these steps. To the extent that you develop a pathway for doing evangelism, you will be keeping leaders outwardly focused, and they will in turn multiply the missional mind-set throughout the church.

Missional Catalyst 3: Ministry outside the Church

A church that is concerned about evangelism must define ministry as activity outside the church as much as, if not more than, activity inside the church. Two truths about pastoral leadership immediately create a conflict of interest when it comes to defining the term *ministry*. The first truth is that pastors are the key influencers in defining what *ministry* means in the life of the church. The second truth is that pastors are responsible for the day-to-day operations of the church as a volunteer-driven organization. Therefore, when defining ministry, pastors tend to overemphasize the ministry activity that takes place within the walls of the church. This is usually unintentional and is driven by the urgency of the needs the pastor sees. The church always needs more greeters, small-group leaders, Sunday school teachers, nursery workers, and youth trip chaperones. The pastor may be focused on recruiting a finance committee chairperson or someone to build a new web site. Over the course of time, church members become accustomed to a limited perspective on ministry, and the leadership culture becomes too inwardly focused.

From a theological perspective most pastors would never limit the world of ministry to internal church needs. But, practically, pastors may find it difficult to define and encourage ministry outside the church, which could include ministering in the local prison, establishing small groups in the workplace, or building relationships with unchurched neighbors.

I (Will) realized my own limited perspective one day when I was meeting with Steve, a group leader in my church. I coached Steve, who at the time was leading a service group in the area of children's ministry programming. It was one of the most volunteer-intensive roles I have ever supervised. I met weekly with Steve and he poured six to eight hours into his role every week. Although Steve really enjoyed his place in children's ministry, he was also passionate about a prayer ministry he was leading at work. As a vice president in a large company, Steve held an effective and evangelistic weekly prayer meeting at lunchtime in one of the conference rooms.

One day the thought hit me: *I (representing the church) do nothing to support Steve in his vital ministry in the workplace. I focus all of my attention on Steve's leadership in the children's ministry.* At that point I realized I was on the verge of committing pastoral malpractice. Without intending to, practically, I was defining ministry for Steve as only the activity he did inside the church. I was not helping Steve keep an outward focus as a leader. From that point on I committed myself to spending as much of my coaching time focused on his workplace prayer ministry as on his children's ministry.

Evaluate how you currently define ministry in your church. Many churches today have gifts assessment classes and ministry placement processes. How heavily are ministry opportunities weighted toward internal church needs? How often are leaders encouraged to pursue new ministry ideas in their respective areas of influence outside the church? When defining ministry, be intentional about staying true to Jesus' call—to raise leaders who will be productive soil, fruitful branches, flavoring salt, and penetrating light.

Missional Catalyst 4: A Large Welcome

The "main event" for most churches is the Sunday morning worship service. It is the time for preaching God's Word, celebrating the sacraments, and performing other expressions of worship. As a fundamentally corporate event, it is a natural time to be internally focused. At the same time, however, the presence of guests and infrequent attendees makes Sunday morning an excellent time to be outwardly focused.

We know of a church that has just finished a three-year ministry evaluation. The church, with one thousand attending on Sunday morning, discovered that more than fifteen hundred people had visited the church only one time in the last three years. What an incredible service and evangelism opportunity!

Over the past decade we have found that effective churches have developed very intentional welcoming systems on Sunday morning, which incorporate a host of ministries, including parking lot attendants, greeters, information centers, registration tables, and ushers. In addition, support services, such as information packets, internal signage, and nursery paging systems, are seen as vital. Needless to say, a welcoming system creates more opportunities for service, but most important, it creates a leadership culture that is outwardly focused.

A year ago I (Will) visited a church on Sunday morning for a guest perspective consultation. Driving into the parking lot (the church was meeting in a school) thirty minutes ahead of time, I noticed about seventy cars parked more than a hundred yards away from the building. Because the leaders and other volunteers who came to set up the church and serve on Sunday morning wanted guests and other attendees to feel welcome, they left the best parking spots for them. This was a great example of an outwardly focused leadership culture.

Missional Catalyst 5: Engaging the Assimilation Process

This catalyst closely follows the one previously mentioned. Engaging the assimilation process means that leaders and members interact with disconnected and inactive *members* of the church as well as with *guests* of the church. If you rely only on church staff to recruit, you will hit a bottleneck in the assimilation process. Let's use small groups as an example. In some churches the small-group leaders expect the church to provide all of the leads for potential group members. In other churches group leaders are expected to be proactive in inviting others to their group. Which church do you think will have the most people in small groups?

One church does "escape-connect-invite" training. They actually role-play the process of inviting a disconnected person who has attended the worship service into a small group. "Escape" is the first step and refers to the process of escaping from a conversation with someone you already know during the time before or after the worship service. Then you connect or engage a person you do not know. Next you invite the person to join a group, if he or she is not already involved in one. The critical window of time in which to do escape-connect-invite is called the "ten-minute mingle." Every leader in the church knows that the ten-minute mingle is the golden opportunity of the week to expand the ministry of their small group.

Of course your church may not have small groups, but it does have a second step in the assimilation process. Whatever that step is—Sunday school, Class 101, men's or women's Bible studies—make sure to train and motivate your leaders to help others through the assimilation process.

Missional Catalyst 6: A Model for Personal Evangelism

We hold firmly to the assumption that you can teach what you know, but you can reproduce only what you are. Nowhere is this more applicable than in training people to be evangelistically intentional. When people see their leaders sharing their faith, rather than just hearing that they should be more active in sharing their faith, they are much more inclined to do evangelism. As a leader, you must ask yourself: *Am I spending time with unchurched people? Am I engaging the lost through service evangelism? Am I praying for people on my "most-wanted" list?*

If the top leaders in the church are not pursuing these goals, how will a contagious outward focus trickle its way down through all levels of leadership? If, however, the top leaders are doing these activities, they should be careful to talk about their efforts, equipping and inspiring others. One church staff prays weekly in staff meetings for lost friends. This is an accountability step that helps staff personally. Also, they talk about these same lost friends with the leaders they lead. Obviously this helps pass on the missional focus that the staff is cultivating in their own lives.

Missional Catalyst 7: Time for Missional Pursuits

Nearly every church could actually do more by doing less. Usually churches inundate their people with church activities to the point of quenching missional pursuits. Even if leaders' hearts are on fire to reach others, in many churches their time is all taken up with church activities. On average, churches consistently offer six to eight weekly ministry opportunity categories, such as the following:

1. Sunday morning worship
2. Sunday morning adult Bible study
3. Sunday evening event
4. Weekday small group opportunity
5. Wednesday evening event
6. Special weekday class or seminar
7. Ministry team, committee meeting, or service event

Churches want more members building intentional relationships with lost people, but by the time these members attend four to seven church events each week, maintain a career, and try to sustain a vital marriage and family life, there is little time for getting to know a neighbor who is far from God.

We recommend that churches figure out the three most important weekly venues, prioritize and promote the "big three," and give the people back their time to connect with the lost. Believers need to be set loose into the world to reach the world. Don't hold them captive in the walls of the church.

Questions for Reflection and Discussion

1. Does your church tend toward a cause-dominated leadership culture or a community-dominated leadership culture? Why?
2. What metaphor in this chapter represents the current strength of your church and/or the leadership development process? What metaphor represents the greatest weakness?
3. How does the church evaluate a potential leader's responsiveness to authority?
4. Review the seven missional catalyst statements. Which one represents your current church strength? Which one represents what your church needs to develop most?

6

How Early Churches
Developed Leaders

What the Church Teaches Us
about Leadership Development

The first-century church ministered in ways that can guide and influence the leadership-development process of the twenty-first-century church. When we use the term *early church*, we're referring to various first-century bodies, glimpses of which we find in Acts and the Epistles. At that time the apostles and others were in the beginning stages of constructing the church and thus building their leadership-development processes. They were in the midst of pouring critical new foundations and erecting on them ministries, such as leadership development. What follows is a study of how some leaders, who represented or led the churches, developed their leaders.

In chapter 4 we saw that Jesus' development of his disciples consisted of the following steps: recruitment, selection, training, and deployment. As we study Acts and the Epistles, we can piece together the same elements. While these are descriptive, not prescriptive, they do provide for us a most helpful pattern that can serve our churches in building our leadership-development house in the twenty-first century.

The Recruitment of Leaders

How did leaders of the first-century church find future leaders? They recruited them, proactively going after them. For this study, we define *recruitment* as the process of finding potential leaders for ministry at some level in the church. The Savior recruited leaders by personal invitation (Matt. 9:9; Mark 1:16–20). He also directed his disciples to recruit leaders through prayer (Matt. 9:36–38).

Only a few passages in Acts provide us with glimpses of how the early church approached emerging leaders. Though not binding on today's church, these methods serve as windows through which to observe their leadership-recruitment practices. One is Acts 15:36–41 where Paul and Barnabas are about to begin their second missionary journey. An important decision was who should be a critical part of their ministry team. Verse 37 says that Barnabas wanted to take John Mark. However, Paul thought this was unwise because John Mark had deserted them during their prior journey (v. 38). The two parted company over this issue. Barnabas took John Mark and went in one direction, while Paul recruited Silas and went in a different direction (vv. 39–41). This may suggest that past ministry performance was a criterion for leadership selection, at least from Paul's viewpoint.

In Acts 16:1–3 Timothy joined Paul's team. The passage says only that Paul wanted to take him along on the second missionary journey. As in the cases of John Mark and Silas, Luke doesn't explain precisely how Paul recruited Timothy. It's likely, though, that he used the same method Jesus did—personal invitation. If Paul wanted to take Timothy along, he probably invited him. Verse 2 tells us that the Christian brothers in the churches at Lystra and Iconium "spoke well of him." This would suggest that good character and recommendation were important to the process as well.

It's evident that Paul was in the leadership recruitment business, for he recruited leaders constantly while on his missionary travels. Even if Paul used a specific recruitment method, unless Scripture mandated it, that practice would not be binding on the church. Consequently we have no prescriptive passages that dictate a recruitment process in today's church. The Holy Spirit leaves this up to each church. However, prayer, good character, and the recommendation of others are essentials in the process, and personal invitation will always be near the top of a good leadership-recruitment approach.

The Selection of Leaders

Selection is the determination of who among the church's recruited leaders will actually become involved in the church's leadership. Scripture indicates that various groups and individuals were part of the church's proactive selection process. First, the congregation selected leaders. For example, in Acts 6:1–6 the Twelve instructed the Jerusalem congregation to select seven men as leaders who would be responsible to administer the daily distribution of food to its widows. In Acts 15:2–3 the church at Antioch selected Paul and Barnabas with others to go to Jerusalem to discuss with the leaders there whether Gentiles needed to be circumcised for salvation. In verse 22 the church was part of a group that sent Paul, Barnabas, and others to Antioch to inform Gentile Christians that circumcision wasn't necessary.

Second, the Holy Spirit selected leaders for ministry. In Acts 13:1–4 the Holy Spirit selected Barnabas and Paul to go on the first missionary journey. The text says that the Spirit accomplished this by speaking to the church through a prophet. Also, in Acts 20:28 the Spirit made or selected the elders of the church at Ephesus as overseers to shepherd its flock.

Third, God used certain individuals in the church to select leaders. For example, Paul and Barnabas chose elders in Acts 14:23. The apostles and elders with the whole church at Jerusalem also were involved in sending Paul and Barnabas to the Gentile Christians to clarify the gospel (15:22).

Paul directed Titus to appoint elders (Titus 1:5), and he instructed Timothy, in 1 Timothy 5:22, how to select them. This passage is instructive for leadership selection because Paul advises Timothy not to ordain elders too quickly. In the context of the book, this would seem to indicate that someone should carefully explore the background and qualifications of a potential elder before selecting him for the position.

It is clear in Scripture that elders, who were the first-century equivalent of today's pastors, and deacons had to meet certain qualifications to be leaders in the church. In 1 Timothy 3:1–7 and Titus 1:6–9, Paul sets out specific character qualifications for elders. It would appear that all these character qualities fit under the heading "above reproach."[1] Also, Peter outlines some qualifications for elders in 1 Peter 5:1–3. Then, in 1 Timothy 3:8–13 Paul establishes character qualifications for deacons and their wives. Apparently deacons had an office in the church, but Scripture doesn't clarify what it was.

The principle is that there are important character qualifications that potential elders and deacons must meet to become actual leaders. Not just anyone could be a leader in the New Testament church. Here the selection process narrows. It's imperative that the church's elders and deacons meet the qualifications in 1 Timothy 3:1–13; Titus 1:3–9; and 1 Peter 5:1–3. In 1 Timothy 3:2 Paul says, "Now the overseer must be . . ." The qualifications he enumerates apply to elders or pastors in the twenty-first century just as they applied in the first century. However, the church has the freedom to establish certain character qualifications for other leadership positions that aren't dictated by Scripture, as long as they don't contradict Scripture. Such passages as Acts 6:3, 5 and 2 Peter 1:3–8 provide some guidance.

To some degree or other, many of these passages inform a church's or denomination's polity or government. Every church invests power in some person or group of people, and that's not wrong. The organization's polity directs how it handles its power. Various groups use these passages to support widely divergent views of church polity, ranging from control by one individual (a pastor or a bishop), a board (deacons, elders, trustees, and others), or the entire church, whether large, mid-sized, or small.

The brief study above indicates that the churches in the New Testament held various views of polity. Despite what some would have us believe, no one view prevailed. Most likely there were varying practices. The local church exercised the polity that was most appropriate to its particular situation. Consequently we can conclude that God gives each organization freedom in how it selects its leaders, except in the case of its elders and deacons. Polity, therefore, is situational.

The Training of Leaders

The Gospels teach us that the Savior cultivated and grew leaders. After his death, resurrection, and ascension, the church took on this responsibility, as demonstrated in the lives and ministries of some of its leaders. Thus, not only did the church recruit and select emerging leaders, it trained them as well.

One example is Priscilla and Aquila's training of Apollos. Acts 18:24–26 tells the story of Apollos, who was a leader in the early church and had a thorough knowledge of the Scriptures. Verse 25 explains that some person or group, apparently in the church, had trained him as a leader, for "he had been instructed in the way of the Lord." However, his knowledge was lacking, as he knew only the baptism of John. Thus Aquila and his wife, Priscilla, invited Apollos into their home where they "explained to him the way of God more adequately" (v. 26). Their role in Apollos's development as a leader was to sharpen or fine-tune his knowledge of Scripture in a particular area—"the way of God." The result was that God used him powerfully in ministry in Achaia and probably beyond.

Another example is Paul's training of Timothy. In 2 Timothy 2:2 he instructs Timothy: "And the things you have heard me say in the presence of many witnesses entrust to reliable men who will also be qualified to teach others." Paul directs one leader, Timothy, to develop other leaders. Paul's own ministry of leadership multiplication spans several generations of leaders.

Leadership Multiplication in 2 Timothy 2:2

Paul
↓
Timothy
↓
reliable men
↓
others

Certain key words in the passage alert us to the qualifications for good leaders. The first is that a potential leader must be competent. Paul uses the term *qualified*. In 2 Corinthians 3:5 *qualified* is translated by the term *competent*. It says that God makes us competent. Competent leaders are good at what they do, displaying leadership skill and ability. In turn this competence leads to personal confidence that doesn't involve pride (it's okay to know what you do well as well as what you don't do well). Godly competence results in a godly confidence based on God's work in and through us.

A second qualification of leaders is trustworthiness. They must be trustworthy, faithful, or reliable. If people don't trust you, you cannot lead them. The leaders of the early church had been entrusted with the things Paul had said. The things that Timothy heard Paul say or teach refer to "sound teaching" (2 Tim. 1:13). This includes the gospel (v. 11), among other things, which was to be accompanied by "faith and love in Christ Jesus." Trust is vital to any leader's ministry for the Savior. In Titus 1:7 Paul tells Titus, another leader, that an overseer (the first-century equivalent of today's pastor) is "entrusted with God's work."

Potential leaders must prove faithful and reliable. They are individuals who won't fade in the ministry stretch. They won't disappear on you. When you look up from all your efforts for the Savior, they're still there, ministering alongside you. Matthew 25:14–30 teaches that faithful servants are people who, because they understand God's goodness, pursue his purposes despite the risks.

A third characteristic of leaders is that they are teachers. Paul told Timothy to entrust future leaders with "sound teaching." This would involve teaching them the truths of Scripture, because they, in turn, "will also be qualified to teach others" (2 Tim. 2:2). Leaders are not only learners; they are also teachers. They teach others. Leaders would be wise to have at least one apprentice to whom they're teaching the truths of Scripture and other ministry concepts that will contribute to their future success as leaders in the church.

Finally, this passage in 2 Timothy rests on a critical assumption. The assumption is that leaders are teachable. The unpardonable sin of those involved in leadership development is their not being teachable. You can't teach unteachable people, because they think they know it all, they don't listen (Prov. 12:15), they're proud (13:10), and they lack follow-through. Their slogan is "Don't bother me with the facts; my mind is already made up!" They're the exact opposite of a man like Apollos in Acts 18.

Therefore, Paul teaches that the four essential qualities of a potential leader are competence, trustworthiness, faithfulness, and teachableness.

One further question remains. How did Paul accomplish this training? Scripture isn't clear. However, it appears that his practice was to train leaders by taking them along with him on his travels, as was the practice of the Savior. Paul always surrounded himself with a team (see Acts 13–20). Most likely these weren't only veteran leaders, such as Barnabas, but some were emerging leaders. Consequently he trained leaders primarily if not exclusively in the context of ministry, using a team approach.

The Deployment of Leaders

Once the church has recruited, selected, and trained its leaders, it's not finished. There is at least one more step—deployment. Deployment involves placing the right leaders in the right place (context) at the right time. The leader's placement is his or her ministry assignment or appointment, where the leader will lead and minister.

Several passages describe the church's leadership deployment practices. In Acts 6:1–6 God used the Twelve to direct the placement of the seven men who would be responsible for administering the needs of the church's widows. In Acts 13:1–4 the Holy Spirit selected Barnabas and Saul for ministry by speaking through a prophet, and they were sent on their first ministry assignment—the first missionary journey.

The Holy Spirit also placed the Ephesian elders in the position of overseers to shepherd the flock (20:28). Next, the church at Antioch selected Paul and Barnabas as well as others and appointed them to go to Jerusalem (15:2–3). In verse 22 the apostles and elders, with the whole church, sent Paul, Barnabas, and others to Antioch.

These passages demonstrate that the Holy Spirit deployed leaders in their ministries through the apostles, prophets, elders, and the congregation. Since God used a variety of methods to deploy leaders in the first century, evidently no one correct practice exists. So the church today, as in the first century, is free to deploy its leaders as wisdom dictates.

One important ingredient to deployment is prayer. The early church in Acts valued prayer highly. Prayer wasn't an option or an elective for them. A constant throughout the Book (1:14; 2:42; 4:31; 6:4; 12:5; 13:3), prayer is a vital part of the church curriculum. And the church in Acts made a point of praying and fasting for its leaders. For example, after the Holy Spirit designated Paul and Barnabas as missionary leaders in Acts 13:2 and prior to their deployment, verse 3 says that the Jerusalem church fasted and then prayed for them. Paul and Barnabas began their incredible time of ministry with prayer.

On that same journey, Luke records in Acts 14:23 that Paul and Barnabas returned through Lystra, Iconium, and Antioch, where they appointed elders or pastors. Then, prior to the new leaders' deployment, Paul and Barnabas commended them to the Lord, after fasting and praying for them.

Jesus prayed for his disciples prior to or at the time of selecting them (Luke 6:12). The evidence in Acts suggests that the church prayed for its leaders at least when it deployed them. Though the Scriptures (Acts) do not say so, we suspect that the church bathed the leadership-development process in prayer from start to finish.

It's instructive to note that most if not all of the church's training principles and practices mirror those of the Savior. Jesus and the early church recruited, selected, trained, and deployed their potential, emerging leaders. They didn't work with just any so-called leader who happened to come along. They expected leader trainees to meet certain qualifications. These principles and practices will prove most important and informative as we think through and develop our processes for building our church leaders in chapters 7–13. Also, they'll provide the biblical foundation that will help guide us through the process, serving both to drive and direct it.

The Church's Leadership Training Steps

Recruitment

Selection

Training

Deployment

Questions for Reflection and Discussion

1. Compare the training of leaders outlined in this chapter with the process the Savior used as described in chapter 4. What do they have in common? How are they different? How do you explain any differences or similarities?
2. Do you think Jesus' practices may have influenced the development of leaders in the early church?
3. What has the process in this chapter taught you about the leadership-development process used in your church? What does Scripture require of you, and where do you have freedom in training your leaders?

Part 3

Moving from Foundation to Finish

The Process for Developing Leaders

7

Who Will Read the Blueprints?

The Personnel for Developing Leaders

As you watch a house being built, you quickly realize how important people are to the process. If you're not convinced, just ask any builder. They'll tell you that having the right people on the job results in a well-built house that requires minimal maintenance. Having the wrong people, however, results in shoddy construction and lots of warranty work.

In this chapter we turn our attention to the people who are key to leadership training. Peter Drucker has well said, "People determine the performance capacity of an organization. No organization can do better than the people it has."[1] In his book *Good to Great*, Jim Collins writes, "The executives who ignited the transformations from good to great did not first figure out where to drive the bus and then get people to take it there. No, they *first* got the right people on the bus (and the wrong people off the bus) and *then* figured out where to drive it."[2] The obvious point is that the right people are critical to the process.

Now that we have in place the necessary preparation for leadership development (part 1) and have established some biblical priorities and practices that offer guidance for training leaders (part 2), it is time to discover the process of leadership development.

In this chapter and the next two, we uncover the leadership development process, answering the important training question, What bases must we all touch to train leaders for the church? When you take your church through the process, the outcome will be different from that of another church, because you're different from every other leader and so is your ministry and its culture (values, traditions, heroes, and so on).

While leadership development is all one process, it naturally falls into two parts. One part comprises the people involved in leadership—the leadership personnel—whom we discuss in this chapter. The other part encompasses the leadership procedures that we cover in chapters 8–10. *Who* is as important as *how*—the personnel are as important as, if not more important than, the procedures. Without the right people on board and involved in the process, leadership development won't happen.

Before starting a leadership-development training program, you must take five steps:

1. It's imperative that you determine if the ministry's empowered leadership supports the process.
2. Recruit someone, a champion of the cause, to take responsibility for and lead the process.
3. This leader will need to recruit and develop a lay-leadership team for assistance in developing, implementing, and administering the process.
4. You must arrive at a consensus definition of leadership.
5. If you desire to develop leaders at every level of the ministry, you must determine what those levels are.

Support of the Empowered Leadership

Step 1: Determine if the empowered leadership will support the leadership-development process.

Step 2: Recruit someone to initiate and lead the development process.

Step 3: Recruit and develop a lay-leadership team.

Step 4: Arrive at a consensus definition of leadership.

Step 5: Identify the various leadership levels in your ministry.

The first step involves determining if the empowered leadership will support a leadership-development process. Within a congregation, the empowered sources are people or things, such as the budget, that have the authority and the power to influence or impact the ministry in a significant way.[3] We'll consider four.

Step 1: Determine if the empowered leadership will support the leadership-development process.

- **The lead pastor must be on board.**

The lead pastor must be on board. One of the empowered people in the church is its pastor or senior pastor. The pastor must own the leadership-development process and be accountable for it. He must bear the responsibility for it, intentionally support it, and be enthusiastic about it if it is to be effective. Because the lead pastor wants his legacy to consist of competent, Christlike leaders who will take the ministry into the next few decades, he will be committed to leadership development.

Pastors demonstrate ownership by their involvement in the process. They become involved because leaders are learners, and if they ever stop learning, they stop leading. However, as we have seen, leaders are also teachers, because teaching and learning are inextricably intertwined. Leaders teach what they learn, and if they ever stop teaching what they're learning, they stop leading. So it's natural for them to support and be heavily involved in the training of leaders and building a leadership legacy.

If the pastor resists, drags his heels, or shows no interest in raising up this and the next generation of leaders, it won't happen. This may be the case with the pastor who is a strong teacher or preacher. This person may be a gifted teacher who loves to study and proclaim the Scriptures but doesn't value training leaders, either because he values proclamation over leadership training, or because he knows how to preach but not how to train leaders. This is a core values issue. When the senior leader has no ownership, either the movement doesn't get started to begin with or it quickly dies for lack of direction and momentum.

For example, a church board member once invited me (Aubrey) to come and help his church do strategic planning. However, the pastor, who is a friend, really didn't see the need for strategic planning. He believed that preaching and teaching the Bible are the most important parts of ministry, and those were his strengths. I conducted one planning session and sensed his lack of enthusiasm and support for the process, even though the board members responded most enthusiastically. They went so far as to e-mail me several times, asking for dates when I might be available to return. However, the opportunity never happened. It died for lack of a second—the pastor's second to the motion.

Step 1: Determine if the empowered leadership will support the leadership-development process.

- The lead pastor must be on board.
- **The leadership board must be on board.**

The leadership board must be on board. A second empowered source is the church's governing board. In many ministries the governing board is more influential than the pastor. There are two extremes. On the one hand, the pastor directs the church, and there may or may not be a board. If the board exists, it may function as the pastor's rubberstamp. On the other hand, the board leads the church and hires a pastor to do what they aren't comfortable doing: preaching, teaching, weddings, funerals, and other clergy-related functions. This latter extreme is characteristic of many small churches in North America and parts of Europe.

Regardless, if the governing board makes or is involved in making strategic decisions, it must favor the leadership-development process—the board must be on board. In churches in which the board runs or heavily influences the running of the church, the board as well as the pastor should approve and even cast the vision for the leadership-development process. If the board doesn't see the need for and the value of leadership development, the implementation of such a process will be difficult at best.

Step 1: Determine if the empowered leadership will support the leadership-development process.

- The lead pastor must be on board.
- The leadership board must be on board.
- **The leadership staff must be on board.**

The leadership staff must be on board. A third empowered source is the leadership staff. In ministries with voluntary or paid leadership staff, the staff must back the vision for a leadership-development process if it is to be effective. They must be on board, involved in the process and mentoring emerging leaders.

When we implemented a leadership-development process at my (Aubrey's) church, a number of the staff were excited because training leaders had long been their passion. Thus they were quick to get on board. However, if equipping leaders isn't a value and it means more work for some staff, they may resist the implementation of such a process. They'll drag their feet and somehow never get around to training leaders. After all, who needs more work? This is often the case in a highly task-oriented ministry.

How then do we get the staff on board? The following are suggestions for encouraging staff to buy into the process:

Take a kingdom perspective. Challenge staff people to reproduce themselves in future leaders for the sake of the kingdom and not only for their church. The people whom they take time to train will someday use their training to make a major contribution to the cause of Christ. In a sense, the trainees take a part of the leader's competence with them.

Help staff see that when they train leaders, those leaders become a part of the staff's leadership legacy. When staff retire from ministry, these emerging leaders will carry the leadership torch in their place.

Once trained, emerging leaders will provide competent, skilled help that will take some of the ministry load off the staff person. Two are smarter than one and can accomplish far more than one. This assistance should make up for the time it takes to train the aspiring leader.

The newly trained leaders can sub for staff when they are away. The realization that there won't be a pile of work waiting for the staff person when he or she returns from vacation, a retreat, or conference should be encouraging.

Training leaders should be part of the staff leader's role description if the church expects its leadership staff to develop emerging leaders. This makes staff accountable for the leadership-development process.

Five Reasons Staff Should Train Leaders

1. Training leaders who will minister in other churches embraces a kingdom perspective.
2. Training leaders leaves behind a significant leadership legacy.
3. Training leaders leads to teamwork and more ministry productivity.
4. Training leaders provides for better ministry coverage.
5. Training leaders results in their achieving good staff evaluations.

A church often has others who can train and mentor leaders besides the staff. Most churches have gifted, nonstaff lay leaders. For example, Lake Pointe Church in Rockwall, Texas, has several CEOs of major companies in the Dallas–Fort Worth Metroplex who are deeply committed believers and are willing to mentor emerging leaders. The wise church will recruit those who are qualified and involve them in the leadership-development process. Then the ministry doesn't expect the staff to do all the training and mentoring but shares it with other leaders whom God has brought to the church.

Step 1: Determine if the empowered leadership will support the leadership-development process.

- The lead pastor must be on board.

- The leadership board must be on board.

- The leadership staff must be on board.

- **Nonpositional leaders must be on board.**

Nonpositional leaders must be on board. In some churches, other highly influential but nonpositional leaders may actually lead the congregation. For example, it's common for a patriarch or matriarch to be the leader in a small church. It's usually an older man or woman who has been a member of the church since its inception. Even when there's a pastor, church members will look to the matriarch or patriarch to lead the church. They know that these people have the church's best interests in mind and that they'll be there when needed, long after the pastor has moved on to another ministry.

Many times the best way to influence these leaders is through informal relationship-building experiences. Go out of your way to keep them "in the loop" through one-on-one meetings and informal encounters. Discuss your ideas with them and get their input. Pray with them on a weekly basis. Before you move forward with the leadership-development process, be sure that these leaders, especially those who play the role of patriarch or matriarch, are well informed and on board. Otherwise, the process probably will come to a dead end.

Step 1: Determine if the empowered leadership will support the leadership-development process.

- The lead pastor must be on board.

- The leadership board must be on board.

- The leadership staff must be on board.

- Nonpositional leaders must be on board.

- **The budget must be on board.**

The budget must be on board. A fifth empowered source is the budget. The pastor and board must actively seek the necessary resources to conduct the leadership-development process. This is a budgetary issue. Will the necessary funds be a line item in the ministry's budget? Will the decision makers put the ministry's money where it counts? Will they back up the leadership-training vision with the necessary funding? (We know of one medium-sized church that sets aside twenty thousand dollars a year for staff leadership training.) It's surprising how reasonably priced and worthwhile these kinds of training experiences are. Regardless, any necessary expenditure will test whether the ministry truly values leadership development. Any ministry's budget reveals what that ministry values.

How can the ministry invest in leadership development? It can use funding to provide its leaders with good training materials, such as books, periodicals, cassettes, and tapes. Some churches develop their own leadership resources, such as a leader's newsletter or cassette tapes recorded in-house for leadership training. A ministry could send its people to seminars and conferences on leadership and other pertinent ministry areas. It could bring in consultants or trainers to advise its leaders and train its people. (We suspect that in the future more churches will have a consultant who will coach the leadership staff in an ongoing relationship.) The church also could use funds to provide some compensation for internships and residencies. Finally, it could fund a part-time or full-time position for a pastor or director of leadership development.

The best situation is to have all of the empowered sources in a church in favor of the leadership-development process. Though it depends on the situation, if the pastor votes against the process, you may be wasting your time going any further. If the board or staff says no, you may want to continue to work through the process, realizing, however, that their responses will severely hamper the results. If most or all aren't on board, you should postpone the process to another time.

A Leader of the Process

Step 1: Determine if the empowered leadership will support the leadership-development process.

Step 2: Recruit someone to initiate and lead the leadership-development process.

Step 3: Recruit and develop a lay-leadership team.

Step 4: Arrive at a consensus definition of leadership.

Step 5: Identify the various leadership levels in your ministry.

The second step before starting a leadership-development training program is to recruit the right person to champion the cause and take responsibility for designing and implementing the training process. You must answer several questions: Who will train the ministry's leaders? Has the leadership assigned the responsibility for this process to a leadership staff or nonstaff person? Who will implement the process? Who will take direct responsibility for leadership training? Who will carry the torch?

Step 2: Recruit someone to initiate and lead the leadership-development process.
  • **The senior pastor could lead the process.**

The senior pastor could lead the process. In most smaller churches, the pastor or senior pastor will have the vision for training and raising up leaders. Consequently he may assume the role of leader of the process. Some pastors may feel the role is so important to the future of the church that they will include it as a permanent part of their job description and ministry in the church. Other pastors, also placing value on raising up and training leaders, may prefer to train another staff person or highly qualified lay person to take this responsibility, because he or she can give it more time or is more gifted to equip leaders. The pastor who leads will need to decide this issue early in the process.

In small churches the person who leads the process will face two problems. The first is the time crunch. Far too many small churches practice the twenty-eighty rule. Twenty percent of the people (most often leaders) do 80 percent of the church's ministry in addition to their personal responsibilities. In addition, pastors spend much time on pastoral responsibilities: preaching, visitation, counseling, administration, and numerous other time consumers. Where will they find time to mentor leaders? How can they include leadership development in their schedule if they are already up to their necks in ministry?

The second problem is apathy. For a variety of reasons, some people simply resist the furtherance and work of the church. How might the small church deal with these problems? Here are some suggestions.

The pastor and the church's leaders must determine what their priorities will be. The contention of this book from the beginning is that, while every church has its priorities, leadership development must be at or near the top. Leadership is the backbone of the church; it's the hope and future of the church. Pastors must work through this concept with their board and congregation and attain their understanding and support. Then, for example, if a pastor fails to visit an older member and that member complains to the board, the board will back the pastor, because they understand that the time spent in leadership development will eventually leverage more ministry, including visiting older members. The same applies to the other leaders in the church. Their leadership and training of leaders must take priority over less critical, time-demanding functions.

The pastor and the church's leaders must adopt a recruitment mentality. Every person has the necessary gifts and talents to minister in his or her church. The problem according to one survey is that few pastors and church leaders ever personally challenge congregants to get involved. Often people won't respond to announcements from the pulpit or in the bulletin, but many will respond to a personal, one-on-one invitation. You'll recall from chapter 4 that the Savior modeled this in Mark 1:16–20.

When you catch people accomplishing some ministry-related function, invite them to do it in the church. Most people serving in smaller churches know others who are capable of doing ministry functions. Ask them to draw up a list; then you can approach the people individually. It's imperative that pastors and lay leaders discipline themselves to approach people in their congregation, challenging and inviting them to minister in Christ's church.

Address the reasons people (the so-called apathetic 80 percent) aren't involved in ministry. Some have had a bad ministry experience in the past; some need encouragement; others have had no biblical teaching on spiritual gifts and God's design for ministry and no training; many lack confidence in their ability to serve. These are not overwhelming or insurmountable hurdles. An aspect of good leadership is addressing and overcoming them.

Busy pastors and lay leaders must adopt a team mentality. The Scriptures teach that all of us working together are better than some of us trying to do it all (1 Cor. 12:12–31). It's imperative that leaders in the church build ministry teams. A healthy team can accomplish far more than an individual. If we are to minister and lead well, we do our church a favor by pursuing others to join our team and minister alongside us. They will relieve us of some of the ministry load and free us up so that we can train leaders as well as take an occasional day off or a much needed vacation.

Solving the Time Crunch and Apathy Problems

1. Place leadership development at or near the top of the ministry's priorities.
2. Adopt a ministry recruitment mentality.

3. Address the reasons people in the church are apathetic about ministry involvement.
4. Adopt a ministry team mentality.

Step 2: Recruit someone to initiate and lead the leadership-development process.

- The senior pastor could lead the process.

- **A lay or staff pastor could lead the process.**

A lay or staff pastor could lead the process. The best scenario for successful leadership development is the church that has a staff pastor or lay pastor of leadership development who has no other responsibilities. This person's job is to see that leadership training is accomplished. But many ministries don't have the necessary funds for such a staff position. Some might, however, be able to combine this position with another, such as Christian education director, pastor of mobilization, small-groups leader, youth pastor, or some other position. If this isn't feasible, a highly skilled nonstaff person could take the position as his or her ministry in the church. Eventually, if the process produces good leaders, the church may understand the benefit of employing a part- or full-time person for the position.

If the pastor plans to raise up another person to lead the process, he should work through the following questions:

- Will this be a staff (paid) or a nonstaff (nonpaid) position? If nonpaid, do you have plans to make this a paid position in the future? If so, when? Should this ever be a paid position?
- Do you prefer a man or a woman or does it matter?
- Will the person who leads this process have a title? Having a staff person with a title sends the message that the church not only values but provides training for its ministry leaders. Some possible titles are Pastor or Director of Leadership Development, Pastor or Director of Leadership Training, or Pastor or Director of Equipping. In some cases a title may not be possible, as in the case of a staff person who has multiple responsibilities.

Step 2: Recruit someone to initiate and lead the leadership-development process.

- The senior pastor could lead the process.

- A lay or staff pastor could lead the process.

- **Determine the qualifications.**

The ministry must determine the necessary qualifications if it hopes to find the most qualified leader. The following are some potential qualifications. No one will meet them all, so you must prioritize them. Also, as you attempt to find the right person, remember that God is sovereignly working behind the scenes to help you. (Matthew 20:23 seems to teach that places of ministry and reward are sovereignly directed by God.) You're not alone in the process.

- The following Scriptures may prove helpful in determining qualifications for the position: Acts 6:5; 1 Timothy 3:1–13; 2 Timothy 2:2; Titus 1:6–9; 1 Peter 5:2–3; 2 Peter 1:5–8.
- The candidate should embrace fully and believe he or she can embody the ministry's core values, mission, vision, and strategy. The ministry must determine if leadership is in reality a core value.
- The candidate should have a vision for training leaders. For example, a vision for this position could be to develop the premier leadership-development process in North America, training leaders not only for this ministry but for other ministries as well. This is a kingdom perspective.
- Determine the ideal divine design for this person. What spiritual gifts does he or she need? Is the spiritual gift of leadership a requirement? (Some argue that it takes a leader to train leaders.) What natural gifts would be helpful (a natural gift of leadership)? What must this person be passionate about (developing leaders)? What personal profile (DiSC) temperament is preferable, if any? What MBTI temperament is preferable, if any? Are there any other design requirements or preferences?
- Determine if the candidate must have a good knowledge of the leadership field. Does he or she need to be current with new developments and well read in leadership?
- Determine the necessity of the candidate's having a history of developing leaders in this or other contexts, such as in the corporate world.
- Other qualifications that are required by your ministry.

Step 2: Recruit someone to initiate and lead the leadership-development process.

- The senior pastor could lead the process.
- A lay or staff pastor could lead the process.
- Determine the qualifications.
- **Identify the responsibilities of the position.**

Next you must identify the responsibilities of the position. What is expected? To whom will this person report? The ministry must articulate a ministry description for this position so all are on the same page with their expectations. You may want to include the following in the ministry description: title, profile, and summary of the position; a list of responsibilities; and the individual(s) to whom this person reports and with whom he or she works.

The following is a sample of what a completed ministry description for this position might look like. It's important to note that the person designing and implementing the process as well as the person administering it should use this description. Once the process is established, you may need to tweak the description. For example, you may want to drop some goals and replace them with other goals. It may be beneficial to select someone with strong administrative gifts and abilities for the position so that he or she can regularly evaluate the process and improve it.

Sample Ministry Description

Ministry Title: Pastor of Leadership Development

Ministry Profile: The Pastor of Leadership Development should have the abilities or gifts of leadership, discernment, and administration. This person is expected to create, develop, and refine the process of leadership development and then administer it. This person should have a passion for emerging and existing leaders.

Ministry Summary: The Pastor of Leadership Development is responsible for developing, refining, and administering the church's leadership-development process, which includes discovering, developing, and deploying leaders.

Ministry Goals:
 • Cast the vision for leadership development
 • Design an overall, intentional, systematic leadership-development process
 • Oversee the implementation of the process
 • Raise up and develop a lay-leadership training team to help lead and operate this process
 • Influence the church culture so that leadership becomes and remains a visible core value
 • Keep abreast of what is taking place in leadership development in America and abroad
 • Understand the leadership needs of the ministry

Line of Authority: The pastor of leadership development will report to the senior pastor and work with the pastor of lay mobilization.

A Lay-Leadership Team

Step 1: Determine if the empowered leadership will support the leadership-development process.

Step 2: Recruit someone to initiate and lead the development process.

Step 3: Recruit and develop a lay-leadership team.

Step 4: Arrive at a consensus definition of leadership.

Step 5: Identify the various leadership levels in your ministry.

The third step is that the leader recruits and trains a lay leadership team to assist him or her in developing, implementing, and administering the training process.

The rationale for the team is that the director of the training can't develop and implement the process alone. Ken Blanchard says, "None of us is smarter than all of us."[4] We would add that none of us is more talented than all of us. Even in a megachurch there probably will not be the opportunity of having another paid staff person on the team to assist the pastor or director of leadership development. Perhaps later, when more people value the development of the church's leaders, this will change. For the present, the director will need to recruit a team of people from the congregation. Ultimately this may be a better strategy than having several paid staff because involvement of the laity will give them ownership of and thus more commitment to the process. This team of people will vary in size from one or two in small churches to as many as eight or twelve in larger churches.

As directors of leadership development implement and accomplish the training of the lay leadership team, they must understand that they are modeling for the staff and congregation the entire leadership-development process in embryonic form. Since this is their area of ministry expertise, they are examples to the staff and congregation of how the process works.

Step 3: Recruit and develop a lay-leadership team.

- **Consider using a focus group.**

If the ministry is fairly large, you may want to begin with a focus group. Then you can transition to or raise up the team later in the process. The advantage of the focus group is time, since you can form this group, which will provide temporary help, in a matter of days. Should you opt for the focus group, you will need to address the following:

- When will you recruit this focus group? Most likely the best answer is in the next few days. The leader of the training process will need help right away, so the focus group should be formed in the very early stages of the process.
- What are the group's qualifications? First, do members of the focus group need to be Christians? Some think that an unbeliever, who is interested in and good at leadership, would give the team a valuable perspective. Thus they would welcome input from and dialogue with the non-Christian. Others would limit the focus group to

Christians, believing that unbelievers wouldn't have anything to offer in such a setting.

Second, do the group members need to have a genuine interest in leadership training in the church context? The obvious answer is yes. It's doubtful that a person without any interest would last or make a significant contribution to such a team.

- What is the focus group's ministry mission? A ministry mission is necessary because it clarifies the group's goals and then they know what is expected of them. Here is a sample to guide your thinking: "The Leadership Focus Group serves to provide input, make contacts, and promote the leadership-development process in its early stages until a leadership-development team is formed."

The group will supply some initial ideas and identify church members who are passionate about and gifted in leadership and could serve on the leadership-development team. They also will cast vision for the process and give it the necessary emotional support during its infancy.

Step 3: Recruit and develop a lay-leadership team.

- Consider using a focus group.
- **Shape the leadership-development team.**

It is critical to guide the shaping of the leadership-development team. The persons responsible for leadership training must raise up a leadership team to assist them in the development and implementation of the process. The following are some vital questions that will affect such a team.

- When will you recruit this team? The answer is as soon as possible. Should you have a focus group, it serves during the interim to transition from no team to a fully functioning team.
- How many people should you have on this team? You will need at least two people in a small church and not more than twelve in a large church. Experience dictates that a team of more than twelve people becomes cumbersome and functions poorly. It seems certain that the Savior had a reason for not attempting to pour his life into more than twelve disciples.
- What are the qualifications for this team?

  1. They should be members of the church in good standing. Membership should signal commitment to the church, its identity,

and what it stands for. A member in good standing should be of sound moral character.

2. They need to be in general agreement with the church's statements: core values, mission, vision, strategy, and doctrinal beliefs.

3. The team should be diverse. As much as possible, it should be made up of people of different generations (Builders, Boomers, Busters, and Bridgers), gender, race, and so on. This will provide for greater input and representation of opinion. However, all members will need to agree with the ministry's values, mission, vision, and strategy. Otherwise, this diversity could prove chaotic. Rather than pull together, they could easily pull apart.

4. It would be good if the members are not only interested in leadership training but have some passion for it. This results in greater commitment to the team's mission and lower turnover.

5. Each member must be willing to set aside the necessary time to serve this team. A number of opportunities and obligations constantly compete for people's time. Time for the team must be a priority.

6. These team members must not be enforcers but challengers of the status quo. This implies that they will be creative. They are what we refer to as "early adopters" in the change process. They should be those who risk thinking outside the box and coloring outside the lines.

- What is this team's mission? What do you want them to do? Stating the mission will give the team direction and bring all who are involved together, encouraging unified expectations. The following is a sample mission statement: "The leadership-development team will assist the director of leadership development in developing, implementing, and administering the leadership-training process."

- Who will recruit this team? Who will suggest potential team members and assist in recruiting them? There are several options:

  1. The pastor or director of leadership development—the person in charge—must lead the recruitment effort.

  2. In a small church the pastor or senior pastor likely will be involved but doesn't have to be. If he isn't involved, make sure he approves of the suggested recruits, as he may have some vital information about them that you don't.

3. You might involve other leadership staff, such as the director of ministry involvement, in the recruitment process.
4. The focus group could be involved.

- How will you recruit this team? Personal invitation is a good option. You may want to get the recommendations of the pastor and other key leaders. Or use a churchwide assessment process that includes measures of such characteristics as gifts, passion, and temperament, through which potential members may be identified. Another method is to go on reputation. Who in the ministry has a reputation for wisdom, discernment, a good eye for emerging leaders, and other necessary qualities?

A Consensus Definition of Leadership

Step 1: Determine if the empowered leadership will support the leadership-development process.

Step 2: Recruit someone to initiate and lead the leadership-development process.

Step 3: Recruit and develop a lay-leadership team.

Step 4: Arrive at a consensus definition of leadership.

Step 5: Identify the various leadership levels in your ministry.

The fourth step in identifying the personnel to carry out leadership development will not take long, but it may be the most important. If the ministry is to develop leaders, it must know what a leader is. It must know what it is attempting to accomplish. Without this knowledge, how will it know if or when it has accomplished its goal? This calls for a definition of leadership.

In chapter 1 we defined Christian leaders as servants who use their credibility and capabilities to influence people in a particular context to pursue their God-given direction. At this point in the process, you will need to write your own definition of a leader. Then you will be prepared to move to the next step that requires you to apply this definition to the potential leaders in your ministry.

If you are the senior pastor, you can provide this definition, but be sure to ask for the input of your leadership team. Let them get their fingerprints on it. It's important that you reach consensus and gain their ownership so that everyone is on the same leadership page. The same is true if you function as a lay or paid leadership staff person who is in a support role but responsible to direct the leadership-training process for the ministry. You will need to confer with the senior leader on the definition.

The point is that everyone needs to be using the same definition or you will arrive at different destinations. This necessitates consensus. Consensus doesn't mean that all on the team agree with the final definition. This may not be possible. Neither does it mean that everyone compromises. Everyone is unhappy with a compromise definition. It means that the team agrees to disagree. You will go with the majority definition and those who don't approve of it will agree to use it as a working definition.

The following are some definitions that may help you arrive at your own definition of leadership:

Leadership is figuring out what needs to be done and then doing it.

Leith Anderson[5]

Leadership is a dynamic process in which a man or woman with God-given capacity influences a specific group of God's people toward His purposes for the group.

J. Robert Clinton[6]

Leadership is the ability to influence others based upon one's character, capabilities, and the clarity of the ministry's direction.

Lewis Cooper[7]

In essence leadership appears to be the art of getting others to want to do something you are convinced should be done.

James Kouzes and Barry Posner[8]

Leadership is influence, the ability of one person to influence others.

J. Oswald Sanders[9]

Leadership involves influencing one's peers as a team to carry out the purposes of the church.

Steve Stroope[10]

Leadership is mobilizing others toward a goal shared by the leaders and followers.

Gary Wills[11]

Perhaps one of these definitions or a combination thereof will help you arrive at yours. If not, then you will need to research other definitions and rework them until you arrive at one you can own. The adoption and clarification of a definition focus the group and bring unity to the development process.

Identifying Leadership Levels

Step 1: Determine if the empowered leadership will support the leadership-development process.

Step 2: Recruit someone to initiate and lead the leadership-development process.

Step 3: Recruit and develop a lay-leadership team.

Step 4: Arrive at a consensus definition of leadership.

Step 5: Identify the various leadership levels in your ministry.

The fifth step is to identify the various levels, layers, or types of leadership in your ministry and the leaders of each. If you have completed step 4—come to a consensus definition of leadership—this step will not be difficult. From the start, this book has emphasized the importance of not only training leaders but training leaders at every level of the ministry, as Moses did in Exodus 18:21: "But select capable men from all the people—men who fear God, trustworthy men who hate dishonest gain—and appoint them as officials over thousands, hundreds, fifties and tens."

Here is where the planning team discovers and determines the various layers of leadership in the church. The mistake that most books on leadership development make is to focus solely on leadership at the upper level (the pastor or the professional pastoral team), while ignoring all the other levels of the ministry. This is comparable to erecting a five-story building and focusing all your attention on the top floor. The problem is that the top floor is dependent on all the other floors for support. Ignoring them in the construction process may result in the top floor joining all the other floors in a pile of rubble at ground level.

Identifying your ministry leaders takes you back to the definition of leadership you developed in step 4. Then take the following steps.

Step One: Identify all the Church's Ministries

First, write down all the church's ministries as they are or as you foresee them. If you are a small church, it may be helpful to include the names of those serving in these ministries. The following are some examples of church ministries:

- small-group ministries, such as adult Bible fellowships, cell groups, or Sunday school
- age-graded ministries, including youth, children, preschool, and nursery
- worship ministries, including choirs, bands, praise singers, and instrumentalists
- interest-oriented ministries, including men's, women's, singles, young marrieds, and recreation
- counseling ministries, such as support groups, addiction recovery, and lay counseling
- welcome ministries, such as ushers, greeters, parking lot attendants, registration areas, and information centers
- missions ministries, including service projects, church planting, and short- or long-term world missions
- special ministry "franchises," such as Stephen Ministry, Al Anon, Alpha, and Awana
- leadership ministries, including small group coaches, division leaders, deacons, elders, trustees, and boards

Step Two: Identify the Leaders in Each Ministry

Second, review the list and determine who your leaders are in each ministry. Here is where you will apply your definition of a leader. You are looking for people who are not currently holding leadership positions; some will be easy to identify and others won't. You'll have to consider the degree of influence a person has in some of these cases, and you would be wise to consult with those who lead the ministry areas in which individuals serve. They'll give you perspective as well as insight.

Steps one and two result in a long list of ministries and possibly the names of leaders. What do you do with all this information? The answer is step three.

Step Three: Configure the Leadership Positions into Leadership Levels

Step three focuses on the leadership positions in the ministries and not the ministries themselves. In this step you organize or configure these leadership positions into leadership levels so that you can train leaders at each level. This is similar to what Moses did at the advice of his father-in-law in Exodus 18 and brings order to the list of positions and names. This configuration or organization is what we call leveling, layering, typing, or classifying the leaders. I prefer *leveling*, but this term could leave some leaders feeling inferior to others. You'll need to select the term that best fits your situation.

Edgar Elliston and Timothy Kauffman in *Developing Leaders for Urban Ministries* provide several ways for typing leaders.[12] I have included an example of the process in the following section. You may find it helpful to refer to it for clarification as you read the rest of this chapter.

You will need to arrive at some criteria for establishing the different levels. The following are sample criteria. You may want to use one or a combination of them:

- professionally trained and not professionally trained
- leaders of ministries and leaders of leaders
- leaders with churchwide influence and leaders with ministry-specific influence
- paid and unpaid
- full-time and part-time
- leaders with budget responsibility and leaders without budget responsibility

You must decide which leaders in your ministry fit each type or level. Some leaders may shift from one level to the next. For example, a level 2 small-group leader may become a staff person at level 4. However, the goal for leaders isn't to move from one level of leadership to another; it's to grow within their level.

Some people may operate at two different levels at the same time. An example could be an elder (who may have churchwide influence) who also teaches Sunday school (classwide influence).

An Example of the Leveling Process

The following is an example of leveling leaders, using some of the criteria above.

Level 1 leaders. These are all people who are nonprofessional, nonvocational leaders who volunteer to serve God and the church at the entry level of ministry. They exercise influence over a small, focused group on a part-time basis. These could include Sunday school teachers, nursery workers, children and youth workers, ushers, greeters, choir directors, leaders of singles ministries, Stephen Ministry leaders, leaders of men's and women's ministries, and Al-Anon leaders. Any apprentices in training also would be included here.

Level 2 leaders. These people are nonprofessional, nonvocational leaders who volunteer to serve alongside the leadership staff. Another designation would be paraprofessionals. In their positions they exercise more influence and need more advanced leadership skills than those at level 1. They could include small-group leaders and their coaches; board members (elders, deacons, trustees); adult Bible fellowship leaders; and possibly adult Sunday school teachers and lay counselors, as well as any apprentices who serve with them.

Level 3 leaders. These people are potential or part-time staff. They may or may not be paid or may work their way into a paid position over time. They are emerging leaders who are preparing for vocational ministry. Consequently they will have or be in the process of receiving specific vocational training for their ministry tasks. While their influence may be limited, it will be growing as they begin to minister to people. All of this will change when they complete their official training, because they will take over their own ministry in the church or leave to do ministry elsewhere. Examples would be future church planters and revitalizers and interns and residents who train with the leadership staff at level 4.

Level 4 leaders. People at this level are paid vocational workers who minister full-time. They exercise broad influence and some may have more power than leaders at the other levels. These leaders include pastors, executive pastors, associate pastors, assistant pastors, pastors of leadership development, pastors of missions, pastors of worship, pastors of Christian education, pastors of mobilization, children's pastors, youth pastors, singles pastors, zone pastors, life phase pastors, pastors of spiritual life, pastors of recreation, and professional church counselors.

You may wish to categorize these four levels into mid- and upper-level leadership. For example, you could identify level 2 and 3 leaders as mid-level leaders and level 4 as upper-level leaders. In your ministry context, you may need to identify more than four levels of leadership or fewer. Two helpful samples are in the last chapter of this book. Use them to guide you as you identify the various levels of your ministry.

Questions for Reflection and Discussion

1. Do you agree or disagree with Peter Drucker's observation that "people determine the performance capacity of an organization"? Why?

2. Do you believe that the empowered leadership in your ministry will support the leadership-development process? Why or why not?
3. Who might you choose to lead the development process? Why?
4. Who would be good members of a lay-leadership team? Why?
5. What is your definition of leadership?
6. Identify and articulate the various levels of leadership in your ministry.

8

Putting the Process in Motion

The Procedures for Developing Leaders, Phase 1

Not only are contractors dependent on their construction personnel, they also must employ the right procedures in building a house. These procedures consist of various steps that must take place at a certain time and in a certain order. To get out of step could spell disaster for the entire project. For example, the plumbers must lay down the necessary pipes before the foundation is poured. And the electricians must put the house's electrical wiring in the walls before other workers cover them with sheetrock.

Chapter 7 dealt with having the right personnel to build your leadership-development house. We learned that without the right people in place, the entire process is in jeopardy from the start. Emerging leaders will reflect the training or lack thereof of those who develop them.

This chapter and chapters 9, 10, and 11 will take leader-trainers through the five steps that are vital to the leadership-development process. Step 1 is the leadership discovery step in which you locate your emerging leaders. Step 2 is the launching step in which you place your discovered leaders in the proper ministry. In step 3, the development step, you grow your leaders. It's so important that we have devoted chapters 9 and 10 to it. Step 4 focuses attention on evaluating your leaders as well as your entire leadership-development process, and in step 5 you reward your leaders.

Steps in Leadership Development

Step 1: Discover Leaders

Step 2: Launch Leaders

Step 3: Develop Leaders

Step 4: Evaluate Leaders

Step 5: Reward Leaders

Discover New Leaders

Step 1: Discover new leaders for development.

Step 2: Launch new leaders into their positions of leadership.

Step 3: Develop new and current leaders for ministry in the church.

Step 4: Regularly evaluate your leadership-development process.

Step 5: Regularly reward those in the leadership-development process.

The development of your ministry's leaders begins with discovery. It's an essential step to leadership development that consists of three ingredients: recruitment, exploration, and assessment.

Step 1: Discover new leaders for development.

- **Recruit**

Recruitment

Recruitment is essential to leadership development because it helps the ministry *discover* new leaders among its new and/or uninvolved members. Thus it provides a fresh supply of leaders for the church without which the ministry would begin to decline and eventually grind to a halt. Both the Savior (chapter 4) and the first-century church (chapter 6) recruited leaders for ministry.

We define *recruitment* as *the never-ending process of inviting potential leaders into ministry at the various levels of the church.* Several important issues are part of this definition. First, recruitment is a process that is never ending. As long as the church exists, it will need leaders. Thus the church must not only plan to be in the recruitment business but be good at it.

Second, recruitment is extending an invitation to new leaders. In every church a number of people are standing on the sidelines or sitting in the stands, watching others do the ministry. As we have said, there are numerous reasons for this. Some people are new members who haven't had time to get into the game. Others have experienced failure or burnout, or they lack confidence in themselves and their abilities. However, the main reason people stand on the sidelines is that they have never been *asked* to get into the game! Recruitment is moving all these people from wherever they are to where God wants them to be—on the ministry playing field.

Third, these new leaders will have influence at a particular level of the church. Though some of these people may already exercise influence in some way, they haven't been officially recognized as leaders in the church and aren't being trained as such.

We have already seen, as we looked at the ministry of Jesus and the early church in Acts, that Scripture doesn't prescribe a specific method or process for recruiting the church's leaders, except for prayer. In his book, James reminds us that we do not have some things because we don't ask for them (4:2). Sometimes we miss the obvious. We don't have leaders and we lose sleep wondering where we'll find some, when all along God invites us to ask him for them. The Savior directed his disciples to pray for harvest workers in Matthew 9:36–38: "When he saw the crowds, he had compassion on them, because they were harassed and helpless, like sheep without a shepherd. Then he said to his disciples, 'The harvest is plentiful but the workers are few. Ask the Lord of the harvest, therefore, to send out workers into his harvest field.'" This invitation grows out of his compassion for the lost and his desire to see them come to know him. Leaders are critical to people coming to know the Savior. Thus prayer is a vital recruitment ingredient.

Jesus also invited his disciples to join his team. As we bathe the recruitment process in prayer, it also would be wise to personally approach and invite people to leadership involvement. Otherwise, some may apply who aren't leaders or who don't qualify as such, and we have to go through the difficult process of turning them down. Regardless, each local church has the freedom to develop its own recruitment process as long as it includes prayer and doesn't violate Scripture in some way.

Thinking through a unique recruitment process will raise some questions that each church must answer. Here are a few: Where will your leaders come from? (Can they apply? Do they have to be invited?) Who will find them (staff, small-groups coaches, leaders, others)? How will they find them (church assessment, recommendations from other leaders, other methods)?

WHO WILL RECRUIT LEADERS?

In general, the goal is for everybody to recruit leaders. The ministry should seek to develop a leadership-recruitment mentality. Its leaders need to be talent scouts who are recruitment sensitive, always scanning the ministry landscape on the lookout for emerging leaders. Since each person in ministry must seek to reproduce himself or herself, leadership recruitment is everybody's job. With this in mind, the ministry could ask or at least encourage every leader at every level to have an apprentice, intern, or resident. The pastor of leadership development or the individual responsible for training leaders, department heads, leadership staff, teachers, and ministry leaders should always be a recruiter for the cause.

The key to creating a recruitment mentality is to emphasize its importance with the current leaders at each level. There are several ways to accomplish this:

- Expose them to other well-known leaders who highly value leadership and the recruitment of leaders. These would be men such as John Maxwell and Bill Hybels who have stressed this at their leadership conferences and summits. Challenge your people to listen to their tapes.
- Regularly cast a vision for recruitment—talk about it all the time.
- Be sure to tie recruitment to the biblical concept of discipleship. Leaders must know the spiritual motive behind recruiting and not just the organizational motive.
- Honor those who recruit leaders. Treat them as ministry heroes. Use them in sermon illustrations and as positive examples when casting vision.
- Include recruitment as a regular item in every worker's evaluation process. Ask him or her, "How many leaders did you recruit this quarter?" What gets evaluated gets done.
- Make training on how to recruit people a key component of the leadership-development process. This can be done through role playing, providing scripts, and practicing the script with leaders. During leadership training, regularly ask existing leaders to share how someone challenged them to become a leader.

WHO WILL BE RECRUITED?

Who is the recruitment pool? The answer is twofold. First, people from within the church—members or, the better term, partners—will be recruited. (The ideal is people who have been members for at least a couple of years.) When the church is encouraging its attenders to higher commitment through membership, it is a good time to recruit leaders also. As current leaders recruit new members, they should assess their potential as future leaders.

The uninvolved membership also serves as a rich source for leadership recruitment. Invite those who have chosen not to be involved but have leadership ability to train for leadership. In addition, the church must not ignore recruiting and training its young people to be future leaders. Why not begin training them now?

Existing leaders also will recruit people from outside the church. These could be students with minimal experience who may be undergoing theological training at a college or seminary. These students could serve an internship in some area of leadership. Potential staff persons are another source of leaders. These are promising people who may have theological training, past pastoral experience, or both. Perhaps they have pastored a church but feel they need more training before pastoring again. They could serve a residency. The church might recruit them as future church staff or train them and send them out as church planters or revitalizers or in other functions.

How Will Leaders Be Recruited?

Leaders will be recruited by two actions: aggressive listening and bold, consistent asking.

Aggressive listening is the first key action in recruiting leaders. It involves paying attention to what people are saying. In general, current leaders must be in radar mode 24/7, scanning the horizon and taking in all of the data that potential leaders are sending their way. Recruiters should be looking for any indication of undiscovered leaders—people who draw the attention of existing leaders, who are seen taking the initiative, who give 110 percent, or who clearly embrace the mission, vision, and values of the church.

Paying attention is not enough, however. It must be followed up with investigative work. Aggressive listening also involves probing with good questions to discover the untapped leadership potential in others. A leader may ask another leader, "Mary seemed very effective in organizing the retreat weekend. Has she planned a lot of events before?" A leader may probe with a new church member, "Bill, I heard that you were recently promoted to plant manager. I sense that you're a seasoned leader. Have you exercised your abilities in churches before you came here?"

One very effective form of aggressive listening is brainstorming with other leaders. This involves discussing emerging leaders with the top three to ten existing leaders in the church organization. It is not uncommon for a leadership team to have different experiences and points of view on people. Therefore, a group discussion can bring much synergy, clarity, and efficiency to the identification of potential leaders. Imagine, for example, if several elders agree, based on various experiences, that Joe is a prime leadership candidate. This can increase confidence and speed up the process of approaching Joe as an emerging leader. In addition, the outcome of a group discussion may provide helpful insight for *not* approaching someone as a potential leader.

While the team approach is very effective, at other times a current leader will discuss potential leaders with someone else, such as the director or pastor of leadership development or another responsible person, before issuing an invitation. In either case, the discipline of aggressive listening will speed up the process of discovering new leaders.

The second key activity in recruiting leaders is bold, consistent asking. Asking must be bold in the sense that leaders call emerging leaders to the transcendent cause of kingdom work. The real problem in recruiting leaders is often not their lack of commitment. The missing element can be the lack of a vast, compelling vision, a sense of the immensity of the task at hand.

Asking also must be persistent. Leaders must keep asking potential leaders until they get a decided yes or no. Most people won't make a significant life investment into leadership after just one ask. Because recruiting is a process, many people will need time and repeated invitations to cross the leadership line. Therefore, unless there is a clear no, the door remains cracked for you to ask again at an appropriate time in the future.

In general, there are two major categories for asking: personal address and organizational address. Personal address is when a leader speaks to an individual in an effort to recruit, based on an established relationship. Organizational address is when the church as an organization makes known its need for leaders.

The personal address is always better and will yield more results because it happens in the context of familiarity, trust, and warmth. Any professional in marketing will tell you that word of mouth is by far the best advertising. This is true in the church and especially true in the development of leaders. Because the personal ask is so important, it is imperative that every leader use it in recruiting new leaders.

When inviting a potential leader to step up to the leadership plate, there are several types of appeal that the recruiting leader can use. The four basic types of appeal are need-based, relationship-based, significance-based, and vision-based.

A leader may make an appeal based on ministry needs. For example, "Ellen, we have a constant need for new leaders. You have been coming to the church for a while, and we are convinced that you would make a good leader. Would you consider leading in a ministry area?" Another leader may leverage a personal relationship, "Hey, Jack, I have really enjoyed getting to know you, and I appreciate your commitment to our small group. Would you consider becoming an apprentice leader in the group?" If a leader observes leadership gifts in another, it is easy to make an appeal based on divine design and personal significance: "By the way, Sue, I noticed how well you initiated the discussion tonight. Have you ever considered using your skills in a leadership role at the church? I think that you would be an effective ministry director." And finally, there is the vision-based appeal: "Our dream is to launch twelve churches in the next three years. Steve, would you consider being one of the core group members of a new planting initiative?" A good recruiter will use all of the different appeals at different times and with different people in the ministry.

The organizational address is another form of asking, which includes such things as advertising, announcements, invitations from the pulpit, creative programming, and ministry placement systems that all point out opportunities to become a leader. Frequently I (Will) recommend to churches that they include a check box on their communication card (a tear-off sheet that is part of the worship bulletin) that says, "Send me information about becoming a leader." Another recommendation is inviting from the pulpit the church-at-large to leadership-training events. When potential leaders register, enter their names in a database and identify them as potential leaders. Special training events will introduce them to your leadership-training process and expose them to your leadership culture.

While the organizational address is less effective than personal address, it is still very important. It will always produce some direct response all by itself. For example, if people are new to the church and happen to be seasoned leaders, they may respond to an organizational address before they have been personally invited. This speeds up the process of assimilation into leadership.

Organizational address supplements the word-of-mouth relationship-based recruiting. For example, an individual may have received numerous personal invitations from a friend without ever responding. Then an organizational address may encourage him or her to actually attend a leadership event. Often it takes several impressions before the commitment is made.

Finally, regular, repeated organizational addresses keep the importance of leadership before the congregation. When people hear an organizational address enough times (at least seven), they realize the significance of what is announced.

The How of Recruiting

Key Recruiting Action	What to Do
Aggressive listening	Pay attention 24/7 Probe with questions
Bold, consistent asking	Cast a compelling vision Ask until they say no Use personal address through need-based, relationship-based, significance-based, and vision-based appeals Use organization address

Exploration

Step 1: Discover new leaders for development.

- Recruit

- **Explore**

After a potential leader is recruited, exploration must take place. Exploration is important because it's that part of the discovery step when the newly recruited emerging leader and the ministry enter into dialogue over the leadership-development process and the prospective leader's possible involvement in that process.

Exploration is the twofold process when newly recruited leaders discover more about the church's leadership-development process and the church discovers more about the prospective leader. It's a process that likely will take place over several meetings as the prospective leader asks questions about leadership development and the ministry has questions for him or her. Also, the ministry representative may want to schedule meetings for the potential leader with others in the ministry. For example, if the prospective leader desires to lead a small group, he or she could meet with the small-groups coach or a small-group leader. During these discussions, the prospective leader will discover and learn more about the church's leadership development, such as its vision, qualifications, expectations, process, benefits, and other pertinent information.

As church leaders discover more about the prospective leaders, they are gathering vital information that will direct the potential leaders' future ministry in the church as well as qualify them for ministry, and, perhaps in some cases, disqualify them.

Scripture doesn't directly address the topic of exploring leaders. For example, in Acts 13:1–3 the Holy Spirit worked through prophets and teachers to direct Paul and Barnabas on their first missionary journey. The implication is that it simply happened with little discussion between the participants, but the text doesn't go into much detail. There may have been more interaction and discussion than is recorded. Regardless, the lack of biblical imperatives leaves the church free to explore as they see fit, as long as it's done wisely.

The exploration process touches three areas: It raises some questions that the church must answer; it examines the emerging leader's qualifications; it relates the benefits of being a leader.

QUESTIONS FOR EXPLORATION

First, the church must determine who will lead the exploration process. This could be any number of people or a combination of them. In a small church, this person may be the senior pastor. When the church has a director of leadership development, this person could lead the process.

In a larger church, the senior pastor, because of time constraints, probably would be unable to fill this role. Thus the pastor or director of leadership development, someone on the leadership development team, the pastor or director of lay mobilization, or an area supervisor could lead the exploration process.

The ministry also should decide if one person handles the exploration process for everyone else (a centralized approach) or if different people will lead the process at each of the church's leadership levels (a decentralized approach). Then they must decide who the person or persons will be. In many cases the size of the church will dictate the approach.

Next the ministry must decide how the process will be accomplished. The ministry representative doing the exploration should conduct an interview with the prospective leader that covers the following:

- introduction of himself or herself if unknown to the recruited leader
- questions that will elicit information about the recruit, such as where the person lives, marital and family status, vocation, reason for attending the church, and any other background and current information
- the church's vision for developing its leaders
- explanation of the leadership-training process and the ministry's expectations of its leaders
- the benefits of being a leader
- exploration of the prospective leader's interests
- arranging for interviews with others, if necessary

QUALIFICATIONS FOR LEADERSHIP

The church may want to call on a ministry representative to explore potential leaders' qualifications for leadership. In some cases, especially in a small church, current leaders usually know if people meet leadership qualifications before any recruitment takes place. If some people don't meet the qualifications, the exploration goes no further. Here's an important point: It's much easier not to select people at this early stage in the process than it is to remove them later when they're firmly entrenched in leadership positions. Be sure to pray and ask for God's wisdom in this matter (James 1:5–6).

The following are some possible qualifications or disqualifications. Work through them and decide what is important to your ministry. Write them in question form and have potential leaders respond to them (see a sample church leadership questionnaire in appendix B).

Here are some qualifications of a potential leader. He or she should be

- A Christian.
- A person of good character. You'll need to determine the character qualifications for each leadership level.
- A person of good reputation in the community. Check with the local authorities, if necessary. This is an imperative if the person will work with children.
- Teachable. While the potential leader may not articulate this, it is usually obvious if someone thinks he or she knows it all. This is usually a sign of some deeper emotional issue. You may find that you're wasting your time with such a person because he or she, deafened by presuppositions, won't listen to you. Therefore, you need to explore this issue up front, especially with those at the higher levels of leadership. You could do this by requiring references and asking about the prospective leader's teachability. In many cases, you won't discover that the person isn't teachable until he or she is already in the process. This would be grounds for probation or dismissal. Some people may be open to the teaching of certain leaders and not others, so an alternative to probation is having the person work with someone with whom he or she feels comfortable.
- Committed. People show their commitment through church membership and ministry involvement. The prospective leader may have a reputation for commitment or lack thereof.

- Able to agree with the ministry's statements—core values, mission, vision, strategy, and doctrine.

- A person with good personal habits and background. Questions to ask here are, Does he or she use tobacco or drink alcoholic beverages? Is he or she divorced or separated from a spouse? While these may not be disqualifiers, you should be aware of them. Is there any history of domestic violence? Are there any areas of possible disqualification of which the church needs to be aware?

What will you do with those who aren't qualified? If such a person pursues becoming a leader, you will need to meet with him or her and explain the problems. If handled gently and properly, this could be a life-changing experience for the person who desires to be a leader, challenging him or her to grow in the deficient area. If the person is agreeable, you could map out a strategy for improvement. If he or she reacts adversely, this confirms your decision that the person isn't qualified for leadership.

BENEFITS OF LEADERSHIP

Finally, the ministry representative should explore with the potential leader the benefits of leadership. In 1 Timothy 3:13 Paul mentions two benefits of being a deacon. The first is a high standing. Paul may be referring to divine rewards in this life and the life to come, or he may be referring to esteem and respect from those whom the deacon leads and ministers to in the church community. The second is "great assurance in their faith in Christ Jesus."

There are other benefits as well, such as the privilege of serving Christ by serving people (Matt. 20:26–28) and a sense of self-worth and significance because of the value of what is done for Christ.

Assessment

Step 1: Discover new leaders for development.

- Recruit

- Explore

- **Assess**

Once the prospective leader has qualified and accepted a leadership position, his or her readiness for leadership must be assessed. It is a most important part of discovery because it helps potential leaders uncover and then act on their divine design. Assessment also will help the church develop and then deploy its leaders.

Assessment *helps Christians discern and reaffirm how God has uniquely designed them to serve him.* Assessment involves the discovery of a person's spiritual and natural gifts, passion, temperament, and other vital aspects of who he or she is. Assessment aids Christians who are not aware of how God has designed them for leadership and ministry to discover that design. Some Christians are vaguely aware of their design based on past ministry experience. Assessment serves to reaffirm that design as well as uncover new areas of ability.

The New Testament addresses assessment primarily from the perspective of spiritual gifts. It provides several lists of spiritual gifts (Romans 12 and 1 Corinthians 12) or gifted people (Eph. 4:11–13). It also commands believers to exercise their gifts (1 Cor. 14:1; 1 Tim. 4:14; 2 Tim. 1:6). Otherwise, Scripture grants the church much freedom in how it assesses its people for ministry.

The concept of assessment raises several important questions that each church must address.

WHO ASSESSES LEADERS?

The ideal is for every church to have a formal, systematic assessment process in place. A pastor or director of lay involvement or mobilization would lead this process and one or several lay volunteers would staff and operate it. Not only would the director and volunteers serve to assess or help assess a congregation, but they also could help train other leaders in the assessment process. If such a process is not in place, it will need to be developed by a pastor, ministry department leaders, ministry team leaders, or those trained in assessment.

WHO IS ASSESSED?

The recruited potential leaders who aren't currently involved in the church are assessed. They have completed the exploration phase and are ready to have their God-given design for ministry assessed.

WHAT DOES THE ASSESSMENT PROCESS ENTAIL?

This process consists of the three Ds: design, direction, and development. The emphasis of assessment is on the first D—design—but they all work together. Design is vital to one's direction, and direction dictates how one develops. A person's design consists of a number of components. The general areas are giftedness (spiritual and natural), passion, and temperament. Other areas for assessment include in-depth looks into past experience, spiritual maturity, prior and present leadership experience, reputation, recommendations, and prior and present training.

There are several good resources and tools that will help you assess individuals for ministry and leadership roles. I (Aubrey) have written a book on divine design called *Maximizing Your Effectiveness,* which covers these areas in more detail and provides assessment tools. Two church-based assessment resources are *Network* by Willow Creek Community Church and *SHAPE* by Saddleback Community Church.[1]

After assessment is completed, the ministry will enter these people with their designs into the church's computer for ministry matching and ultimate ministry assignment.

The leadership covenant is another important assessment tool. A leadership covenant is a written expression of the spiritual commitment that the church asks of the leader. While leadership qualifications reflect the spiritual maturity required to lead and the leader's role description reflects the responsibility of the leader, the leadership covenant reflects the predisposition of the heart and spiritual commitment of the leader. The covenant is a unique indication of the emerging leader's readiness to lead. As you might imagine, a potential leader may fulfill all of the leadership qualifications, know his or her design for ministry, and be ready to perform the responsibilities, but still not be ready to make a spiritual commitment to leadership. Obviously this is a key point of discernment before launching a leader.

The content of the leadership covenant depends on the ministry context and values of the church. When I (Will) work with churches in developing a covenant, the first thing I look for is an existing definition, internal to the organization, of what a mature disciple looks like (or whatever language describes the accomplishment of the church mission). If the church has a definition, I encourage them to structure the covenant around it. The basic reason for this is that the church, in launching an emerging leader, is implicitly saying to its people, "This person is a worthy model to follow." (Think about the seriousness of this for a minute!) Therefore, the covenant ought to align with any preestablished definitions. The following is a sample covenant.

Sample Leadership Covenant

Salvation
_____ I have trusted in Christ alone for my salvation and I realize that my standing with Christ and value as a believer are based not on my performance but on God's grace.

Ephesians 2:8–9 For it is by grace you have been saved, through faith— and this not from yourselves, it is the gift of God—not by works, so that no one can boast.

Spiritual Growth

_____ I will seek to grow toward being a fully devoted follower of Jesus Christ by having a consistent time alone with God through prayer and Bible study.

2 Peter 3:18 But grow in the grace and knowledge of our Lord and Savior Jesus Christ. To him be glory both now and forever! Amen.

Small-Group Community

_____ I will lead my group into biblical community (prayer, Scripture, care, and service). I will serve with a leadership team including a leader, apprentice, and host. I will lead my group to actively participate in appropriate planning and training meetings.

Acts 2:42–47 They devoted themselves to the apostles' teaching and to the fellowship, to the breaking of bread and to prayer. Everyone was filled with awe, and many wonders and miraculous signs were done by the apostles. All the believers were together and had everything in common. Selling their possessions and goods, they gave to anyone as he had need. Every day they continued to meet together in the temple courts. They broke bread in their homes and ate together with glad and sincere hearts, praising God and enjoying the favor of all the people. And the Lord added to their number daily those who were being saved.

Service

_____ I will enlist and equip others in the group to serve God according to their gifts.

1 Peter 4:10 Each one should use whatever gift he has received to serve others, faithfully administering God's grace in its various forms.

Stewardship

_____ I will cheerfully, generously, and regularly give to God through the local church. The biblical starting point for financial stewardship is a tithe (10 percent) to the local church. I will seek to be a good steward of any money used by my ministry group.

Malachi 3:10 "Bring the whole tithe into the storehouse, that there may be food in my house. Test me in this," says the Lord Almighty, "and see if I will not throw open the floodgates of heaven and pour out so much blessing that you will not have room enough for it."

Name _____   Group _____

Signature _____   Date _____

Launch New Leaders

Step 1: Discover new leaders for development.

Step 2: Launch new leaders into their positions of leadership.

Step 3: Develop new and current leaders for ministry in the church.

Step 4: Regularly evaluate your leadership-development process.

Step 5: Regularly reward those in the leadership-development process.

Launching new leaders into leadership positions is important because it helps to assure that people who are gifted as leaders are ministering in leadership positions for which they are gifted. Christians can't do or be anything they want; to serve effectively, they must be in positions commensurate with their divine design. *Launching, then, involves the right people putting the right leaders in the right place (context) at the right time.*

We discovered in chapter 6 that the Holy Spirit places leaders in their ministries through such vehicles as the congregation, apostles, elders, and others. While Scripture describes, it doesn't *prescribe* a specific placement process. Therefore, each church is free to design one that works best for it. As long as it doesn't violate Scripture, God will use it to place his people in ministry.

Who Is Launched?

The people who have gone through the recruitment, exploration, and assessment stages of leadership discovery are ready to be launched in their ministry position. As you will recall from chapter 7, there are several levels of leaders who will be launched in various placements.

Level 1 leaders are the largest group. They are volunteers with little formal training and may serve the church as Sunday school teachers, learning center teachers, nursery workers, greeters, ushers, audio-video technicians, drama people, choir directors, band members, music people, counselors, and in many other areas.

Level 2 leaders are those who will serve the church along with the staff. This is a smaller group of paraprofessionals who are volunteers with some training. They may serve as small-group leaders or church board leaders (elders and deacons).

Level 3 leaders are those who plan to enter the professional ministry as staff, missionaries, church planters, and in other capacities. They would include promising, gifted lay people, interns, and others.

Level 4 leaders serve the church as staff. This is a small group of paid professionals, which would include all the pastors of a church.

Who Launches Leaders?

The minister or director of mobilization, a staff person, a ministry area director, or another leader could place level 1 leaders into a position. He or she could send people to a specific ministry according to their design, for example, Sunday school, Stephen Ministry, or music ministry. These newly deployed level 1 leaders would serve initially as apprentices, working under a trained, more experienced person. In some cases, when a person is designed to minister in an area that is not yet a ministry in the church, the person who launches the leader will help him or her begin or plant such a ministry when the timing is right.

For level 2 leaders, the pastor or director of leadership development, the leadership staff, the board, or small-group leaders will usually do the deployment. The pastoral staff will select and place leaders from within or outside the congregation. The board and staff will select and deploy new board members. Each current small-group or Sunday school leader could directly or indirectly deploy an apprentice leader.

The pastor, pastoral staff, and the board (in some cases) could select and launch level 3 leaders. The pastor, certain staff (for example, an executive pastor), the chairman of the board, as well as others could oversee the selection and placement of level 4 leaders.

What Is the Right Ministry?

Context is whom and where a leader leads—primarily, the people and their circumstances. Proper context is critical to leadership because effective performance depends on the proper match between the leader's style of interacting with followers and the degree to which the situation gives control and influence to the leader. The wrong context can prove devastating. For example, sometimes seminary placement officers have allowed those who are least experienced and are testing their ministry wings to accept pastoral positions in struggling, often dysfunctional situations, which may prove disastrous. Other, more experienced pastors usually avoid such situations. Laypeople placed in the wrong ministry context also can experience discouragement and ineffectiveness.

The director or pastor of mobilization or the persons responsible for launching may want to give prospective leaders several placement options (contexts) within their leadership level. Here are some of the questions they must ask and answer:

- Is there a ministry context in the church where this person fits?
- What if this person has a design for which there is no present ministry? Would we design a new ministry for him or her? If not, what would we do?
- Will the new leader minister within or outside the facility where the church meets? Some churches minister outside the walls of their facility as well as within them. An example is an inner-city ministry that provides a soup kitchen, an alternative school, and job training and placement.

- What if the emerging leader fits several ministry contexts within or outside the church? Could he or she visit several different ministries where there is a match, talk to the people leading and ministering in those areas, and then decide on one of them? If the first choice doesn't work out, the person could try another.

In most situations, a ministry needed the leader yesterday. Leaders are in constant demand, and most will be scooped up quickly. However, the divine design process may reveal that no position and context exists for some people at the present. An option in these situations is to begin or plant a ministry that they will lead. However, those responsible must decide when the time is right for such a venture. That's not always easy, but knowing that God has raised up a leader is a good indication that the time is ripe for the new ministry.

Questions for Reflection and Discussion

1. Who could or should recruit leaders in your ministry?
2. Who will be recruited in your ministry? Will you recruit from outside the church?
3. Who will assess leaders in your ministry? Do they know how to do assessment? If not, how will they learn?
4. Which leaders will be assessed? Will you use any of the resources suggested in this chapter?
5. How do the leaders in your church compare to those at the various leadership levels in this chapter? How do they differ?

9

How to Grow Leaders

The Procedures for Developing Leaders, Phase 2

At this point in the leadership-development process, you've thought through and are working your way through steps 1 and 2—discovering and launching emerging leaders at every level of the church. Now you're ready to take the next step—developing your leaders. The questions are: How do we develop leaders? How do we move them from where they are to where they need to be to lead most effectively in Christ-honoring ministries within and outside our churches?

Develop New and Current Leaders

Step 1: Discover new leaders for development.

Step 2: Launch new leaders into their positions of leadership.

Step 3: Develop new and current leaders for ministry in the church.

Step 4: Regularly evaluate your leadership-development process.

Step 5: Regularly reward those in the leadership-development process.

The following general process will help you design a unique leadership-training process for your specific ministry situation. As discussed in chapter 1, all leaders have a need to grow and develop in terms of their character, leadership knowledge, skills, and emotions. Since no one will ever arrive at perfection in these areas, he or she must constantly strive to grow and develop. The mark of good leaders is that they're always learning and thus growing spiritually, intellectually, experientially, and emotionally.

It's important to note that this is step 3, not step 1. We've observed that most of those who have designed leadership-training processes usually begin and end here. However, these processes struggle for survival because they have neglected to properly select the personnel to do the leadership development and they have not realized the importance of the discovery and launching of new leaders. Also, if they don't do steps 4 and 5—regularly evaluating and rewarding leaders—they've not touched all the bases that are necessary for sustaining the life of the process.

Leadership development is the process of helping leaders at every level of ministry assess and develop their Christian character and to acquire, reinforce, and refine their ministry knowledge and skills. As a process, leadership development is never ending, because leaders are learners and if they ever stop learning, they stop leading. Potentially, leadership development focuses on leaders at every level in the ministry, because all leaders in the ministry need training. It involves assessment of leaders' character and helps them know where they are in their personal character development and where they need to grow.

Leadership development concerns acquiring new leadership knowledge and skills. Leaders are learners as well as teachers, so they should keep up with and update their leadership knowledge and skills in their areas of ministry. They must continually assess and refine their current knowledge of leadership and their skills for leading and discard any practices that may prove unbiblical or culturally irrelevant for their ministry in the twenty-first century.

The Scriptures prescribe the training of leaders, as we have seen in 2 Timothy 2:2 where Paul instructs leaders: "And the things you have heard me say in the presence of many witnesses entrust to reliable men who will also be qualified to teach others." Scripture also provides numerous examples of leaders, such as the Savior, Paul, Timothy, Aquila, and Priscilla.

However, the Bible doesn't prescribe how leaders are to be developed. Again this means that the Holy Spirit has left the process and structure up to each local church. As long as it doesn't violate Scripture, each ministry has the freedom to design a leadership-training process tailor-made for its leaders.

A characteristic of churches that are training leaders is that they have some kind of development process in place. The structures may be different, but the training occurs. And in this training, churches have a distinct advantage over seminaries. They provide for immediate application.

Training Dynamics

The rest of this chapter and the next turn your attention to the three dynamics that we believe are necessary to train leaders. The first dynamic involves the four core leadership competencies—character, knowledge, skills, and emotions. The second dynamic involves the four means for training—learner-driven, content-driven, mentor-driven, and experience-driven. And the last dynamic involves the sixteen training venues, which we will cover in chapter 10. For a thorough process of leadership development, all levels of leadership must address these dynamics.

Step 3: Develop new and current leaders for ministry in the church.

* **Four core leadership competencies**

Four Core Leadership Competencies

Leaders must become proficient in four core competencies—character, knowledge, skills, and emotions. Apparently, more than twenty-five years ago, one of the first Army leadership-training manuals coined the expression that best summarizes the first three competencies: "Be, know, do." We would add a fourth—feel, which involves the emotions. All four areas impact deeply the kind of learning that must take place before leaders can consider themselves competent.

BEING

Character reflects the very heart and soul of the leader. It is soul work that develops the leader's Christlikeness from core to crust. Psalm 78:72 says that David shepherded (led) his people with "integrity of heart," a good description of godly character.

In the introduction to this book, we commented that America in general and the church in particular are facing a leadership crisis. We have heard Howard Hendricks say on several occasions that the great crisis in America today is a leadership crisis and the great crisis in leadership is a crisis of character. Leaders must be people of good character. In the circles of theological education, character development in students is often assumed, and this is often a problem. Educators stress the importance of character development but assume that students are working in this area—a poor assumption that has proved disastrous for some of our top Christian leaders.

After the collapse of such notable corporations as Enron and Arthur Andersen, even the corporate world has begun to emphasize the importance of good character and servant leadership.

The importance of character raises several questions for leaders: Who must leaders be to lead effectively at each level of the ministry? What are the character requirements for each level of leadership? Who do people expect the leader to be? Scripture provides us with some general character qualities. Passages such as 1 Timothy 3:1–7; Titus 1:6–9; and 1 Peter 5:2 provide the church with the characteristics for elders, who would be equivalent to today's pastors. First Timothy 3:8–13 provides the character qualities for deacons. In 2 Peter 1:3–9 Peter appears to address all Christians, stressing certain qualities. Acts 6:3–5 provides some requirements for early church leaders, and Galatians 5:22–23 presents the fruit of the Spirit, which should characterize every Christian's behavior.

Some other necessary character qualities that we dealt with in chapter 4 are found in 2 Timothy 2:2, such as competence, trustworthiness, and teachability. We consider teachability vital. As we've already implied, a lack of teachability is the potential leader's cardinal sin. It quickly disqualifies him or her from leadership in any area, because leaders must always be learners.

We encourage leader-trainers to develop character audits to use with their trainees for measuring their character development.

KNOWING

Knowledge impacts the leader's intellect, emphasizing his or her ability to acquire and process content or information. Whether old or new, knowledge of the ministry area is essential for leaders.

Competency is based to a great degree on knowing what to do. In God's preparation of Moses for leadership, he specifically taught him what to do (Exod. 4:15). This is where seminarians come up short far too often. They are trained well in crucial areas, such as languages, theology, and church history, but receive little training—if any—in leadership. A seminary student once said that his biggest struggle as a pastor-leader was knowing what to do.

The key questions regarding the leader's knowledge are: What are the basic knowledge requirements at each leadership level of this ministry? What must one know to lead at his or her level? Those responsible for developing leaders at the various levels must carve time out of their busy schedules to answer these crucial questions.

To identify all the knowledge components for leaders at the various levels is beyond the scope of this book. That information would fill several books. Regardless, you may need some help in thinking through what is important in your ministry. The following should get you started:

- Leaders must know God (Romans 6–8).
- They must know themselves (their divine design, strengths, and weaknesses).
- They must know people (this involves the use of tools, such as the Personal Profile and the Kiersey Temperament Sorter for training purposes).
- They must know how to study the Bible and have a general knowledge of the Bible and theology.
- They must know how to pray.
- They must know and agree with the organization's statements (core values, mission, vision, strategy, and beliefs or doctrine).
- They need to know how to think and plan strategically.
- Those at higher levels must know how to preach, raise money, develop staff, and perform weddings, funerals, and baptisms.

DOING

The leader's skills affect the leader's actions or behavior. In Psalm 78:72 we read of David's leading his people with "skillful hands" as well as with "integrity of heart." Leaders must be able to put into practice what they learn. They may have leadership knowledge, but can they lead? Can they turn theory into practice? The key skills questions are: What must one be able to do to lead a ministry? What skills must one have to function well at each level of leadership? What habits are necessary for effective leadership and ministry? Again, leaders at each level must answer these questions for the people they train.

The following are some general leadership skills you should be aware of. The first are the hard or task skills, such as how to cast vision, pray, discover and develop core ministry values, develop a ministry mission statement and strategy, and teach and preach the Bible or a Sunday school lesson. In appendix D we have listed these in the form of a Task Skills Inventory that you can use with developing leaders.

The soft or relational skills include knowing how to listen, encourage, mentor or coach, resolve conflicts, network, counsel, motivate, take risks, solve problems, and build trust. See the Relational Skills Inventory in appendix E.

FEELING

Simply stated, your emotions are your feelings. Leaders' emotions are their heart work, reflecting what they feel. Scripture has much to say about emotions, beginning in Genesis when Adam and Eve experienced shame due to their sin (Gen. 3:11–12 compared to 2:25) and extending through Revelation, where John, when describing the New Jerusalem, writes, "He will wipe away every tear from their eyes. There will be no more death or mourning or crying or pain, for the old order of things has passed away" (Rev. 21:4).

A leader's emotions affect his or her mood. And research as well as ministry experience tell us that the leader's mood is most contagious, spreading quickly throughout a ministry. A good mood, characterized by optimism and inspiration, affects people positively. However, a bad mood, characterized by negativity and pessimism, will cripple the ministry and damage people.

The key emotions questions for leaders are: What emotions are liabilities for your ministry? What emotions must you deal with to create a better climate for ministry? Again, it's beyond the scope of this book to go into great detail regarding the leader's emotions. However, the following overview should help catalyze your thinking in this area.

To develop emotional well-being and establish a spiritually healthy climate for ministry, leaders must cultivate their own emotions and those of the people with whom they minister. To understand and manage their own emotions, leaders must take four steps:

1. Learn to recognize what emotions they are feeling.
2. Identify the emotion, for example, anger, anxiety, sadness, fear, shame, discouragement, surprise, joy, love.
3. Begin to manage the emotion.
4. Explore why they are experiencing certain emotions.

Once leaders begin to understand their emotions, they must learn to manage them. To accomplish this, they need to remember that they can't control being swept away by their emotions, because the emotional mind often overrides the rational mind, such as when we lose our temper. However, they can control how they respond to or handle the emotions they are feeling. They can recognize them and deal biblically with them in the power of the Holy Spirit.

Leaders must not only be aware of and work on their own emotions but also recognize others' emotions and help them manage them as well. This is commonly referred to as empathy. Most of us have been in situations in which an emotionally unhealthy person, whether in a leadership position or not, affects a ministry context negatively. It's imperative that leaders deal with these people for the sake of the ministry as well as the individual. How do leaders accomplish this? In much the same way they work with their own emotions, they apply the above four steps to the troubled person.

When leaders recognize others' emotions, they also need to manage them. This is done by helping individuals learn how to manage the feelings they experience and can be accomplished through example and by working one-on-one, using the same approach that leaders use to manage their own emotions.

The assumption here is that the people in our ministries want help. When the person needing help is emotionally and/or spiritually dysfunctional and not willing to work on the issues, the leader, though attempting to help him or her, should be ready to refer the person to professional help.

Core Leadership Competencies

Character (being)	Soul work
Knowledge (knowing)	Head work
Skills (doing)	Hand work
Emotions (feeling)	Heart work

Having briefly explained the four core competencies, we now want to attach a warning label to what we've said. A distortion in learning can happen if we overemphasize any one of the elements over the others. Character is a must, but without knowledge and skills, one's ministry is severely limited. The leader may be a nice guy but doesn't know what he is doing. Knowledge without skills is dry intellectualism. As we've already said, this is a major problem in our seminaries, where faculty and students can be disconnected from the real world of the church and much learning is merely theoretical. A skill without knowledge is mindless activity or mere busywork, and skills without character can lead to mere task-oriented ministry. Finally, emotions without knowledge lead to frustration. The leader knows something is wrong but doesn't know what it is or how to get relief. Good leader-trainers teach their emerging leaders to integrate and balance as much as possible the four elements at their respective leadership levels.[1]

Step 3: Develop new and current leaders for ministry in the church.

- Four core leadership competencies
- **Four training types**

Four Training Types

We must examine the means we have for training leaders because they will aid us in better cultivating leaders who are competent in their character, knowledge, skills, and emotions. There are four means that we've labeled Types 1–4 training.

TYPE 1: LEARNER-DRIVEN TRAINING

Type 1 training is where emerging leaders take responsibility for their own growth, so that the emerging leader is ultimately responsible for his or her own training. This is self-training for the purpose of self-development in character, knowledge, skills, and emotions. It may be planned or unplanned and may occur at any point throughout the week, depending on the leader's schedule.

This private, personal preparation asks, What can leaders do on their own to learn how to function well or competently in their ministries? Here are some suggestions:

- Read books and periodicals on leadership and their ministry areas.
- Listen to tapes and view videocassettes by prominent leaders who teach ministry knowledge and skills.
- Make appointments with and interview experienced, competent leaders.
- Attend classes, seminars, and conferences that focus on leadership and ministry development.
- Visit churches in their geographical area that God is blessing, observe what they do, and ask lots of questions.

The emphasis of self-directed training is that leaders pursue these opportunities on their own initiative or at the suggestion of a leader-trainer.

TYPE 2: CONTENT-DRIVEN TRAINING

Type 2 training focuses on the transfer of knowledge. *Content-driven* means that someone other than the learner has structured a body of information that determines the basis for the training experience. Thus a predetermined outline, lesson plan, or curriculum guides the training process. This training usually takes the form of a lecture or a one-way communication from a knowledgeable person to one seeking that knowledge. Most seminars, classroom settings, and conferences are venues for content-driven training. Practically speaking, most leadership training falls into this category, since gaining a basic knowledge of the ministry task at hand is an important starting point for any ministry leadership.

Content-driven training comes in all shapes and sizes. The content may be relatively focused and presented in a three-hour seminar. Or the content may be comprehensive enough to require a three-year curriculum. Also, the nature of the training varies widely on the continuum of formal versus informal. Informal training, on one end of the continuum, includes a myriad of church-based and volunteer-led training. Formal training, on the other end, includes accredited degree programs and even seminary training.

Informal content-driven training takes place any time a church, parachurch, or individual develops training content and teaches others in the local ministry context. Usually this training takes place in short time periods, is planned and supervised, and does not result in a degree or academic credential. The training is offered so that a church or parachurch ministry can intentionally train its people for leadership and ministry.

An example of informal training is when the pastor or a staff person uses a classroom setting to teach emerging leaders about the church. The emphasis is on ministry content or information more than actual experience. The leader might cover the church's history, any denominational affiliation, polity, theology and philosophy of ministry, core values, mission, vision, strategy, doctrinal position, and so on. Another example is when the pastor, staff member, or a professor from a nearby college or seminary teaches a class of interns or volunteer leaders Bible study skills, various books of the Bible, systematic theology, church history, how to preach and teach the Bible, Christian education, spiritual formation, missions, or any number of other subjects.

Formal content-driven training of staff and potential staff is often used to prepare them for leadership and ministry. Colleges, universities, and seminaries provide this formal training, which usually culminates in a diploma or degree, such as a master's of ministry (M.Min.), a master's of divinity (M.Div.), a doctor of theology (Th.D.), a doctor of ministry (D.Min.), or a doctor of philosophy (Ph.D.) degree.

Leaders must ask if formal training is vital to their ministry preparation. Classical programs that attempt to prepare future pastors for ministry provide in-depth training in such areas as Bible, languages, theology, and church history. Some organizations, especially the mainline denominations, may require a theological degree from an accredited school to pastor one of their churches. Thus formal education serves to credential prospective leaders in these ministries.

Some serious disadvantages of formal content-driven training are that it tends to be too academic, ignores leadership training and people skills, tends to be out of touch with the culture, and doesn't involve the student in enough hands-on ministry experience. In addition, most programs still require that the emerging leader move to where the institution is located to pursue training. In their research, Kouzes and Posner rated formal education and training a "distant third" in comparison to hands-on "trial and error" experience and training with other people, such as coaches and mentors.[2]

Schools have designed and adopted the master's of ministry and the doctor of ministry programs for those in professional ministry. Also, some schools are adopting distance-education programs that allow emerging leaders to stay where they live and minister in their home churches while pursuing an academic degree. However, at the time of this writing, it is unknown how far the accredited ministry community will go with distance education.

Some churches have responded to the need for leadership by selecting their own people from within the church—people who have proven themselves capable leaders—rather than taking a chance with a seminary graduate who has little experience. With this trend in mind, future leaders who pursue formal training would be wise to invest themselves heavily in hands-on ministry while attending school.

TYPE 3: MENTOR-DRIVEN TRAINING

The third type of training takes place when an emerging leader works intentionally and closely with a mentor or coach. The focus is on the trainer, and this distinguishes it from the other training types. For example, someone such as the pastor of leadership training brings together aspiring leaders with proven leaders and the latter train the former directly or indirectly. The coach or mentor could use an actual hands-on experience or a classroom context or both. The coach is there for the emerging leader and advises and directs him or her.

The oversight of a good and godly mentor is invaluable to an emerging leader. In my (Aubrey's) experience, although I've learned much from poor leaders about how not to lead, good leaders who have modeled servant leadership, challenged me, trusted me, and been willing to spend quality time with me have been the most instructive. Prospective leaders would be wise to identify servant leaders in their communities and form a mentoring relationship with some of them. Initially, when asked to be a mentor, a leader may refuse, but we advise the emerging leader not to take no for an answer. Be persistent. Show the potential mentor that you are serious and you see in him or her much that you could learn.

Good mentoring involves the following four processes.

1. *Instruction*. Mentors must provide their people with the knowledge necessary to lead at their particular level in the ministry. This encompasses the second core competency, knowledge or head work, but by no means excludes the other three (character, skills, and emotions). The emerging leader needs instruction in all four core competencies. The mentor will be able to use his or her own experience to provide some of the knowledge that the trainee will need to lead at his or her ministry level, but the mentor will use books, seminars, and the expertise of other staff as well.
2. *Modeling*. Conveying knowledge alone isn't sufficient. When possible, good mentors model what they are teaching their students. Modeling moves the student from theoretical understanding to observation of actual or simulated ministry experiences. This emphasizes the third core competency, skills, but doesn't exclude the others.
3. *Observation*. Not only do good mentors instruct and model competent leadership and ministry, they observe emerging leaders as they attempt to follow what the leader has modeled. They let the developing leaders lead and minister, involving them in the process.
4. *Evaluation*. Good evaluation, when the trainer evaluates how the trainee is progressing, is sprinkled throughout the mentoring process. After emerging leaders have ministered, they need to know how well they accomplished a particular task. Periodically the mentor also will assess their overall performance. In particular, the mentor looks for the trainee's strengths more than his or her weaknesses, which makes for an encouraging experience for the student.

TYPE 4: EXPERIENCE-DRIVEN TRAINING

The emphasis in type 4 training is on actual hands-on experience—the doing of ministry. In this case potential leaders are taught to lead and serve effectively through actually practicing and experimenting with skills in a context in which the leader is doing ministry, such as leading a small group, counseling a troubled person, visiting the sick, teaching a class, conducting a baptism, consoling the bereaved, welcoming visitors to the church, presenting the gospel to a lost person, and many other experiences.

You can't learn leadership by simply being in a classroom or a seminar. It's best learned while you are involved "up to your elbows" in ministry in which you can apply and evaluate classroom or seminar instruction. In their book *The Leadership Challenge*, Kouzes and Posner refer to studies by the Honeywell Corporation and by the Center for Creative Leadership and to their own studies and conclude, "What is quite evident from all three studies is that, whether you are talking about managing or leading, experience is by far the most important opportunity for learning." They continue, "There is just no suitable surrogate for learning by doing."[3] They conclude, "The first prescription, then, for becoming a better leader is to broaden your base of experience."[4]

However, you cannot limit experience-driven training to the hands-on ministry alone. Learning takes place in a context or environment where ministry is going on, and this context, which includes such concepts as people's values, personality, attitudes, perceptions, and so on, contributes to experienced-based learning. The environment includes spontaneous interactions and unplanned relationships that contribute to the overall atmosphere of the church or ministry and influence the aspiring leader. Much of this environment is intangible, like the collective enthusiasm of the people or a clearly demonstrated value for excellence.

The uniqueness of the environment is that it is always influencing people, and most don't realize it. The church or parachurch ministry should be aware of how the environment subconsciously trains its people for leadership and ministry. Keep in mind that environment consists of everything that trainees are exposed to and learn from during their training time. Much of it takes place in the ministry context. For example, learning takes place—even though we may not be conscious of it—when we're worshiping, attending a board meeting, or simply standing around and talking with people after a ministry event. Things that are said or the way that they are said reveals how people feel about the church's pastor, other leaders, programs, and key areas of ministry. All of this results from mere exposure to the environment. We will explore this more in chapter 13 when we look at leadership culture.

Questions for Reflection and Discussion

1. Which of the four leadership competencies is most developed among your current leaders? Which is least developed? How about in your own life?
2. Do you agree with the chapter's emphasis on the need to develop in the area of emotions? Why or why not? Does this frighten you? If so, why?

3. Do the four training types make sense? Can you think of any other possible types?
4. Which training type do you tend to operate in as a default mode?
5. What degrees have you earned? Do you plan to pursue any advanced degrees? Why or why not?

10

Designing the Leadership-Development Process

The Procedures for Developing Leaders, Phase 3

Now we come to the heart of the leadership-development process—the actual design of the process for your church. Before you can begin your design, however, you must be aware of all of the training venues at your disposal. We like to think of them as building blocks or, in keeping with the building metaphor, the structural two-by-fours of the building. In this chapter we will discuss the following sixteen venues: classroom, small group, turbo group, apprenticing, one-on-one, coaching, consulting, self-led, huddle, seminar, conference, getaway, retreat, workshop, rally, and benchmarking.

The venues fall into one of two broad categories—process or event oriented. Process-oriented venues always involve multiple meetings and may occur over weeks, months, or years. Event-oriented venues are always one-time occurrences.

As we explore each of these venues, keep in mind that the four leadership competencies—character, knowledge, skills, and emotions—and the four training types—learner-driven, content-driven, mentor-driven, and experience-driven—were covered in chapter 9 for a reason. Each training venue is unique in terms of which competencies it may touch and which training types it utilizes. After we do an overview of the venues, we will look at how to select the ones to use in your church or ministry.

Training Venues

Process Oriented	Event Oriented
Classroom	Huddle
Small group	Seminar
Turbo group	Conference
Apprenticing	Getaway
One-on-one	Retreat
Coaching	Workshop
Consulting	Rally
Self-led	Benchmarking

Step 3: Develop new and current leaders for ministry in the church.
- Four core leadership competencies
- Four training types
- **Process-oriented venues**

Process-Oriented Venues

Classroom

The classroom is a training-venue staple for many churches. The obvious features of the classroom are its limited size—usually three to fifty people—and the one-way communication environment—usually driven by seating configured in rows. The most important consideration with the classroom is a caution: Do not overly rely on classroom training. Because it is the easiest venue to provide, many churches rely exclusively on it. The downside of classroom training is the inherent limits on relationship building, interaction, and ministry exposure.

An example of classroom training is a class I (Will) attended at Dallas Theological Seminary, taught by Howard Hendricks. There were approximately thirty students who met for thirteen weeks, and each class lasted seventy-five minutes. The class was content-driven (I did receive some fantastic content!); however, thirteen weeks later, I had not developed any significant relationships with other students or with the teacher. Even though this class served my professional training well, it did not provide for the relationship building and ministry exposure I also needed.

When is the classroom format appropriate? Use it when there is a need to cover a large amount of information. For some people, in certain seasons in life, it may be more convenient to meet in a series of weekly classes. Also, a classroom can be a nonthreatening entry point for beginners. Remember, if you rely on the classroom, try to make it conducive to interaction and make sure you provide complementary training venues that will promote relationship building.

The following chart is the first in a series of charts that provide an overview of each venue. See the entire chart in appendix F.

Venue 1	Classroom		
Definition:	A group of individuals meeting in a one-way communication environment for ongoing instruction		
Role of Leader:	Teacher		
Chart Key:	● High ○ Variable ○ Low		

Competencies				Training Types				Characteristics												
Knowledge	Skills	Character	Emotion	Content-driven	Learner-driven	Mentor-driven	Experience-driven	Relational	Interactive	Inspirational	Modeling	Broad content	Focused content	Beginner friendly	Time intensive	Long-term	Flexible scheduling	Preparation logistics	Cost
●	○	○	●	●	○	●	○	○	○	○	○	●	○	○	○	○	○	○	○

Small Group

The second training venue is the small group of three to twelve individuals meeting in a relational environment for training. The small group can meet for any length of time—four weeks or an entire year or more—and on average each meeting lasts for an hour and a half to two. A small group will usually meet in a home or in a classroom with seating arranged in a circle (for discussion and interaction).

The obvious strength of the small group is that it provides the opportunity to build relationships. While this strength limits the amount of information covered, the information that is taught tends to make more of an impact because the application of the ideas can be discussed and debated during the meeting. The key aspects of character and emotional development are possible because of the sharing, accountability, and prayer that can take place in a small group. Also, if the leader-in-training plans to lead a small group in the future, valuable modeling is taking place as well.

There are a number of downsides to the small group. One, of course, is its time-intensive nature, especially if it continues for more than eight weeks. Often the leadership responsibilities for existing leaders preclude their investing their time in a small-group community just for the leadership development of emerging leaders. Also, as relationships flourish and as special needs in the group arise, it is more difficult to stay on task when covering content. Finally, keep in mind that a small-group environment is a little more intimidating as an entry point for prospective leaders.

An illustration of small-group–leadership training is a group of seven group leaders I (Will) led for a year. We met weekly either in a restaurant, where there were minimum distractions, or in a home for about two hours a meeting. Three of the men were existing group leaders, and four were emerging leaders. The content of the group was focused on personal spiritual formation, with significant time provided to discuss issues occurring in each leader's group. Several lifelong relationships developed in that group, even though many of the men have since moved geographically.

A small-group format is particularly good when leaders have a need for emotional support because of their personal life or the season of the ministry they are leading. A small group works well for leaders who are taking a break from their leadership post for a short time. In general we have found short-term groups (four to eight weeks) to be the best for training, especially if the members of the group are concurrently active in leadership.

Venue 2	Small Group		
Definition:	A group of three to twelve individuals meeting in a relational environment for ongoing training		
Role of Leader:	Facilitator/teacher		
Chart Key:	● High ◉ Variable ○ Low		

Competencies				Training Types				Characteristics												
Knowledge	Skills	Character	Emotion	Content-driven	Learner-driven	Mentor-driven	Experience-driven	Relational	Interactive	Inspirational	Modeling	Broad content	Focused content	Beginner friendly	Time intensive	Long-term	Flexible scheduling	Preparation logistics	Cost	
◉	○	●	◉	◉	○	●	○	●	◉	○	◉	●	◉	○	●	◉	●	●	○	

Turbo Group

A turbo group is a specialized small group of three to twelve individuals meeting short-term in a relational environment. The purpose is focused training with the goal of launching group members into leadership. A typical duration for a turbo group is eight to twelve weeks. The turbo format emphasizes focused content on leadership and modeling. The goal is to impart all of the critical information that the individual needs to get started in leadership. Usually there is a launch date or deadline that makes the quick learning of the necessary information essential. Typically a portion of the group time is dedicated to the leader's modeling the kind of leadership the members will be exercising. Also, it's common for the group members to practice leading the group. This allows a unique feedback dynamic as everyone gets the chance to evaluate everybody else as they take a turn practicing group leadership. Because group members will be leading in the near future, there is a heightened responsiveness to feedback and skills development.

There are two primary limitations to the turbo group. The first is that the shorter duration and the modeling focus limit the amount of content covered. The second limitation is that a skilled, experienced leader is needed for the group to function well. Because modeling is taking place, the strengths and weaknesses of the group leader will be duplicated.

An illustration of a turbo group is a gathering of six emerging coaches (leaders of small-group leaders) that I (Will) led for eight weeks. Each meeting lasted two hours. The content included specific information that each person needed to function as a coach. There was also a significant focus on skills development. One of the key functions of a coach is to visit a group meeting and to evaluate the leader in a debriefing session after the meeting. Observation and evaluation skills are critical. During the turbo group sessions, over the course of the eight weeks, each group member took a turn leading the group. During the last thirty minutes of each group meeting, the entire group evaluated the performance of the group leader. The group evaluation led to exponential learning and skill development for this key skill set.

The turbo group is a strong option for leadership development. It is particularly useful in high-growth environments or any time a group of leaders launches at one time. For example, a church that is launching a small-group ministry for the first time should consider turbo groups. In one setting in which I (Will) worked, the church launched five new discussion groups that corresponded to the Sunday morning teaching series. In this case, the church prepared five new leaders through the turbo-group process.

Venue 3	Turbo Group	
Definition:	A group of three to twelve individuals meeting in a relational environment for short-term, focused training with the goal of launching group members into leadership	
Role of Leader:	Facilitator/teacher	
Chart Key:	● High ◐ Variable ○ Low	

Competencies				Training Types				Characteristics											
Knowledge	Skills	Character	Emotion	Content-driven	Learner-driven	Mentor-driven	Experience-driven	Relational	Interactive	Inspirational	Modeling	Broad content	Focused content	Beginner friendly	Time intensive	Long-term	Flexible scheduling	Preparation logistics	Cost
○	○	◐	○	●	○	◐	○	◐	◐	○	◐	○	●	○	○	○	◐	◐	○

Apprenticing

Apprenticing is when an individual performs a ministry leadership function, in a learning role, under the direct supervision of an experienced leader. This venue is especially effective because the on-the-job nature provides experience-driven learning, and the supervision of an experienced leader provides mentor-driven learning. Most professions or avocations that require specialized skill development require some form of apprenticeship. Think for a minute of the diverse arenas that use apprenticeships—music, cuisine, martial arts, academics, trades—the list could go on and on.

The word *apprenticeship* shares a common root with the term *apprehend* and conveys the meaning of seizing new understanding and ability. The effectiveness of the apprenticeship is directly related to the close proximity of the teacher and learner. In fact, one dictionary definition highlights this close relationship with the definition "binding to or putting under the care of a master."

Every church should seriously consider apprenticing as a training venue. The great thing about apprenticing is that it can take place anytime ministry is occurring. In other words, every event and activity that your church is currently doing provides a built-in opportunity for apprenticing. Therefore, no extra time or cost commitment is required. Also, apprenticing is unique in its ability to touch on all four levels of learning (knowledge, skills, character, and emotions) as a result of the life-on-life context. It is particularly effective for learning skills.

In fact, for every significant skill we have ever learned, we can picture corresponding faces of the men and women who provided training and modeling.

Another strength of apprenticing is the high motivation of the learner. If you teach an emerging leader "five keys to leading small-group prayer" in a classroom setting, he or she is liable to fall asleep. But if you share the same content the evening before the person is scheduled to actually lead a small-group prayer time, he or she will be completely attentive.

You may wonder, if apprenticing is so effective, why don't more churches use it? The difficulty of apprenticing is the intentionality it takes to do it well. It requires planning and patience in the ministry setting itself, as well as a long-term, intensive time commitment on the part of both the apprentice and the master. When churches do have apprenticing venues in place, one of the greatest challenges is connecting leaders with apprentices. We have found that the recruiting of the apprentice is best driven by each individual leader.

Many churches use apprenticing throughout their small-group structure, and the primary benefit is that every small-group meeting becomes a training session. One important limitation in this instance is that both the strengths and weaknesses of the leader get duplicated in the apprentice. As a result, a church should be careful not to rely solely on apprenticing for training, even though it has such clear and unique benefits.

An illustration of this venue is a church that strongly encourages small-group leaders or Sunday morning Bible fellowships to have apprentices as a part of the group leadership team. One church I (Will) work with has approximately forty small groups. About 50 percent of the groups have a clearly identified apprentice. During training events, group leaders are encouraged to bring apprentices, even to the point that special tickets are provided as tools for invitation. Individual coaching and one-on-one meetings always keep the recruiting of an apprentice at the top of the discussion list. When a group grows and is ready to multiply, a new group is formed and the apprentice leader launches into his or her own ministry. One of the first responsibilities of the emerging group leader is to repeat the process by finding an apprentice for the newly birthed group.

Venue 4	Apprenticing
Definition:	An individual performing a ministry leadership function in a learning role, under the direct supervision of an experienced leader
Role of Leader:	Mentor/coach

Chart Key:	● High ◐ Variable ○ Low

Competencies				Training Types				Characteristics												
Knowledge	Skills	Character	Emotion	Content-driven	Learner-driven	Mentor-driven	Experience-driven	Relational	Interactive	Inspirational	Modeling	Broad content	Focused content	Beginner friendly	Time intensive	Long-term	Flexible scheduling	Preparation logistics	Cost
●	●	●	●	○	○	◐	◐	◐	◐	○	●	●	○	◐	●	●	◐	◐	○

One-on-One

A one-on-one venue is simply two individuals meeting in a relational environment, not in the ministry context, for training. The primary benefit of the one-on-one venue is the extreme flexibility for the two individuals to meet. They can meet anywhere at any time in a formal or informal learning setting. Because one-on-one is relationship intensive, the opportunity for character and emotional development is also present.

The primary limitations of a one-on-one venue are the time commitment and the relative "inefficiency" of the trainer's time, because it does not multiply the time, knowledge, and experience of the trainer beyond one person at a time.

The beauty of one-on-one meetings is the opportunity for unstructured and informal training initiatives at the discretion of the trainer. In my training role in the local church, I (Will) look for leaders who need special support and attention and schedule one-on-ones with them. The one-on-one meeting is a great tool for capturing teaching moments. At other times, I use a one-on-one approach in a more structured manner, encouraging every leader to meet one-on-one every month with the leader above him or her in the organization. This helps to provide a regular connection through listening, training, and support with every frontline leader in the church.

Venue 5	One-on-One
Definition:	Two individuals meeting in a relational environment for training
Role of Leader:	Mentor/friend
Chart Key:	● High ◐ Variable ○ Low

Competencies				Training Types				Characteristics											
Knowledge	Skills	Character	Emotion	Content-driven	Learner-driven	Mentor-driven	Experience-driven	Relational	Interactive	Inspirational	Modeling	Broad content	Focused content	Beginner friendly	Time intensive	Long-term	Flexible scheduling	Preparation logistics	Cost
●	●	●	●	○	○	●	○	●	●	○	○	○	○	○	○	●	●	○	○

Coaching

While *coaching* is a broad term, we are referring here specifically to an outside professional who focuses on the personal and leadership development of a higher level church leader. The coaching process is unique in how it accomplishes leadership development. The coach works not by providing answers per se but by asking questions through which the leader gains new insight and takes new actions.

Howard Hendricks defines coaching as "helping people do what they don't want to do, so they can become what they want to become." This is a great definition, especially in an athletic context. But for a church leadership context, we would tweak the definition to be: "helping people discover what they could not discover on their own, so they can become what they want to become."

While executive coaching has continued to flourish in corporate settings in the last decade, we see surprisingly little occurring in the church. This is unfortunate, because if the point leaders in the local church stop growing, leadership development at every level is stifled. We encourage every senior pastor reading these words to seriously consider finding a coach. There are several ways to do this: Ask other pastors who may have used coaches, ask business leaders in the congregation, call The Malphurs Group (see contact information at the end of this book).

Coaching as a specialized one-on-one meeting is very flexible. In fact, much coaching takes place over the phone (usually in an hour or less) and can be accomplished through a long-distance relationship. Coaching can be structured as frequently as desired and for as long as the leader needs it. For example, a coach can meet on a quarterly basis in a relationship that lasts for years or on a weekly basis in a relationship that lasts for several months.

The primary limitation of coaching is the cost involved, as professional coaching comes with a wide range of fees. However, the church could include this as a line item in the budget under the pastor's professional development. Also, the church might consider using a coach before hiring the next staff person. In helping or advising the leader in better carrying out ministry, the coach would actually be relieving some of the workload. Also, the coach could help clarify what position the next staff hire should fill. Compared to the costs of another staff person (salary, benefits, and so on), a coach is much less expensive. We address this further under the next venue—consulting.

Venue 6	Coaching		
Definition:	An outside professional who focuses on the personal and leadership development of a higher level church leader		
Role of Leader:	Coach		
Chart Key:	● High ◉ Variable ○ Low		

Competencies				Training Types				Characteristics											
Knowledge	Skills	Character	Emotion	Content-driven	Learner-driven	Mentor-driven	Experience-driven	Relational	Interactive	Inspirational	Modeling	Broad content	Focused content	Beginner friendly	Time intensive	Long-term	Flexible scheduling	Preparation logistics	Cost
○	◉	●	○	○	◉	●	○	●	●	◉	◉	○	●	◉	○	●	●	○	●

Consulting

Consulting is when an outside individual immerses himself or herself in the church culture to bring specialized knowledge for organizational and leadership development. The distinction between a coach and a consultant is that the consultant brings expertise in a certain arena. For example, this expertise may be in strategic planning and mapping, marketing and communications, leadership development, capital campaign fundraising, or some other skill. We believe that the effectiveness of the consultant comes when he or she is willing to commit the time needed to know and understand the organization.

A consultant can play a vital role, especially at critical seasons in the life of the church. These seasons include confronting growth barriers, navigating high-growth rates, facility changes, relocation, pastoral leadership changes, and directional changes. Having the right knowledge during these times will significantly impact the scope of the church's ministry for decades.

In some cases a consultant can augment church staffing. The primary benefits are that the consultant works only on important, nonurgent issues, unlike other pastoral staff; the consultant incurs no overhead cost, such as health insurance and other benefits; and the length of the consulting contract is flexible. We believe that both professional coaching and consulting will play increasingly vital roles in the future of church staffing, especially in leading-edge churches with strategic thinking, because churches are recognizing that objective consultants see the issues more clearly and they bring insights from diverse experiences. Their counsel shortens the learning curve for churches as they go through the critical seasons mentioned above.

The primary limitation of consulting is the cost, which is highly variable. But today's leaders and their churches must ask if they can afford *not* to bring in a consultant. Check references on consultants before hiring them, and don't be afraid to pay more for the right kind of expertise. As with many things, you get what you pay for. In addition, make sure that the consultant is theologically trained. What you and they do together is deeply theological, and the typical corporate consultant comes up short here. Of course, we recommend that you consult with The Malphurs Group in these areas (www.malphursgroup.com).

Venue 7	Consulting
Definition:	An outside individual, immersing himself or herself in the church culture to bring specialized knowledge for organizational and leadership development
Role of Leader:	Consultant/facilitator
Chart Key:	● High ◐ Variable ○ Low

Competencies				Training Types				Characteristics											
Knowledge	Skills	Character	Emotion	Content-driven	Learner-driven	Mentor-driven	Experience-driven	Relational	Interactive	Inspirational	Modeling	Broad content	Focused content	Beginner friendly	Time intensive	Long-term	Flexible scheduling	Preparation logistics	Cost
●	◐	○	○	●	◐	○	○	○	○	○	○	●	●	◐	◐	○	○	○	●

Self-Led

Self-led venues are those in which a potential leader trains himself or herself. In the last chapter we describe this under the learner-driven training type. The primary tools are books, audiocassettes or CDs, and the Internet.

The best part of using self-led venues is the flexibility. For example, a leader can listen to a tape while driving to work. This is very significant, because it is a way for the church to deliver pertinent information to leaders without having another meeting or adding another time commitment.

An illustration of a self-led venue is a cassette tape that a church produces in-house for quarterly leadership training. The church staff plan the content of the training, which focuses on the skills for leading people into biblical community. While the conversation is recorded, the pastors discuss the training topic with one another. The product is a thirty-five-minute tape of fun and informal conversation that brings practical leadership training to each group leader—at his or her own time and convenience. Along with the training, leaders get to know their pastors better while hearing stories from their experiences.

There are few limitations with self-led training. Even if your church doesn't have the resources to make its own audio training (highly unlikely in developed countries today), you can create a leadership library of books and cassette tapes for leaders to check out. Another option is a leadership newsletter that leaders can read on their own time. One drawback is that the leader who is self-led may not be receiving feedback concerning his or her ideas and practices. This venue should be used with another venue in which there is give-and-take with a more experienced leader.

While we have not personally developed web training, there is no question that it is a key tool for the future. Last month I (Will) took a six-hour defensive driving course on the Internet. Rather than going to a six-hour class, I completed the course in the evenings over five or six days at my own convenience.

Venue 8	Self-Led
Definition:	A leader initiating his or her own learning
Role of Leader:	Learner
Chart Key:	● High ○ Variable ○ Low

Competencies				Training Types				Characteristics											
Knowledge	Skills	Character	Emotion	Content-driven	Learner-driven	Mentor-driven	Experience-driven	Relational	Interactive	Inspirational	Modeling	Broad content	Focused content	Beginner friendly	Time intensive	Long-term	Flexible scheduling	Preparation logistics	Cost
○	●	●	●	○	●	○	○	○	○	○	●	●	●	○	○	○	●	◐	○

> Step 3: Develop new and current leaders for ministry in the church.
>
> - Four core leadership competencies
>
> - Four training types
>
> - Process-oriented venues
>
> - **Event-oriented venues**

Event-Oriented Venues

We now turn to the event-oriented venues.

Huddle

A huddle is a specialized small group of three to twelve individuals with common ministry responsibilities that meets in an interactive environment for training. The distinguishing feature of the huddle is the gathering of leaders who share similar ministry responsibilities. A huddle, for example, may consist of a group of children's Sunday school teachers or student small-group leaders or finance committee members. Meeting once or at periodic intervals, a huddle is useful because it allows for training, sharing, discussion, and problem solving around ministry-specific issues. A huddle can be a time for encouragement and celebration among the leadership community. It also can serve as a skills-development time for ministry-specific skills.

An example of a huddle is a gathering of small-group hosts—the people in small groups who provide an environment, usually their home, in which the small groups meet. During this huddle there was training and discussion about creating an ideal small-group environment in the home. Child care was the most significant challenge for the hosts, so they developed several child-care strategies. As they shared their favorite horror stories of wild pets and coffee-stained sofas, the hosts connected with one another. It was a very valuable equipping time for this specific group of leaders.

Venue 9	Huddle
Definition:	A group of three to twelve individuals with common ministry responsibilities meeting in an interactive environment for training
Role of Leader:	Coach/facilitator
Chart Key:	● High ◉ Variable ○ Low

Competencies				Training Types				Characteristics												
Knowledge	Skills	Character	Emotion	Content-driven	Learner-driven	Mentor-driven	Experience-driven	Relational	Interactive	Inspirational	Modeling	Broad content	Focused content	Beginner friendly	Time intensive	Long-term	Flexible scheduling	Preparation logistics	Cost
●	●	○	○	○	○	○	○	○	○	○	●	○	●	○	○	○	●	○	○

Seminar

The seminar is a relatively large group of individuals who meet in a one-way communication environment for one time of focused instruction. The seminar differs from the class in two primary ways. The seminar services a larger group, and the seminar is a one-time event. As a one-time event, it is usually more time-intensive than a class, lasting anywhere from three hours to an entire day.

A seminar may be a venue either that the church provides for itself or that an outside organization offers in the area. For example, churches and denominations invite us to do a number of seminars each year on various topics, such as strategic planning, church planting, and other vital areas of leadership.

Seminars have many benefits. They are relatively easy for a church to plan and are low cost. If your church does not have an adequate room to host a seminar, you could hold it at a local hotel or other public meeting place. Through a seminar, a church is able to provide focused content to many people at one time. This maximizes the time of the trainer and allows the ministry to target individual topics effectively. The seminar is also a very good entry point for emerging leaders. The low interaction makes it less threatening, and the one-time nature makes it easier to schedule than some other training venues. Because seminars are commonly used in the business world, the *seminar* label itself has an appealing ring to people.

Use seminars when your goal is to deliver content to a large number of people. You might use a seminar in a large church for new leaders training. A three-hour introductory seminar for potential leaders could be called Leadership 101 or New Leaders Training.

Also, a church should take advantage of seminars sponsored by outside organizations that come to your area. One church that I (Will) worked with sends all its leaders to a time-management seminar every year.

Venue 10	Seminar
Definition:	A large group of individuals meeting in a one-way communication environment for one time of focused instruction
Role of Leader:	Teacher
Chart Key:	● High　　◐ Variable　　○ Low

Competencies				Training Types				Characteristics											
Knowledge	Skills	Character	Emotion	Content-driven	Learner-driven	Mentor-driven	Experience-driven	Relational	Interactive	Inspirational	Modeling	Broad content	Focused content	Beginner friendly	Time intensive	Long-term	Flexible scheduling	Preparation logistics	Cost
●	○	○	○	●	○	○	○	○	○	○	○	○	●	●	●	○	○	○	○

Conference

A conference is a large group of individuals who meet in a one-way communication environment for instruction from a teacher, usually a notable leader. Conferences are larger than seminars and involve multiple days of training.

Conferences have popped up everywhere over the past few decades. Several of the prominent megachurches have led the way by hosting leadership-training conferences. Two of these are Willow Creek Community Church and Saddleback Community Church. However, a host of churches all over the country offer church-based conferences that may attract three thousand to fifteen thousand people in weekend attendance.

There are numerous benefits to using this venue.

- A local church-based conference provides a wonderful vision-casting opportunity. Leaders can see the giant potential of their local church.
- Leaders can network with those from other churches.
- The opportunity for leaders to spend several days off-site usually brings refreshment and new insight.
- Traveling together provides special team-building opportunities for a church's leaders. Traveling and eating together, going to entertainment, and just hanging out can be special times for leaders who attend conferences with their colleagues.

- Many conferences provide very useful, focused training in small, breakout seminars.

We highly recommend conferences for leadership development, because no event can catalyze the commitment of an emerging leader as a conference can. Recognizing the value of conferences, some church staffs will take forty or fifty volunteer leaders across the country to attend a church conference. In one case, the church paid five hundred dollars of the seven-hundred-fifty-dollar total trip cost for leaders who wanted to go. The church was convinced that it was the best investment it could make in the life of its leaders. We agree.

The limitations of conferences include scheduling, necessary travel, and cost. We recommend that a pastor or other leader attend conferences first to discover which one will work best for his church. Once you select a conference, you must recruit people early to attend and you must decide if the church is going to offset the cost for lay leaders.

Venue 11	Conference
Definition:	A large group of individuals meeting in a one-way communication environment for instruction from a teacher, usually a well-known leader
Role of Leader:	Teacher/vision caster
Chart Key:	● High ○ Variable ○ Low

Competencies				Training Types				Characteristics											
Knowledge	Skills	Character	Emotion	Content-driven	Learner-driven	Mentor-driven	Experience-driven	Relational	Interactive	Inspirational	Modeling	Broad content	Focused content	Beginner friendly	Time intensive	Long-term	Flexible scheduling	Preparation logistics	Cost
●	○	○	○	●	○	○	○	●	○	●	○	●	○	○	●	○	○	●	●

Getaway

A getaway is a group of individuals who meet off-site for one day of training. The site should be between forty-five and sixty minutes away (close enough to drive round-trip in one day, yet far enough to be a true getaway).

The getaway has many advantages.

- It allows for a diversity of training types and venues. You can literally use any of the other venues mentioned in this chapter. For example, imagine a day consisting of an hour-long large-group seminar, which then divides into multiple, forty-five-minute small-group sessions. Then, after lunch and free time for one-on-one discussion, the last two hours of the day are spent in several workshop options.

- A getaway can help forge leadership community. Something happens when leaders "rub minds" together with one another in a daylong event. There is the cross-pollination of ideas, and new relational chemistry develops. Much of this happens through relationship building during the informal and in-between times.

  During one getaway that I (Will) led, I remember feeling humbled by this observation. I realized that the primary benefit of the getaway was not my prepared teaching but the spontaneous sharing and learning that happened leader-to-leader after my talk was over. (In fact, this motivated me to provide less one-way communication in getaways and to create more interactive learning environments.)

- A getaway is an excellent venue to train new leaders and potential leaders. New leaders assimilate into the leadership culture quickly in a getaway environment (for the reasons mentioned above). A new leader track can be planned for this purpose.

- A getaway can be downright fun. Prepare team-building activities or recreation (appropriate to the gender and age) for your leaders. The hour after lunch is a good time for activity.

The three limitations of a getaway are planning, expense, and time. A daylong event like this takes considerable logistics planning (facility selection, registration, travel, meals, training materials, child care, and so on). It also incurs expense that will vary depending on location.

The other limitation is the fixed time. The schedules of some leaders will mean they will miss it. Therefore, plan in advance and recruit early. Provide early registration incentives if you are charging something for the getaway. We recommend charging people to attend because it creates commitment and raises expectations as well as helping to pay for the facility and food.

Venue 12	Getaway
Definition:	A group of individuals meeting off-site for training for one day
Role of Leader:	Variable

Chart Key:	● High ○ Variable ○ Low

Competencies			Training Types				Characteristics											
Skills	Character	Emotion	Content-driven	Learner-driven	Mentor-driven	Experience-driven	Relational	Interactive	Inspirational	Modeling	Broad content	Focused content	Beginner friendly	Time intensive	Long-term	Flexible scheduling	Preparation logistics	Cost
○	○	○	○	○	●	○	○	○	○	○	○	○	●	●	○	○	●	○

Retreat

A retreat is a group of individuals who meet off-site for training over multiple days. A retreat differs from a getaway by adding the overnight experience. This effectively amplifies the strengths and limitations of the getaway—increased relationship building and increased preparation logistics and cost.

Many churches use an annual retreat effectively in the leadership-development process, because the strength of this venue is its ability to accommodate a variety of training experiences. If you choose this venue, the selection of facilities is critical. Never book a facility without doing an on-site visit or receiving a recommendation from a trusted individual.

Venue 13	Retreat
Definition:	A group of individuals meeting off-site for training over multiple days
Role of Leader:	Variable
Chart Key:	● High ○ Variable ○ Low

Competencies				Training Types				Characteristics											
Knowledge	Skills	Character	Emotion	Content-driven	Learner-driven	Mentor-driven	Experience-driven	Relational	Interactive	Inspirational	Modeling	Broad content	Focused content	Beginner friendly	Time intensive	Long-term	Flexible scheduling	Preparation logistics	Cost
●	○	○	○	○	○	●	○	●	○	○	○	○	○	●	●	○	○	●	●

Workshop

A workshop is a relatively small group of individuals meeting over a period of time in a skills-focused, interactive environment for training. A workshop will usually last a half-day to a day and will focus on a specific ministry skill. Some examples of workshops are those emphasizing life-application teaching, church marketing, and leading from a personal mission statement.

The key difference between a workshop and other training venues is that the participants of a workshop move beyond hearing something to actually doing something. For example, in the life-application teaching workshop, those attending would actually work as a group to craft a teaching series. There is a high degree of interaction with others in the workshop and with the instructor. Because of this, I (Aubrey) prefer the workshop to the seminar and conference venues when training leaders.

I (Will) am currently planning a workshop with leaders involved in the welcoming system or "first impressions" ministry of their church. During the workshop, we will look at the facility maps of the different churches and chart where parking attendants and greeters should stand. We will discuss and work on role descriptions for the various team members and role-play and practice the type of interaction that should happen when a guest walks through the doors of the church.

In the local church, short workshops for leaders can be very effective. You can do workshops on a wide variety of topics, such as inductive Bible study, preparing a Bible lesson, mentoring, conflict resolution, recruiting, and vision casting. When planning a workshop, make sure the topic is an issue that your leaders are currently confronting.

The first challenge of having a workshop is finding an experienced trainer. Because the trainer will be modeling behavior as well as providing skill-based training, he or she must have more to offer than knowledge. The trainer must be good at what he or she does. The second challenge is time. Taking a day to learn a specific skill is a big commitment for busy church lay leaders. Consequently it may be wise to bring in a well-known person, who is a recognized expert in the particular skill, to do the training for you.

Venue 14	Workshop
Definition:	A relatively small group of individuals meeting over a long period of time in a skills-focused, interactive environment for training
Role of Leader:	Trainer

Chart Key:	● High	○ Variable	○ Low

Competencies				Training Types				Characteristics												
Knowledge	Skills	Character	Emotion	Content-driven	Learner-driven	Mentor-driven	Experience-driven	Relational	Interactive	Inspirational	Modeling	Broad content	Focused content	Beginner friendly	Time intensive	Long-term	Flexible scheduling	Preparation logistics	Cost
●	●	○	○	○	○	●	●	○	●	○	●	○	●	●	●	○	○	●	○

Rally

A rally is a group of individuals meeting in a one-way communication environment for celebration-based training that is focused on past accomplishments or future expectations. This venue may seem a little unusual, but it is a critical type of training that often gets overlooked.

The distinction of this venue is that it targets the heart—the goal being motivation and inspiration. The primary role of the trainer is to champion the cause and cast the vision, and the primary benefit of a rally is that it reminds leaders why they sacrifice. Day in and day out, our lay leaders make an enormous commitment, often with little thanks. The leadership-development process must take leaders' morale into consideration and plan intentional venues that will serve to fill the leaders' emotional tanks.

A rally could be a "vision night." Bill Hybels practices this venue at Willow Creek Community Church. Once a year there is a special gathering when the pastor opens his heart about the future direction of the church. Many other churches hold a very effective vision night.

Another example of a rally is one that I (Will) recently led. We had just finished a semester-long training of five turbo groups for coaches. At the end of the semester we leaders planned a final event of which the trainees were unaware. We set up a room to look like the stage of a television game show that was popular at the time—*Who Wants to Be a Millionaire*—even with lighting and sound effects. When the turbo group members arrived, they realized they were contestants on the game show as we asked review questions about the coaches' training. Afterward we cast the vision of the essential role of the coach and thanked them for their commitment to the training. The bottom line is that we filled their emotional tank with a fun and motivating time together.

There was a day when I (Will) would have secretly heaped negative judgment on a training venue like this. Through experience, however, I have learned that touching the heart and providing laughter are vital aspects of the leadership experience. Don't overlook your leader's heart.

Venue 15	Rally		
Definition:	A group of individuals meeting in a one-way communication environment for celebration-based training, focused on past accomplishments or future expectations		
Role of Leader:	Vision caster/motivator		
Chart Key:	● High ◐ Variable ○ Low		

Competencies				Training Types				Characteristics												
Knowledge	Skills	Character	Emotion	Content-driven	Learner-driven	Mentor-driven	Experience-driven	Relational	Interactive	Inspirational	Modeling	Broad content	Focused content	Beginner friendly	Time intensive	Long-term	Flexible scheduling	Preparation logistics	Cost
◐	○	○	○	◐	○	○	◐	○	○	●	◐	○	○	●	○	○	○	◐	◐

Benchmarking

Benchmarking is taking a small group of individuals to visit another ministry context for learning and modeling. Benchmarking is one of the easiest and yet most underutilized training venues. Basically, every church within an hour's drive provides a potential benchmarking opportunity. Usually churches are more than willing to allow another church's leadership team to observe their ministries and will share what they know in an effort to multiply their strengths for the kingdom.

The advantages of benchmarking are numerous. It is a no-lose proposition. The stronger points of the church you are visiting provide vision and modeling for your leaders, and the weaker points can bring affirmation to what your ministry is already doing better. On one occasion I (Will) took a children's ministry leadership team to visit the children's ministry at another church. It was effective modeling because they learned some simple and creative ideas that were new and easily transferable. The event was also affirming to the leaders. The church we visited had a similar-size ministry to that of our church with almost twice the paid staff. Consequently our leaders felt like real champions for having "done more with less" over the years. It was a fantastic win-win trip.

The other advantages of benchmarking are the low cost, the team-building dynamic, and the opportunity to take some downtime from the leader's own ministry. For example, it was a great Sunday break for the children's ministry team when we visited another church.

Of course, this leads us to the greatest challenge of benchmarking—having all of your leaders absent while visiting another ministry. This will usually require some creative problem solving, but the extra effort to pull this off will yield much fruit.

Venue 16	Benchmarking
Definition:	A group of individuals visiting another ministry context for learning and modeling
Role of Leader:	Model
Chart Key:	● High ◐ Variable ○ Low

Competencies				Training Types				Characteristics											
Knowledge	Skills	Character	Emotion	Content-driven	Learner-driven	Mentor-driven	Experience-driven	Relational	Interactive	Inspirational	Modeling	Broad content	Focused content	Beginner friendly	Time intensive	Long-term	Flexible scheduling	Preparation logistics	Cost
◐	◐	○	◐	◐	●	◐	○	◐	○	◐	◐	○	●◐	◐	○	○	◐	●	○

Putting the Venues Together

Now it's time to think through how the venues work together in the leadership-development process. A helpful tool for this exercise is the Training Venues Comparison Chart in appendix F. The overriding question to answer for your specific context is which training venues are best to use. In this section we will help you select your top three venues—one primary and two secondary venues.

Select a primary leadership-training venue for your church. It is important for church leaders to agree and understand that the venue they select will be their staple venue. It's important to realize that all of the venues listed in this chapter are not created equal. Some are more suitable as primary venues than others. The following chart is our recommended list of primary venues. Now, based on where you are going as a church, which venue do you aspire to have as a primary venue?

Recommended Primary Venues

Apprenticing

Small Group

Turbo Group

Seminar

Getaway

Retreat

Select two secondary venues. Once you have a primary venue in place, what supplementary venues are required? This is where you need to use the comparison chart. What competencies and training types does the primary venue miss? What other venues would strategically complement the primary one? Based on where you are and where you're going as a church, what are the two best secondary venues for leadership training?

When you've answered these questions and selected the top three venues, you've taken a giant step in putting the leadership-training process in place. We will keep these top three venues in mind as we move to the next two chapters, especially the section on centralized and decentralized training in chapter 12.

Questions for Reflection and Discussion

1. What is the most beneficial training venue you have personally participated in? Why did it benefit you more than other experiences?
2. What venues have you been using in your current ministry setting? Are these venues effective? Why or why not?
3. What new venues are you most excited about implementing? Why?

11

The Finishing Touches

The Procedures for Developing Leaders, Phase 4

There comes a point, in the building of every house, when only the finishing touches are needed. Several types of workers take care of these. One group is the finish carpenters who perform a number of functions, such as installing the trim around the baseboards and cabinets. Another is the finish painters who are responsible for the final touch-up of all painted surfaces.

When building the leadership house, all agree that the third step—developing new and current leaders for ministry in the church—is most critical to the entire process. It's likely that when you as a leader purchased this book, you were looking for the information found in chapters 9 and 10. We encourage you, however, not to stop reading now. There are two final steps that will add the critical finishing touches to your leadership-development structure. The fourth step deals with evaluation of your process. You must ask if the process is getting the job done. Is it developing leaders? And if not, why not? Evaluation serves to trouble-shoot the system and to work out any problems. Regular evaluation dramatically improves the process.

The last step urges you to reward your leaders. Sometimes in the busyness of ministry, we become too focused, especially those of us who are task oriented. In the pursuit of our mission and goals, we can easily forget about our people, particularly our leaders. After all, they're committed, aren't they?

We learn from step 5 that, even when our leaders are committed, they need encouragement and lots of it. So step 5 asks you to lavish encouragement on your leaders by remembering and rewarding them.

You may be thinking that these last two steps don't sound all that important—just icing on the cake. Trust us on this one. If you leave out these steps, they will come back to haunt you later on. And then it may prove difficult to recover lost ground.

Leadership-Development Process Evaluation

Step 1: Discover new leaders for development.

Step 2: Launch new leaders into their positions of leadership.

Step 3: Develop new and current leaders for ministry in the church.

Step 4: Regularly evaluate your leadership-development process.

Step 5: Regularly reward those in the leadership-development process.

After leader-trainers and their ministries have implemented the process outlined in this book, it's imperative that they evaluate it regularly.[1] Every system develops kinks that get in the way of good leadership development. No plan, especially a new one, is free of problems. The key is always looking for ways to improve training. This will mean many necessary tweaks that will serve dramatically to improve the leadership-development process. They will also keep it current with the times.

Most ministries do little if any evaluation for at least two reasons. It makes some people uncomfortable, and they've never done evaluation before. These reasons, among other things, cause ministries to neglect evaluation. But when we fail to evaluate our leadership process (or any process for that matter), it becomes stale, dated, and brittle. In time it will become totally ineffective. When leaders realize what has happened and that they need to get caught up, they find that they will have to implement ten or twenty years' worth of change (deep change) in a year or two, which most people in the ministry will refuse to do. However, constant little tweaks result in the same changes, but they are incremental changes that will incite little if any resistance.

What will you evaluate? You will evaluate the effectiveness of the leadership-development process. That includes the overall process and the people as well as the various parts that make up the process. Is the process actually developing leaders? Some of the people whom you will evaluate are the leader-trainers or mentors and the trainees. You also will evaluate the curriculum, any technology, and other related areas.

Not only will the individuals in the process be evaluated, but they will do self-evaluation. And this should precede any formal evaluation. A question for the leadership staff at the end of the year could be, How many leaders did you equip this past year? Standard questions for trainees could be, What did you like about the development process? What didn't you like about it? How could we do it better next time?

How often will you evaluate the process? Informal evaluation is ongoing. Asking questions such as, How can we train our leaders better next week? suggests weekly evaluation at all levels. This is an excellent approach and could be done informally by the leader-trainer as he or she reflects on and discusses with others what has transpired over the preceding week. It may be obvious that there are things that should be done differently next time. The trainer or coach also could regularly ask the trainees for their input.

Formal evaluation also can be helpful and should take place periodically. When the leadership-development process is first getting underway, it's a good idea to conduct a formal evaluation each quarter. Once the process has been in place for one to two years, the formal evaluation is necessary only twice a year and eventually only once a year at all levels.

How will you evaluate the process? We recommend that, for the formal evaluation, you develop a written format for all levels in which you will want to answer such questions as, What is this person doing well? In what areas does this person need to improve? What would you suggest that he or she do to improve? You would follow this with a verbal evaluation. This could include self-evaluation, evaluation between mentor and trainee, and evaluation by all in a particular ministry or leadership level. Formal evaluation is most effective in situations in which the ministry struggles to do evaluation. It makes it more likely that evaluation will be done.

Formal evaluation is helpful but should bring no surprises if informal evaluation has been taking place all along. Informal evaluation will identify problems and contribute to growth, because it is an ongoing process, taking place, for example, when the leader-trainer catches the leader-trainee doing something well and tells him or her so. When this has been happening before the formal evaluation, the trainee already knows how he or she is progressing.

Somehow any evaluation always gets back to people. It's because people ultimately operate the process as well as design it. Thus we need to say a few words about working with people in evaluation.

We mentioned above that people don't like personal evaluation because it makes them feel uncomfortable. No one likes to hear what he or she is doing wrong, including you and me. Consequently the key to effective evaluation is to focus on what your emerging leaders are doing well. You must determine in your own mind whether your leaders will get better by focusing on their weaknesses or on their strengths. We think the answer is a no-brainer. If leaders improve their weaknesses, at best they move from weak to average in those areas. This isn't too exciting or motivating. If they improve their strengths, however, they become even stronger and enjoy what they're doing in the process. Thus you would be wise to harp on their strengths, many of which likely surfaced in the assessment phase of step 1. Remind them of and celebrate those strengths, point out newly discovered ones, and encourage them to continue to grow in them.

Focusing on strengths doesn't mean that you completely ignore weaknesses, especially the glaring ones. However, you don't dwell on them. Always begin a formal evaluation by focusing on the person's strengths. Then identify a few areas where you think he or she can improve. The former should outweigh and even overwhelm the latter. Then you may want to end the session by returning to the person's strengths.

Who will do the evaluation? It's best that all who are involved in the process evaluate it at every level. This includes the trainees as well as the leader-trainers. The trainers evaluate because they've designed the process and must be in tune with where to tweak it. The trainees evaluate because they are involved in the process and thus are in a good position to give feedback as to the effectiveness of the training in their lives.

What will you do with evaluations? This seems like a strange question and applies only to formal evaluation. However, there is a tendency to ignore the evaluation results. We may do evaluation because we know we're supposed to, but we can ignore the feedback and make no changes. When this happens, evaluation is a huge waste of time and ultimately defeats the purpose of the process. You would be wise to save the evaluations for at least one year for purposes of comparison to look for improvement when conducting subsequent evaluations.

Rewarding Those in Leadership

Step 1: Discover new leaders for development.

Step 2: Launch new leaders into their positions of leadership.

Step 3: Develop new and current leaders for ministry in the church.

Step 4: Regularly evaluate your leadership-development process.

Step 5: Regularly reward those in the leadership-development process.

Who among us doesn't care for some genuine, appropriate appreciation somewhere along the way while we're leading and ministering to people? When you are appreciated, you feel honored. Those who are leading and training to be leaders feel the same way. On the one hand, it's true that appreciation can be overdone and make people very uncomfortable. On the other hand, some appropriate, timely appreciation is better than showing no appreciation at all.

On one occasion I (Aubrey) was taking a group of leaders through the church revitalization or refocusing process that we employ at The Malphurs Group. (To take the church through the process, we ask to work with the church's core leadership. These are the key leaders, mostly laypersons in the church, whom the congregation respects and follows.) These leaders looked tired. Discouragement was written all over their faces. And at one point in the process, one lady commented on how discouraged she was. Her point was that no one in the church ever thanked her for all the hours she spent working with and teaching her Sunday school class. It was a thankless experience. This doesn't have to be. Actually, it must not be! And a good reward system will see that this doesn't happen in your ministry.

In the sample system that we've presented in this book, the level 1 and 2 leaders (see chapter 7) are mostly nonpaid, while the level 3 leaders are compensated in some situations, and the level 4 people are paid staff. Whether or not money is involved, wisdom advises us to reward our leaders for their ministries. In Jeremiah 17:10 God says, "I the LORD search the heart and examine the mind, to reward a man according to his conduct, according to what his deeds deserve." The way to honor and show appreciation is to reward those in the leadership-development process.

Who will reward leaders? Those who are responsible for leadership development and who function in some way as leader-trainers should reward leaders. These trainers include the pastor of the church, the board, leadership staff, and any others who are doing training, including Sunday school teachers and small-group leaders.

How will you reward leaders? There are several ways. One is to make your people heroes. Every culture has its heroes, including the church. For example, in the soul-winning church, they are the evangelists. In the Bible-teaching church, they are the Bible teachers and those who know their Bibles well. At a seminary, they are the scholars. The heroes in the training church are its leader-trainers. We make leaders heroes by using them as positive illustrations in a sermon, telling stories about their contributions, rewarding them in public, and so on.

Some other ways to reward leaders are financial compensation; personal letters, cards, or notes; a framed certificate of appreciation; a plaque; a word of praise or thanks; flowers; testimonies from trainees (and a video of the same); the gift of a Bible, devotional, or commentary on the Bible; an extra day off for staff; tickets to a sporting event; a dinner at a restaurant; and a banquet or celebration event.

Fellowship Bible Church of Dallas, Texas, conducts a celebration called the Billy Awards, named after their senior pastor, Dr. Bill Counts. They have fun as they mimic the Grammy awards. However, as one staff leader confided, while it's done in fun, they all feel honored to be recognized at this event.

How often will you reward leaders? The best answer is every week at every level—at least on an informal basis. This could include a thank-you, a card or letter, and other informal appreciation. Formally, you would be wise to celebrate leaders at least once a year. This could include a leadership banquet.

Questions for Reflection and Discussion

1. Do you believe that it's a good idea to formally evaluate people? Why or why not? Any cautions?
2. Have you ever served on a ministry that conducted formal evaluations of its people? If so, was this a good or bad experience?
3. Do you believe that an evaluation should focus on people's strengths or weaknesses? Why?
4. Do you believe that it is a good idea to reward people for their service? Why or why not?
5. Have you served in a ministry that rewarded its people for their service? Was this a good or bad experience? Why?
6. What ways do you think are appropriate to reward people in your ministry?

12

Home Improvement

Guidelines for Improving the Process

Even though the builder handed you the keys to your house at the closing, you realize that the work on your house isn't finished. You'll have to maintain it. As soon as the building is completed, the bad news is that your house begins to deteriorate. Recently I (Aubrey) spent one Saturday afternoon caulking and painting cracks, putting more insulation in the attic, and adjusting the gutters along the edge of the roof. I installed floodlights in the backyard for illumination at night, and I added several electrical receptacles in the garage. This is all part of maintaining a home and keeping it in good condition.

Developing leaders is no different. Once in place, you must maintain the leadership-development process. At best, the process is complex and even messy (no matter how two authors may try to break it down into neat, clean steps). Relentlessly, repair needs crop up, and you'll find that you will also want to improve the process.

So what are the complex variables of maintaining a leadership development process? What are some of the common improvement projects that you'll want to pursue? We propose five guidelines for maintaining and improving the process that will get you started in the right direction. These are especially helpful if you're just beginning the process. The five guidelines will enable you to anticipate the common challenges that leader-developers face.

Make Disciples

Guideline 1: Don't build a shoe factory and forget to make shoes.

This first guideline makes an important distinction between building leaders and making disciples. Ultimately the reason we build leaders is to make disciples, but the processes are distinct, with leader building subordinate to disciple making.

To make clearer this relationship, we will use an illustration from *The Lost Art of Disciple Making* in which the author, Leroy Eims, compares the church to a shoe factory.[1] He explains that, as the purpose of the shoe factory is to make shoes, the purpose of the church is to make disciples. At the end of the day, if all of the time, equipment, and raw material in the shoe factory do not produce shoes, the factory has failed. Eims argues that the same principle is true of the church. If, at the end of the day, the church, with all of its God-given resources, does not produce disciples, it has failed to fulfill its God-given mission.

The shoe factory metaphor is helpful in understanding the role of the leadership-development process in the church. Leaders are similar to the assembly line in the shoe factory. They are not the final "product" of the church; disciples are. Leaders simply help the church make more mature disciples. Leaders train leaders so that more disciples can be produced. Like the assembly line in the shoe factory, the leadership-development process is not the reason for the church's existence. Rather it is a means to a greater end—making disciples. So then, as you purpose to develop leaders, remember guideline 1: *Don't build a shoe factory and forget to make shoes.*

We have seen churches that think they are excelling at both disciple making and leader building, when in reality they are doing only one well. Some churches make disciples but not leaders, and others make leaders but not disciples. We want to clarify the need to have unique processes for both disciple making and leader building.

When churches design leadership development as a necessary phase of the disciple-making process, they are making an unfortunate mistake. It is unbiblical to assume that all disciples have either the spiritual gift of leadership or unique God-given leadership abilities. So while all leaders are disciples, not all disciples are leaders. If the church makes leadership development the standard for all disciples, it is in effect dishonoring believers who have other gifts, such as teaching, mercy-giving, hospitality, counseling, and so on. Of course, the leadership-development process and the disciple-making process should be related, but they should not be the same process.

If a church tries to build leaders before it is effectively making disciples, it is similar to a shoe factory that plans to expand an existing assembly line before it has ever made any shoes. We recommend focusing energy on the process of making disciples before focusing on developing leaders, because disciple making must come first.

Before deciding on the content of your leadership training, you must define how your church makes disciples. This is essentially helping the team "keep their eye on the ball." If your leaders don't know how your church makes disciples, then who does? And if your leaders don't know, how is it actually happening? We have seen some excellent training content in churches that failed to address this issue. The reality is that a church can provide classes all day long on leadership skills—vision casting, team building, conflict resolution—and your leaders will still be missing the main thing, which is disciple making.

As you select and develop content for leadership development, be careful not to eclipse the more important process of disciple making. If you are the senior pastor, you probably will have to clarify the disciple-making process for yourself and/or your staff, and that's okay. Get it clear, and get it down on paper. Once you do, then feed it to your leaders before you feed them anything else.

The Problem of Nonleaders

Guideline 2: Don't fall prey to the M-myth.

The M-myth will wreak havoc if it traps you. Simply stated, the M-myth is the belief that certain kinds of believers are *necessarily* leaders (please note our emphasis on *necessarily*). These believers are the mature, the mobilized, and the ministry masters. Therefore, the M-myth can be stated in three parts:

1. Mature believers are leaders.
2. Mobilized believers are leaders.
3. Ministry masters are leaders.

To put it bluntly, we have seen many churches hammer some thumbs in leadership development because—following the M-myth—nonleaders were asked to fill leadership roles. Please don't miss this fact: Nothing will repel other leaders more than a nonleader in a leadership role! Therefore, if the church believes the M-myth, construction of their leadership-development process will never begin.

The key to understanding the M-myth is appreciating that very good people are put in leadership roles with very good intentions, but that does not necessarily make them leaders. You should evaluate your current leadership to see if this is the case, and you should keep the M-myth in mind as you proceed to recruit leaders and launch ministries.

Let's take a quick look at the truth about each kind of person in the M-myth. The truth is that *not all of the mature believers in your church are necessarily leaders.* This states in a different way what we have already said—the discipleship process and leadership-development process are two different things. Not all spiritual giants are gifted to lead. Again we want to emphasize that we are not saying that spiritual qualifications are unimportant. But often mature believers are the first to be asked to fill key leadership roles, and they should not be approached *by default* for leadership because they are spiritually mature.

Second, the truth is that *not all mobilized believers in your church are necessarily leaders.* Just because someone volunteers to serve, he or she is not necessarily a leader. Some church environments are so undermobilized that anyone doing work in the church may appear to have leadership qualities. Do not be fooled by this dynamic.

A closely related point to remember is that the leadership-development process is not the mobilization process. Every disciple should be mobilized and every church should have a process to get believers plugged into ministry, but this is distinct from leadership development. How then should the mobilization process and leadership-development process relate to one another as distinct processes? Here are several points to keep in mind:

- *Awareness and training:* Every person coming through the mobilization process should be exposed to the leadership-development process, learning why it exists, how it works, and who is responsible for it. This may be a good time to show the church's organizational chart. As you touch on leader development, it may also be an ideal time to teach briefly from Scripture about the importance of following spiritual leaders. Keep in mind that the people you are mobilizing will soon be assigned to a team or committee with a leader as they plug into ministry.
- *Shared information:* The person responsible for leadership development should have access to the key information garnered through the mobilization process, such as the spiritual gifts, passion, and experiences of people preparing to join a church ministry.
- *Recruitment and follow-up:* Individuals who demonstrate leadership qualities during the mobilization process or through assessment tools are good candidates for follow-up and personal invitation

into leadership. The individual responsible for leader development should have access to this information.

The third truth is that *not all believers with ministry mastery in your church are necessarily leaders.* By ministry mastery, we mean a high degree of competence or expertise in a specific ministry area. For example, an excellent preacher, an outstanding vocalist, or a top-notch counselor does not automatically make a good leader. In fact, the opposite is usually true. When someone displays an unusually high degree of technical competence, his or her greatest contribution is usually in that technical competence, not in leadership.

The point is that the presence of remarkable gifts and abilities should not automatically flag someone as a leader. Ignoring this truth has led to a common dilemma in management referred to as the Peter Principle. The principle points to the tendency of management to promote competent people to the point at which they are no longer competent and therefore less valuable to the organization. Usually that means a nonleader is placed in a role with leadership demands, and he or she does not function well.

One "master" we know is a soundboard technician in a church. He can mix sound with the best, and every Sunday thousands of people benefit from his technical expertise. At one point the church recognized the need to develop the sound team and to recruit and train more technicians. Our friend was the first one approached for team leadership, and he took the role. Six months later he was frustrated and ineffective at leading the team. He was a casualty of the M-myth. Today a real leader leads the team, a person whose technical competence is not as advanced as that of our friend, who remains a team member.

So how can you escape the M-myth in practical ways? There are three things that we recommend you do.

List Leadership Traits

First, make a list of the leadership traits you feel adequately capture the unique contribution that leaders make in the church. By making this list, you and other leaders in the church will keep in mind why mature believers and ministry masters aren't automatically leaders. We recommend that you involve your staff and other top leaders in this process. A good example of a list like this is Bill Hybels's top five leadership traits.[2] The following is the list that he and other staff use at Willow Creek Community Church.

Willow Creek's Top Five Leadership Traits

Influence

Character

People skills

Drive

Intelligence

Remove Nonleaders from Leadership

The second way to escape the M-myth is to identify and remove current nonleaders who are misplaced in leadership roles. This is an extremely difficult process, but it must be done. The responsible person should discuss the change with the nonleader, being open and honest but moving slowly and being sensitive to the nonleader's feelings. The church may want to offer the person a long-term exit strategy or the opportunity to move to another ministry. The leader may even want to take responsibility for making the bad choice of asking the individual to take the position. It is important to remember that the change is being made for the ultimate benefit of the church as well as the individual.

About a year ago the senior pastor of a church we know had the courage to confront the problem of the executive pastor's being over his head with administrative leadership responsibility. The senior pastor spoke the truth in love. Eventually the executive pastor moved to another pastoral role that focused on mobilizing believers in service rather than having staff leadership and leadership-development responsibility. The process was emotionally difficult and bruised the executive pastor's ego, but after nine months he was actually enjoying his new position more than his former one.

Keep Leadership Traits in Mind

The third way to escape the M-myth is to keep your leadership-traits list in mind when you recruit leaders. In some settings you are considered to be leadership material if you have a pulse! Usually, then, the results are disastrous. But if you know the specifics of what you are looking for, you will be able to select the right people.

An illustration of this occurred this afternoon as I (Will) was working on this chapter in a Starbucks cafe. A young man named Rob walked in and interrupted me while I was writing. Rob had approached me about an internship opportunity three months ago. There was no question that he was talented, but the role required specific leadership abilities. At the time, I told him that I was interested in offering him the position, and then I gave him some specific follow-up steps. I was intentionally measuring initiative, which is one of the top traits I look for and expect in leaders. Rob failed the test, and the position had been filled, not by someone more talented but by someone who took more initiative.

Remember that not every mature, mobilized believer is a leader. Even individuals who display mastery of certain ministry skills are not necessarily leaders. You should not attempt to do leadership development unless you can tell the difference. To avoid falling into the M-myth trap, make a list of leadership traits, courageously move nonleaders from leadership roles, and refer to the leadership-traits list when recruiting new leaders.

Centralized and Decentralized Training

Guideline 3: Do both cardio and muscular workouts, not either/or.
The third guideline keeps the body of Christ active with a full-body workout. We use the workout types—cardio and muscular—in reference to centralized and decentralized leadership training in the church, respectively. Cardiovascular workouts develop the heart as a centralized system that supports the entire body including each individual muscle. Muscular workouts develop individual parts of the body—biceps and triceps in the arms, quadriceps in the legs, and so on. Without both kinds of training, the human body will not reach its full potential. And without both centralized and decentralized leadership training, the church body will not reach its full potential.

The analogy is appropriate by virtue of the fact that many people do only one kind of workout. We know people who run or do aerobics (cardio workout) and do nothing else. And we could list several guys who frequent the weight room (muscular workout) but would run out of breath going up a flight of stairs. Likewise there are many churches that do only decentralized or centralized training but not both. In our experience, it is more common for a church to do only decentralized training.

Decentralized training is training specific to a ministry area in the church. This happens when training occurs in areas like children's or student ministry, worship and arts ministry, women's ministry, greeting ministry, and so on. In light of Paul's use of body imagery in 1 Corinthians 12:12–31, we suggest that each of these specific, decentralized ministries is like an individual muscle in the body of Christ.

Centralized leadership training, in contrast, involves all of the leaders in the church, regardless of the different ministry area the leadership may represent. Also, it includes the leaders at every level in the church.

To illustrate the difference, consider two of the examples we used in the previous chapter. The children's ministry benchmarking trip is an example of decentralized training—only the children's leaders attended and the focus was ministry specific. In contrast, a church vision night is centralized, bringing all of the leaders in the church together from all the ministries.

So how do both centralized and decentralized leadership training contribute to the health of the church? The best way to explain this is to describe what happens if you do one without the other.

The Problem of Decentralized Training Only: Effective Parts Do Not Make a Whole

If a church does decentralized training only, the individual ministries will improve but in a way that fragments the church organization as a whole. The effectiveness of the church as a cohesive movement will falter. This occurs because leaders, as the primary influencers, will tend to lose sight of the forest in the midst of the trees. Leaders may start pulling in different directions, and the tendency is to forget the whys of ministry in pursuit of the hows of ministry. Thus tactics become more important than strategy.

This can happen in both large and small churches. Often it involves very passionate lay leaders or staff who thrive on doing their own thing. Their "own thing" may be exactly what God designed them to do, but it should not disconnect them or their ministry from the church at large. If this happens, a leader's passion becomes more important than the church's mission.

It is not that the leader's ministry passion is unimportant—it is extremely important. But the passion for specific ministries must work through a commitment to the church's mission—what the church is ultimately supposed to be accomplishing. The collection of individuals with their gifting and passions must work together, integrated as a whole body in the spirit of 1 Corinthians 12:12–31.

We have heard pastors and consultants talk about this effect in a variety of ways. It has been called a silo effect because individual ministries operate like individual silos, side by side, without any connection.

Describing the fragmented church, Carl George refers to the "sand dollar syndrome."[3] The term comes from the natural design of the sand dollar—several pie-shaped pieces. Others describe the effect as ministries spinning in their own orbits.

Many factors contribute to this problem in the church, and it is not our purpose to explore them here. It is important to understand, however, that if you have only decentralized training taking place, it will contribute to the fragmentation dynamic of the church.

Military training provides a helpful analogy. Imagine an army that had only decentralized training. Highly trained special forces and highly skilled individual soldiers would certainly develop, but the army would be significantly limited if these units did not receive centralized training that would connect them to each other and to the overall mission of the entire force. Individual units need to know how to communicate and coordinate with one another. Decision making must be based on the status of the entire army and the advancement of the mission, not on the status of individual units alone. Like the armed forces, churches need both types of training.

The Problem of Centralized Training Only: A Whole without Effective Parts

The problem of providing only centralized training is that effective parts do not develop within the whole. It is critical to have the parts of the church body in alignment, working together, and moving in the same direction. Once this condition is achieved, it is equally important that each part continue to work effectively and to improve its function. There is no way to focus on the special function of the parts if there is only centralized training.

To use our earlier comparison, centralized training is like a cardiovascular workout. While cardio training helps the heart deliver more blood to each muscle, it does not allow each muscle to develop its unique strength. This requires a different kind of workout. Consequently most gyms have special weight machines designed to isolate muscular movement to develop strength in that part.

Or consider the military illustration. A company or battalion that knows how to work together is essential. But in wartime, every unique skill in the unit must be at its best—from those who use sniper rifles and M-16s to those who use communication and medical equipment. How confident would you feel if you served in an army that provided no specialized training for helicopter pilots, tank drivers, and surgeons?

Finding the Balance: The Whole Is Greater than the Sum of the (Effective) Parts

To reach its full potential, the church must balance centralized and decentralized leadership training. Having reviewed the effects of neglecting one or the other, let's look at the results of having both.

Consider some further advantages of centralized training. First, it's a better system for people who haven't decided on or been placed in a ministry. They can receive training even though they've not yet identified with a particular church ministry. Second, it requires less work from the various ministry leaders. They're not as involved in the training (if at all) as the person heading up the centralized program. Third, a distinct, centralized leadership-development ministry or program provides greater visibility in the church than when training is the responsibility of each ministry. People in and outside the church are more aware of its presence. The program can be advertised or marketed through brochures, announcements in the church bulletin or verbal and video announcements during the service, and other means. Finally, it provides a uniform approach to training leaders: uniform planning, methods, requirements, and standards.

Now connect these advantages to the advantages of a decentralized system, which is better for experienced leaders who are already in a ministry within the church. They don't have to vacate their particular ministry while pursuing the training. Decentralized training also allows for the unique aspects that characterize every ministry and distinguish each from the other. Finally, it involves individual ministries more in the process. They have a greater role and flexibility in training their own people.

The chart below summarizes the benefits of each.

Centralized Training	Decentralized Training
All leaders at all levels	Ministry specific leaders only
Clarifies the church's big picture	Focuses on a single ministry
Mission driven	Passion driven
Fosters church unity	Enhances ministry distinctives
Increases interdependence	Increases effectiveness
Provides uniformity	Provides flexibility
Answers the "why" questions	Answers the "how" questions

The value of both centralized and decentralized training can be summarized in one word—*synergy*. Centralized training keeps the energy that is released in individual ministries aligned with the church's overall direction. Decentralized training keeps the individual ministries strong and effective so that their alignment counts.

The illustration below shows this dynamic. The large arrow represents a church moving in a clear, mission-guided direction. The smaller arrows represent leaders. The smaller bold arrows indicate leaders who are well developed in their particular ministry area. Church 1 with decentralized training has well-developed leaders but they are moving in different directions; some are in line with the church and others are not. Church 2 with centralized training has well-aligned leaders, but they are not as strong in their specific ministry areas. Church 3 is balanced, with aligned and developed leaders.

Building in the Balance

How do you build this balance into your leadership-training process? The first step is to determine the kind of training that is already taking place. Then consider again where you are planning to go. Determine if your existing training venues fall into the centralized or decentralized category. Refer to the primary and secondary training venues that you selected (see chapter 10). This will help you discover your "default" mode of training. Now, to take steps toward designing an intentional balance, consider the following recommendations.

1. To the primary and secondary venue categories in chapter 10, add a new category called "recommended decentralized training venues." Fill in the chart below with the primary and secondary training venues you identified.

Primary Training Venue	Secondary Training Venues	Recommended Decentralized Training Venues

2. Verify that your one primary training venue, as identified in chapter 10, is centralized. (Keep in mind that while apprenticing can fall into either category, it is centralized if it is consistently done throughout the church.) If the primary venue is not centralized, move it on the chart to the new decentralized category.
3. Verify that your two secondary venues are centralized. If they are not, move them to the new decentralized category.
4. If you have moved venues from the primary or secondary venues, scan the venues in chapter 10 and select new venues for your centralized training process.
5. Scan the decentralized training venues and select three for the Recommended Decentralized Training Venues category. (If you already have some here, add enough to make three.) Several venues (in the chart below) are well suited for decentralized training. They tend to be skills focused and event oriented. The skills focus contributes to specific ministry development and the event orientation helps to make implementation more practical.

Recommended Venues for Decentralized Training

Coaching

Huddle

Seminar

Conference

Retreat

Workshop

Benchmarking

6. Keep in mind that decentralized venues can be the same as your primary and secondary venues, and a given venue can be used for either a centralized or decentralized purpose.
7. Use the venue comparison chart in appendix F to help you design your process. This will help you balance the leadership competencies and training types as you build leaders. Please note that you are not limiting yourself to these venues; rather you are prioritizing them so that you can have a well-developed plan and team consensus for developing leaders.

When you complete the chart, you will have identified the top six leadership training venues for your church—three centralized and three decentralized.

The reason we have labeled the decentralized training as "recommended" is very important. It is difficult and limiting to require specific venues for decentralized training. For example, a youth pastor may conclude that a student ministry conference is the best ministry-specific training for his team, but the worship pastor may want to bring in a coach for his team training. Because every ministry has unique training demands, we recommend that churches provide a high degree of latitude to the leaders responsible for their area. At the same time, it is important to think through the desirable decentralized options for your church. This desirability should be influenced by the strengths and limitations of the centralized training that you have selected. For example, if the centralized options are low in the relational category (according to the chart in appendix F), you will want to recommend relational venues for decentralized training.

Here is one example of a church's venues:

Leadership Development at Clear Creek Community Church

Primary Training Venue	Secondary Training Venues	Recommended Decentralized Training Venues
Apprenticing	Getaways	Conferences
	Seminars	One-on-ones
		Huddles

The centralized training is built on the foundation of apprenticing. To supplement apprenticing, the two secondary training venues are getaways and seminars. Getaways happen three times a year in the spring, summer, and fall. Then two seminar days are offered during the year in the back-to-school season and at the beginning of the year. The purpose of the seminars is twofold. First, they provide another entry point for new leaders by offering new leader training. Second, they review key training material for leaders who could not attend a getaway.

The decentralized training includes conferences, one-on-ones, and huddles. Every staff member has money budgeted for attending a ministry-specific conference and is encouraged to recruit other church leaders to attend. Also, every leader meets once a month with the leader above them in the church structure. Finally, leaders who are responsible for other leaders are encouraged and equipped to hold huddles every eight to ten weeks.

A final consideration as you balance centralized and decentralized training is what to do when the two processes conflict with respect to time. This will happen if your church is doing a good job of building leaders with both kinds of training. It will happen when a special student ministry seminar (decentralized) is offered at the same time as a church leadership retreat (centralized). It will happen when a church leader comes to you and sincerely asks, "This year I have to choose between the conference and the retreat. Which one is more important for me to attend?"

In these situations we recommend making the centralized training the priority. We believe the church benefits in the long run by placing unity and alignment first. Also, it is easier to find decentralized training opportunities from organizations outside the church, but it is impossible to replace a significant one-time event that your church puts together itself.

Building the Leadership Community

Guideline 4: Expand the pool at both ends.

The fourth guideline for improving the leadership-development process relates to the building of your leadership community. Think of the leadership community as a group of people in a swimming pool. If the church wants that community to grow, it must expand the pool at both ends—the shallow end and the deep end. The shallow end is where emerging leaders get their feet wet. The deep end is where experienced leaders continue to exercise and have fun. If the church is not constantly expanding the pool, both emerging leaders and experienced leaders will walk by the pool without jumping in because no provision is being made for them.

So whether your church has ten, one hundred, or five hundred leaders, there are two important questions to ask:

- *Shallow-end question:* What can we do to make the leadership community more accessible to emerging leaders?
- *Deep-end question:* What can we do to continue developing the most advanced leaders in the leadership community?

Before jumping right into answering these questions, let's consider why these questions are so important. The illustration below presents a numbering system that John Maxwell uses. It basically numbers leaders on a scale of 1 to 10, with 10 representing the highest leadership ability and experience and 1 representing the lowest.

The illustration also represents two leadership communities. Leadership Community A is the leaders in a church that has intentionally recruited and developed leaders. The leadership community has grown and leveled off a bit after several years. There are numerous leaders, ranging in ability from 3 to 8. You could say this community represents a pool that is four feet deep across its entire length, with no shallow end and no deep end.

Leadership Community A

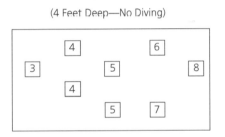

Leadership Community B

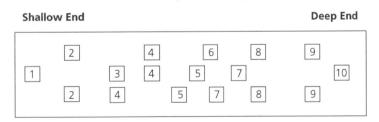

What is the best way for Leadership Community A to continue to grow? To answer this question, let's consider three logical observations.

1. Leaders have an affinity for other leaders.
2. Leaders learn from other leaders.
3. Leaders learn best from more advanced leaders.

With these observations in mind, let's take a look at Leadership Community A. There are not many level 1 or 2 people in the pool. Keep in mind that in the church community at large there are probably more leaders at levels 1 and 2 than at any other level. To these people, the pool may look too intimidating to enter. Therefore, the assimilation of emerging leaders gets stifled.

Also, the lack of advanced leaders in the pool opens the door for other advanced leaders to walk by. There is limited affinity and little opportunity for growth for these leaders.

The lack of advanced leaders in the pool limits the development of leaders at levels 7 and 8 who are already there. Think of the implications. The growth of the entire leadership community is at stake because the development roof affects everyone. If level 7 and 8 leaders stop growing, then 5 and 6 leaders stop growing, and so on.

Now consider Leadership Community B. This church has intentionally taken steps to expand the pool at both ends. Even though this took significant energy and resources, there is a tremendous return on investment potential. There is now room in the pool for a higher percentage of leaders at levels 1 and 2 to enter. Highly developed leaders have more peers with whom to interact. Most important, leaders at every development level have more advanced leaders from whom they can learn.

Building the Shallow End

Now let's answer the question, How do we make the leadership community more accessible to emerging leaders? Here are some recommendations:

- Give an open invitation to centralized venues. At least one of your training venues should be open to the entire church community. This does not mean that just anybody can become a leader, but it does mean that just anybody can come and check things out. If becoming a leader is getting in waist deep, you want some venues where people can watch as they get their feet wet.
- Create a buzz during the open invitation window. When the entire church is being invited to a leadership event, it must become the main focus for the entire staff. It is essential that the staff and key leaders get involved and talk it up.
- Make it an event people won't want to miss. The church should shamelessly add value to the venue to attract as many people as possible. Food and fun are essentials. If you are going to choose one event to demonstrate a commitment to excellence that is off

the charts, this is it. Obviously this may require a financial commitment for the church.

- Have new leaders give their testimonies about becoming a leader. People are inspired when they hear the journey of others. Allow potential leaders to see and hear people with whom they can identify. This also removes some of the ambiguity of the process itself.
- Intentionally address those who are checking things out during the training venue. Welcome and acknowledge potential leaders. You may want to have a discussion time for them alone.

Building the Deep End

Now let's consider the deep end. How do we continue to develop the most advanced leaders in the leadership community? Here are some recommendations:

- Affirm advanced leaders personally. Remind these leaders how valuable they are to the other leaders in the leadership community.
- Go out of your way to create advanced leadership settings. There may be events or times when you invite key lay leaders to be a part of staff meetings or retreats. You may have an informal get-together or create a special forum or focus group for your more experienced leaders.
- Assign special projects to advanced leaders. Let the big dogs eat! Leaders are wired to lead, so don't hold your advanced leaders back.
- Pastors should learn from their advanced leaders personally. This requires much humility but can have a tremendous impact. Think about the stronger leaders in your church. What unique experiences have they had? What unique abilities do they have? When you answer these questions, take the opportunity to learn from them. Interview them or shadow them for a day.
- Use more coaching and consulting. This is important. When your pool doesn't have many level 8, 9, or 10 leaders, you will have to bring them in from the outside to train the lower-level leaders.

Task-Oriented Ministry

Guideline 5: Stay off the task treadmill.
Some ministries that have accomplished much for the kingdom are very task oriented. This sets them up to get caught on the task treadmill,

an ever increasing preoccupation with ministry activity that can kill the leadership-development process.

How does the treadmill dynamic happen? Most often a strong, dominant visionary leader, whom God has burdened with some special task such as reaching an entire community for Christ, starts such a ministry. As the organization grows up around this leader, it becomes highly task oriented, attracting many dominant, task-oriented people whose slogan is "Get the job done for God!" The task becomes all-important and people are recruited to the task with little if any preparation. Many are operating out of their giftedness, taking little time to develop. Often in task-focused organizations, the tasks aren't always done well, expectations aren't met, and the dropout rate is high.

Please don't misunderstand. It's not wrong for ministries to focus on task. Paul emphasizes the ministry task when he underlines the importance that he places on the completion of his own ministry in his lifetime: "However, I consider my life worth nothing to me, if only I may finish the race and complete the task the Lord Jesus has given me—the task of testifying to the gospel of God's grace" (Acts 20:24). If churches didn't focus on task, they would accomplish little for the Savior. However, the key is balance. While no ministry can perfectly balance task with training, its responsibility is to work hard at achieving such a balance.

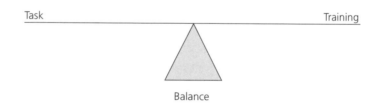

Prone to Failure

Often a task orientation tells leaders the *what* but doesn't provide them with the *how* or *why* of ministry. The organization recruits people to lead, but it fails to adequately prepare them for their work. The following scenario, though extreme, illustrates this abuse. The local community church desperately needs a male Sunday school teacher for a group of junior boys. The last teacher resigned, saying, "I give up!" However, the pastor is able to recruit another unsuspecting soul from the congregation. On the Sunday morning when the new teacher arrives, the pastor points toward the room and says, "There they are. I'll be praying for you." When the teacher frantically asks what he's supposed to do with the class, the pastor looks around and finds a Sunday school quarterly and says, "Here, use this."

When crises emerge, and they will, the staff leader of a task-oriented ministry often resorts to one or more of the following: pleading often to no avail for more full- or part-time staff, depending on the ministry's finances; dropping areas of ministry responsibility—things simply don't get done; or operating in a maintenance mentality—let's just try to get by as best we can—instead of a growth mentality.

Determining If Your Ministry Is Task Oriented

How can you know whether your ministry is task or training oriented? You can use the Personal Profile system, popularly known as the DiSC, to identify your temperament, because some temperaments are naturally task oriented, and this, of course, affects your ministry.

The DiSC works with a four-temperament model. The first is the D that stands for the dominant person—the results-oriented individual who focuses more on accomplishing goals than relating to people. The I represents the influencer—the natural-born leader who focuses more on people and loves to inspire them to action. The S stands for the steady person. Like the I, this person focuses more on people than goals and is very caring and dependable. (If you can't get along with the S temperament, the problem is with you, not them!) Finally, the C represents the compliant temperament. Like the D, this person is goal oriented, but he or she desires to accomplish goals with excellence—the quality-control person. While exceptions exist, Ds and Cs with their focus on goals tend toward a task orientation in ministry. (Cs also realize the importance of training.) However, Is and Ss are more people oriented and thus training oriented. This is summarized in the chart below.

Task Oriented	Training Oriented
D C	C I S

Another method for determining your degree of task orientation is to take the following task-training audit.

Task-Training Audit

   1. The leader
      ___ a. puts tasks first.
      ___ b. puts people first.

2. The budget has
    ___ a. little or no funds for leadership development.
    ___ b. ample funds for leadership development.

3. The organization is
    ___ a. losing leaders and potential leaders.
    ___ b. gaining leaders and potential leaders.

4. The ministry's resources (people, funds, etc.) are
    ___ a. directed toward its ministries.
    ___ b. directed toward developing leaders.

5. Personnel decisions are based on
    ___ a. the organization's needs.
    ___ b. people's needs and fit.

6. Current leaders are
    ___ a. tired and feeling overworked.
    ___ b. refreshed and challenged.

7. Current leaders model
    ___ a. a task mind-set.
    ___ b. a developmental mind-set.

8. The ministry encourages its people
    ___ a. to get the job done above all else.
    ___ b. to pursue developmental training.

9. The organization encourages its upper-level leaders
    ___ a. to challenge their people to set goals and meet them.
    ___ b. to mentor their people.

10. The organization
    ___ a. values setting and achieving its goals.
    ___ b. values training and learning.

Add up the number of a and b answers. If the a answers outnumber the b answers, your ministry is more task than training oriented. If your ministry is task oriented, your people will not be developed to their full potential and leadership development will be stifled. As you implement more training, remember the exhortation from chapter 3—slow down to speed up. By taking the time to develop people, more ministry will be accomplished in the end.

Questions for Reflection and Discussion

1. How well clarified and aligned is your disciple-making process among the staff and key leaders?
2. Discuss how the M-myth may have affected the current church organization.
3. Have you tended to emphasize centralized or decentralized training in the past?
4. Does your ministry need to make the leadership community more accessible to emerging leaders? How can you do this?
5. Does your ministry need to develop your advanced leaders? How can you do this?
6. Share any experiences you have had personally on the task treadmill. How is the church currently doing with respect to the task treadmill?

13

Turning a House into a Home

Creating a Leadership Culture

If this book has served its purpose, it has provided essential information for building a leadership-development process. But to successfully develop leaders, "building the house" is not enough. The physical structure of a house alone does not ensure a livable or even desirable environment. Likewise, the perfect design and implementation of a leadership-training process do not ensure an ideal environment for nurturing leaders.

So what is the difference between a house and a home? Two identical houses can be two very different homes. Why? Because a home is defined more by the people who live in the house than by the structure itself. Every home represents the family members' collection of interrelated values, attitudes, and actions. Clearly, the environment created by these interrelationships has a more profound impact on the people in the house than does the house itself. You may be familiar with some very poor physical structures that are ideal homes. Or you may know of some beautiful mansions that are terrible places to live.

The same is true with leadership development. The training of leaders is defined as much by the people in the process as the process itself. The interrelationships between pastors and leaders and the environment created by these relationships have a profound impact on each leader's development.

Imagine a group of pastors who design a well-thought-through leadership-development process for their churches. Let's also imagine that the churches are identical with respect to denomination, history, membership, budget, and theological background. Now, if each of these pastors implements the same leadership-development process, even with identical venues and training content, the results are probably going to be different, because of the presence or absence of a leadership culture. We believe that a leader's ability to create a leadership culture has a profound impact on the leadership-development process.

Defining Leadership Culture

Even though the term *leadership culture* is often used in leadership circles these days, it is a little difficult to define because the term represents a broad, intangible concept. George Barna offers a definition of culture in the context of leadership development in his book *A Fish Out of Water*. He defines culture as "the complex intermingling of knowledge, beliefs, values, assumptions, symbols, traditions, habits, relationships, rewards, language, morals, rules and laws that provide meaning and identity to a group of people."[1] This definition is helpful, especially as it points to the many components of a "complex intermingling" involved with a group of people.

Before moving on to define leadership culture, let's consider some examples of culture in general. There are as many illustrations of culture as there are groups of people, whether that group is a nation, a company, a church, a club, or a high school.

An ethnic culture can be seen in a church-planting effort in Mexico, where few people arrive for a service at a heavily promoted new time. Thirty minutes later, however, the people show up. In the Mexican culture, starting an event "on time" is not as regular a pattern of behavior as it is in the United States. The perspective on time is one very small expression of how two national cultures are different.

The characteristics of the two corporate giants IBM and Microsoft illustrate differences in corporate culture. IBM, an East Coast–based company, built its culture around conservative values, which have traditionally found expression in a dark suit dress code, an experienced workforce, a drive for excellence, and its "weighty" blue logo (giving rise to the nickname Big Blue). Microsoft, in contrast, a West Coast–based company, is known for very different cultural expressions, such as a young, casual, fast, and flexible work environment. One testimony on Microsoft's web site pictures a young woman who says, "Microsoft reminds me of a college campus because of the open fields and the informal work atmosphere." The Microsoft logo—a colorful flying window—conveys its identity well.

Culture develops on a smaller scale too. For the last three years, my (Will's) two sons and I have participated in the Indian Guides, a program sponsored by the YMCA. The Indian Guides have worked hard to build a culture through which fathers and sons bond in an outdoor context. Clothing (vests, patches, and headdresses), language, symbols, ceremonies, award systems, tribal meetings, camping events, and special outdoor activities all serve to nourish this culture. We have found that this culture has influenced new patterns of thinking and behaving. For example, a hike through the woods is a different experience now because of the way we observe nature with more skill and appreciation.

We can identify a leadership culture in the church, then, by simply noting how the aspects we normally associate with a national entity, corporation, or any interest group apply to a group of leaders in the local church. Thus leadership culture is *a unique interrelationship of values, thoughts, attitudes, and actions within a group of leaders that reproduces patterns of thinking and behaving among them and their followers.*

The Comprehensive Nature of Culture

Let's take a closer look at the elements that make up the definition: *Leadership culture is a unique interrelationship of values, thoughts, attitudes, and actions . . .*

Four terms summarize the comprehensive nature of culture—*values, thoughts, attitudes,* and *actions.* These words are intended to capture the sense of wholeness that culture represents, because culture expresses our deepest thoughts and affections as people (values and thoughts). It is reflected in how we carry ourselves (attitudes). And it ultimately manifests itself in everything we do (actions). It is worth noting the connection between these terms and the leader's developed capabilities covered in chapter 9. The following chart shows the relationship between the terms.

Leader's Developed Capabilities		Leadership Culture
Character (being)	Soul work	Values
Knowledge (knowing)	Head work	Thoughts
Skills (doing)	Hand work	Actions
Emotions (feeling)	Heart work	Attitudes

Culture involves an *interrelationship* between these values, thoughts, attitudes, and actions among the group of leaders. These parts of the culture are always interrelating with each other, creating a dynamic matrix in which thoughts, words, decisions, emotions, conversations, stories, body language, and other dynamics are constantly impacting each other. This is what Barna describes as a "complex intermingling."

The leadership culture is also *unique* to a group of leaders. The nature of the dynamic interrelationship ensures that each culture is one of a kind. Therefore, the leadership culture is an integral part of building identity. In athletics every team has team colors, which provide a practical identification point during the game. Even beyond the game, the colors become a rallying point for team identity and create an emotional association with others (players, coaches, and fans) who share the identity. And, of course, these people enthusiastically show off their team colors.

A leadership culture has the same effect among a group of leaders. Yet in this culture, it is not the color of fabric that makes the distinction, but the fabric of values, attitudes, and actions that sets the group apart.

The reverse side of this observation is an important consideration. If the group of leaders does not have any distinguishing values or patterns of behavior, then the group does not have a leadership culture. Even though most churches have groups of leaders, they do not necessarily have a leadership culture.

A Contagious Dynamic

Leadership culture is a unique interrelationship of values, thoughts, attitudes, and actions within a group of leaders *that reproduces patterns of thinking and behaving among them . . .*

A well-nurtured leadership culture will create a contagious dynamic among a group of leaders. Values are caught, attitudes rub off, behaviors are modeled and imitated. Jesus' strategy to reach the world was focused on a leadership community of twelve men, which is probably related to his priority in establishing a culture at the dawn of the church era. In other words, he wanted his values to be caught, his attitudes to rub off, and his behaviors to be copied. His primary concern was reproducing patterns of thinking and behavior consistent with his character and kingdom living.

The social sciences also confirm the dynamic of behaviors "rubbing off" within groups of people. Elaine Hatfield has researched this dynamic on an emotional level and describes what she calls "emotional contagion." She has made at least three main conclusions. First, people, in conversation and interaction, tend to "automatically mimic and synchronize their movements with the facial expressions, voices, postures, movements, and instrumental behaviors of others nearby."[2] For example, if one person crosses his or her legs or raises his or her voice, it is very likely that others around will follow suit. Or if one person smiles or yawns, it tends to create a domino effect with others in the immediate surrounding.

The second conclusion is that emotional moods and experiences are influenced, moment by moment, by the tendency of these behaviors to synchronize. For example, the raising of voices will, in turn, tend to make all the participants feel curious at first and then irritated. Or frequent yawning and constant playing with pens will tend to generate a feeling of boredom and lethargy in a group.

The third conclusion is that people tend to "catch" one another's emotions. Therefore, a lively, energetic speaker not only entertains the audience but also multiplies the energy among people in the room. Or if one member of a group is depressed, the others are likely to feel downcast as a result of interaction.

These observations point to the contagious nature of behavior and feelings within a group of people. It is this characteristic of groups that allows for the potential to create and guide culture and specifically a leadership culture.

The transfer of thinking and behavior also occurs on a deeper, internal level. When Paul wrote to the Thessalonians, he reminded them: "You know how we lived among you for your sake. You became imitators of us and of the Lord" (1 Thess. 1:5–6). Here Paul describes the transfer of Christlike, ministry-minded values and actions, which the Thessalonians picked up through Paul's modeling. This modeling required a close proximity that is indicated by the mention that he "lived among" them.

When I (Will) was a college student just beginning to practice my faith on a daily basis, I experienced a modeling moment that significantly impacted my life. Once when I walked into my Bible study leader's dorm room, not expecting him to be there, I flipped on the lights and found my friend on his knees praying. No single event could have had a more dramatic impact on my own prayer life, because of the way the activity was concretely displayed in front of me.

In a similar way a leadership culture provides a context for reproducing patterns of thinking and behavior. The time that a group of leaders spends together and the place where this happens form a kind of modeling incubator: Senior leaders model behavior and all group members are affected. Therefore, while the *training process* includes giving out the right kind of information, the *leadership culture* is always giving off signals about what leadership means and about what leaders do.

Influence throughout the Church

Leadership culture is a unique interrelationship of values, thoughts, attitudes, and actions within a group of leaders that reproduces patterns of thinking and behaving among them *and their followers*.

Not only do leaders influence each other, they influence the church community at large. In effect the leadership culture spills over and creates culture within the whole church. This is the primary distinction between a leadership culture and the culture of any other group. If leadership is fundamentally about influence, then the leadership culture is fundamentally about influence in a broader context, namely, the church.

Michael Slaughter describes the way in which he influences the entire church through his investment in leaders (whom he calls trainer-coaches): "The key to radical discipleship [in the church] is the development of trainer-coaches who carry the DNA to the edges of the movement."[3] In other words he focuses on the development of a leadership culture, and the leaders do the rest by carrying the culture "to the edges of the movement."

Creating Leadership Culture

It is one thing to talk about culture and another to create it. We believe that creating a leadership culture is a highly intuitive and subjective process that is profoundly supernatural. However, there are some basic tools and their functions that define the leader's role in nurturing a leadership culture. We can think of the leader as an artist who uses these tools to create his art.

The Leader as Cultural Artist

Creating a leadership culture is more about the art of developing leaders than the science of leadership development. This is suggested by the initial distinction between a house and a home. Many of the chapters in this book—for example, the discussion of the leaders' core competencies and the strengths and limitations of different training venues and the nature of the process itself—cover the science. This chapter is more about the art of developing leaders. Therefore, it is helpful to think about the work of creating culture through the perspective of an artist, who uses particular brushes and brushstrokes to produce the desired effects. Specifically, there are five kinds of brushes for the leader-developer and four different brushstrokes he or she must learn.

The Basic Tools of the Cultural Artist

When an artist paints a picture, he or she uses a wide array of brushes, made of different fibers and in a variety of shapes, each suited to a specific type of work. The cultural artist has several kinds of brushes as well. They can be described as story, symbol, shared experience, space, and Scripture. In a unique way each contributes to the overall picture of the leadership culture.

STORY

Life is narrative. As humans, we are hardwired to live from and respond to the stories of our lives. Imagine, for example, trying to foster intimacy with another person without being able to share a story. It is entirely possible to share facts and data about a person's life all day without really getting to know him or her. Or imagine trying to communicate in an organization without telling stories to make your ideas clear.

Story is an indispensable tool for communicating on a heart-to-heart level things like values, passion, convictions, history, and vision. When God chose to reveal himself through Scripture, he chose the primary form of narrative. And when Jesus instructed the multitudes, he told story after story in the form of parables. Therefore, pastors who want to impact church leaders on the cultural level must become proficient in the use of story.

All preachers are familiar with story as either an illustrative tool or a message construct for the preaching event. But it is also important to view storytelling on a broader level as a tool for creating culture. This requires the identification and development of folklore or special stories that serve as foundational, identity-shaping events within the leadership culture. The telling and retelling of these stories provide texture and color to the culture. For example, every Marine knows the story of the Battle of Chapultepec, which occurred on September 13, 1847, in the Mexican-American War. In the Corps, the story is retold of the courage and self-sacrifice of the NCO Corps who stormed the Chapultepec Castle outside of Mexico City. There they shouldered the weight of heavy casualties as 90 percent of them died taking the Mexican stronghold. To be a Marine means to know this story and to reflect the values of self-sacrifice exemplified in it. Another example is the storytelling at a family reunion. The significant stories of family history are always told and retold with a sense of joy and meaning. They never get boring, unless of course you are an outsider to the family.

The corporate world also understands the importance of story in creating culture. Advertising agencies help organizations develop a corporate story as a marketing and cultural alignment tool. Salespersons are trained to develop a sales approach through persuasive product stories. In *Simplicity,* Bill Jensen's book on corporate communications, the author develops a model to help executives and managers use story as a framework for all kinds of business communications.[4]

At Willow Creek Community Church, Bill Hybels often tells a story that has become part of the "folklore" of that church's leadership culture. The story recounts the interactions of several couples, including Bill and his wife, on a sailboat. Toward the end of the excursion, Bill gets a brief opportunity to share the gospel. In that moment, he contrasts the words *do* and *done.* The "do" represents the philosophy of the world's religions that require man's effort to reach God. The "done," in contrast, represents the gospel and Christ's finished work on the cross. It is a compelling story (and my brief summary doesn't do it justice).

When I (Will) heard the story the first time, I thought it was an excellent sermon illustration. When I heard it a second time a year later, I thought Hybels was running low on good illustrations. But when I heard it a third and fourth time, I realized that the story transcends a one-time sermon delivery because it is a part of the church's folklore. It is a master story that guides and shapes the leadership culture by reaffirming their value for lost people and the first two steps in their particular church strategy—building relationships of integrity and sharing a verbal witness.

Symbol

A symbol is a visible representation of something invisible. For example, a lion is a tangible and visible way of representing the invisible, intangible idea of courage.

Every culture develops and nurtures symbols as a way of expressing values. The bald eagle has represented the strength, courage, and freedom of the United States since 1789. The Battle of Chapultepec, cited earlier, is symbolized by a red stripe on the pants of a Marine officer's dress blues. The red stripe is called the blood stripe to signify the self-sacrifice displayed in battle. Fellowship Bible Church in Little Rock, Arkansas, uses the symbol of a bridge to communicate their vision of "irresistible influence" as they seek to connect people to Jesus. More than two thousand years ago, Jesus sat with his twelve disciples, held up a loaf of bread, and said, "This is my body." And the list could go on.

Since symbols are important tools to both define and reflect culture, leaders who want to shape leadership culture must be intentional in using symbols. Obviously Scripture and church history have provided a wealth of symbolism for Christian leaders to draw from, including the crown jewel symbol of the cross. But leaders must continue to infuse a fresh sense of meaning into our historic symbols and, when appropriate, create new symbols as cultural artists.

I have enjoyed reading Erwin McManus's account of striving to find a contemporary symbol to express the vision and culture of his church. In his book *The Unstoppable Force,* he expressed his appreciation for symbolism: "In every culture you will find essential metaphors that define and shape its ethos. Your symbols hold your secret stories. The metaphor causes an eruption of images, ideas, dreams, beliefs, and convictions all at one time."[5] He then shares the discovery of a symbol that captured the essence of his multicultural vision—a mosaic. The term *mosaic* was eventually used in the name of the church to reflect both its identity and vision. The metaphor reflects at least three components of their culture: the vibrant expression of a multiethnic congregation, the emphasis on personal brokenness lived out in community, and the awareness of a sovereign God who works as the master artist. By using this beautiful and compelling symbol, McManus took a giant leap toward creating a leadership culture in his church.

SHARED EXPERIENCE

The third brush for the cultural artist is shared experience. A shared experience is simply an event designed to reinforce or reflect the leadership culture. Shared experience is very similar to storytelling, but it is more like story writing or story in "real time." The idea of shared experience is broad and limited at the same time. It is broad with respect to the kinds of events and number of people it can include. For example, a shared experience could include a banquet, retreat, coffee shop meeting, religious ceremony, or time on a basketball court. A shared experience can be a unique, dramatic event, such as an appreciation ceremony, or a routine event, such as a staff meeting. But as a leadership tool, the shared experience will have some intent and design behind it. In other words, a shared experience does not happen just because a group of leaders spends time together. It requires planning and purpose.

As Jesus shared experiences with his disciples, he was intentionally creating a leadership culture among them. Calming the storm, feeding the five thousand, and inviting Peter, James, and John to experience the transfiguration (as well as other events) are just a few of the many intentional encounters they had. Then Jesus embeds two essential shared experiences into the fabric of church life—the Lord's Supper and baptism, which maintain a unique level of significance as ordinances (or sacraments) in the church.

Shared experiences create culture because they can shape values, expand perspectives, challenge presuppositions, and enhance relationships. A common shared experience in many churches is the short-term

missions trip during which a small group goes into a cross-cultural environment for a service- or evangelism-oriented project. Time and time
again, people express how an event like this changes their perspective
on life or moves them from their comfort zone.

To one degree or another all of the venues described in chapter 10
are shared experiences. But you should not limit the use of shared experiences to your primary training venues. Here are two other specific
examples of a shared experience.

After I (Will) graduated from seminary, I candidated with several
churches. The choice of my first ministry post was based primarily on
an experience I shared with the pastor. That weekend we spent Saturday
afternoon together, during which he talked about the joys and frustra-
tions of his ministry journey. We spent an hour driving around the
community. He shared his vision for impacting the thousands of lives
around the church and his desire for building a world-class staff. The
same day he introduced me to some of the church leaders with whom
I would be working. In short, God used that day to meld our hearts,
and as we connected, our dreams began to overlap. The whole day was
a shared experience that required planning and preparation. Looking
back, I realize that it was effective because the pastor communicated
his values in very concrete ways. Driving around the community emphasized the value for lost people. The way he introduced me to leaders
highlighted his commitment to leadership development. Two months
later, I was on the staff team.

At one of the churches I served, the leadership was struggling with
burnout, especially after making the transition to two morning services.
Yet one of the stated core values of the church is "sanity." The value of
sanity represents the conviction that life in ministry is not simply about
teaching what you know but reproducing what you are. And who wants
to reproduce an insane life!

A special leadership event was planned as a shared experience to
reinforce the value of sanity. The leaders were invited to an ice cream
shop. After eating a cold treat, the pastor taught on the value of sanity. Afterward large sheets of paper were placed on the ice cream shop
wall in front of the leaders. The sheets represented different ministry
areas (like a large organizational chart). Then each individual received
two sticky-note sheets of paper. After writing their names on the sticky
notes, the leaders were invited to place their two notes on the sheets,
anywhere that they wanted, representing their two *and only two* places
of ministry service.

That night many leaders got frustrated because many were serving
in three to five different ministry areas. But with the pastor's sincere
admonition, and the opportunity to talk as a leadership community

(around large sheets with sticky notes), the shared experience became a true culture-creating event. More than five years later, the leadership community still celebrates the "two sticky rule," as the story is told and retold. More important, leaders have been coached toward healthy involvement. As a result, leaders stay in the game for the long haul rather than flaming out early.

SPACE

Another tool in the cultural artist's hand is space. By space we mean the structure of the physical environment, which includes architectural design, building aesthetics, and the use of space. Even though spatial factors are subtle and often subconscious, they are nevertheless powerful in impacting a leadership culture.

Before a word is spoken, the context of a building's layout or even the arrangement of chairs in a room has spoken volumes about what is important to the leadership culture. A sanctuary design, for example, can reflect a reverent atmosphere or a celebrative atmosphere. A volunteer workspace can emphasize teamwork or individual contribution. An office environment can emphasize peer relationships or hierarchical relationships. There are hundreds of subtle ways that environments communicate value and form culture.

A good illustration of how an environment design reflects cultural values is the difference between a library and a large retail bookstore.[6] Both of these buildings are built to hold books, but each represents a very different culture. A library is a storage facility for information and is designed for efficient access to that information. Usually it is fairly quiet and its architecture and décor are designed to be serviceable. There is no food or music and it is not open late. A bookstore such as Barnes & Noble, in contrast, is designed not for information but for experience. It has comfortable chairs, where you can sit with friends, drink coffee, and listen to music while you read. Unlike a library, you can hang out there late into the evening.

Several times in my (Will's) ministry the impact of building design was clearly felt. At one point our church offices moved, which required building a receptionist's area, the dominant feature of which was a receptionist's window, similar to one at a doctor's office. A locked door separated the rest of the office space from the front door and waiting area, requiring people to come to the little window to "check in" and wait for their appointment.

Within six months we realized that we had communicated a negative message to our leaders, who felt undervalued when they came in (and many leaders frequently did). The design of our office area communicated to leaders that the pastoral staff is very busy and inaccessible and that our time is more important than the leaders' time. This communication was inconsistent with our culture and changes were eventually made to reverse this effect.

SCRIPTURE

The final brush for the cultural artist is Scripture. God's Word is clearly the most significant tool for the task of creating a God-honoring leadership culture. This is where we learn from Jesus how to use the other tools—stories, symbols, shared experience, and space. But even more than telling us about Jesus' example, Scripture is a living and active revelation of God to us. God's Word has power to produce change in the human heart like nothing else. As people within the leadership community hear, study, and respond to Scripture, the complex intermingling of values, thoughts, attitudes, and actions will be affected. At this humbling yet exhilarating point, pastors must relinquish the development of the leadership culture to the hand of God, as God himself works through the Word.

Aside from the preaching event, how do you as a leader teach Scripture in a way that will cultivate leadership culture? The starting point is to distill a list of the passages that have marked your own life. Look for the ones that fuel your passion, enlarge your vision, inform your values, and distinguish your strength as a leader. Own and master these texts. Learn how to share these biblical stories with passion. Then look for opportunities to teach, preach, and vision cast using them.

My life is marked with an enthusiasm to engage people with the gospel. One of my primary motivational passages is Romans 1:16 because of the confidence I can place in God's power, rather than in my ability, as I share the message of grace. As a teacher of the Bible, I maintain a deep affection for Psalm 1. I love to study and restudy this text that so vividly pictures the life that nourishes itself day and night on the "Torah of Yahweh." As a coach-consultant, I still get excited every time I read Exodus 18, where Jethro delivers critical and timely insight as a consultant to Moses. The impact of this one man's objective input led to a reorganization of God's people that transformed their daily lives. It seems that I have studied this passage endlessly, and I love to talk about it. I pray continually that God will help me serve churches in a similar way.

Two well-known Christian leaders today know how to teach Scripture with the purpose of cultivating leadership culture—R. C. Sproul, who is a champion of reformed theology, and Bill Hybels, who is a champion of the evangelistic effectiveness of the local church. I have a tremendous amount of respect for both of these men, who have been formidable evangelical leaders in the twentieth century. Also, both of them have developed a considerable following of church leaders through their respective ministries   Ligonier Ministries and the Willow Creek Association.

Both ministries have a leadership culture, and, more specific, both of these men have developed their cultures around the exposition of certain texts of Scripture. Sproul is a master at expositing the great "holiness" passages of the Bible, such as the Book of Revelation and Isaiah 6. He has built a culture around his passion for God's glory. Hybels, in contrast, is a master at motivating and mobilizing the church with the "search and rescue" passages of the Gospels (lost coin, sheep, and son) and the Great Commission. His passion is for prevailing churches. Both of these men have built a leadership culture around the preaching of core texts.

Four Brushstrokes for Creating Culture

Having considered five brushes for the cultural artist, let's now examine four brushstrokes. It is one thing to have a brush in your hand; it is another thing to use the brush in such a way as to create a work of fine art. If the different brushes are leadership tools, then the brushstrokes are how these tools function in the daily life of the leader.

Artists use several types of brushstrokes when applying paint to canvas. For example, *impasto* refers to the technique of applying oil paint in a thick opaque mass. *Scumbling* involves covering one layer of color with a thin layer of another semiopaque color. Also, different brushstrokes are used for different kinds of subjects in the painting and to show the passage of time. For example, one kind of brushstroke will convey a fleeting moment, while another will convey a timeless moment.

The cultural artist must use different brushstrokes as well. Each type contributes to the culture in a unique way. Let's look at the four key brushstrokes for painting a leadership culture. We call them living out loud, giving people handles, connecting the dots, and turning up the heat.

LIVING OUT LOUD BY MODELING VALUES

The lifeblood of any culture is its underlying values. That is why James Kouzes and Barry Posner write, "Unique values make for unique corporate cultures."[7] In *Corporate Culture and Performance*, John Kotter and James Heskett identify the central role of values when they write that culture represents "values that are shared by people in a group that tend to persist over time even when group members change."[8] Therefore, if we want to impact culture in any way, the impact must take place at the values level.

The most effective way to influence the values of a group of people is through modeling. The key leaders in the leadership-development process, including the senior pastor, must live their values out loud. This is foundational. If a leader uses all of the other key brushstrokes perfectly and forgets about modeling, the attempt at creating culture is at best like building a house of cards.

When James Kouzes and Barry Posner researched effective leadership in organizations, they highlighted the importance of leading by example. Their conclusion is worth repeating:

> Employees look to their leaders as role models of how they should behave. And when in doubt, they believe actions over words, without fail. Every action that a leader takes, or doesn't take, is information about those values and seriousness about those values. People around the leader are always alert to what he or she is doing. Consequently leaders set the example by how they behave.[9]

Michael Slaughter refers to this same process of modeling values as "replicating the DNA" within the organization. He writes, "Leaders are the carriers of the DNA, the shapers of the core values, the influencers. Churches become what their leaders embody. They replicate whatever the leader models."[10]

When it comes to modeling values, the leader is a cultural artist who must utilize the palette of his or her life. Every action, routine, decision, word, tone, and facial expression that comes from the leader is a brush-stroke on the canvas. The leader must be conscious of how daily actions impact the culture and committed to intentional transparency—allowing others to peer into his or her life to see concrete expressions of intangible values. The pastor or leader who understands this will move past any resentment of "living in a fishbowl" to embrace his or her incredible opportunity to influence leadership culture through modeling.

As I (Will) raise my kids, I am often reminded (many times through mistakes rather than successes) that my strongest influence comes from the palette of my life. Recently my three-year-old daughter hopped on a new bike (pink with white tires and purple training wheels) for the very first time. As an avid cyclist, I have a high value for safety and, of course, I want to pass this value on to my children. When I approached my daughter with her helmet and gloves, I anticipated a moment of truth. Would my daughter wear the essential safety gear with enthusiasm or resistance? When she accepted the safety gear with eagerness, I was pleased, and I realized that her positive response came as a result not so much of the verbal request from her father but of her realization that I consider wearing a helmet and gloves important. She had observed me on countless occasions wearing my safety gear when I rode.

So when it comes to leadership and creating culture, pastors must wear helmets before they preach safety. Anything less than living the real deal, day in and day out, will fail to have culture-level impact. For every culture that reproduces missional living, there is a senior pastor who builds intentional relationships with lost people. For every culture that expresses deep community, there are key leaders who pursue accountability. Simply put, a leader will never create a leadership culture with a "do as I say, not as I do" philosophy.

As you seek to improve your own leadership and modeling, consider some of the following questions.

- What are the top five values that I want to cultivate in the leadership culture?
- How does my daily work routine reflect these values?
- How do the kinds of questions I ask other leaders highlight these values?
- What are my regular activities that may not well reflect the cultural values?
- How does my time away from work reflect these values?
- How do I model these values when responding in crisis moments?
- What values do I tend to shortcut when it comes to modeling?
- What values have I modeled successfully in the past but have grown tired of?
- When I'm tired and overwhelmed, which value do I tend to neglect the most?
- Who is the best mentor in my life for modeling values, and how can I spend more time with him or her?

GIVING PEOPLE HANDLES BY IDENTIFYING DISTINCTIVES

Identifying distinctives is a very simple and profound way to create culture. It means labeling ideas and values that are important to the culture. The process of labeling gives people verbal/mental handles to carry around ideas and values that they would otherwise never catch. Because ideas and values tend to stay below the surface of people's consciousness, providing handles for them is important, and once leaders provide them, people can carry and own the ideas of the culture in their mind and heart. If the values are not internalized, the people will never be able to pass them on.

When leaders and consultants talk about values, it is fairly common to discuss "shared values." The very possibility of sharing values requires the identification of those values, the actual unstated values of the organization.

There are two levels of labeling. Ideas and values can have level 1 or level 2 distinctives. Level 1distinctives are the core ideas of the culture and the DNA of the organization. These are the statements that reflect the organization's identity and direction and are the most important distinctives to label. Level 2 distinctives are noncore statements and are secondary in importance. The following chart lists some examples of level 1 and level 2 distinctives.

Level 1 Distinctives	Level 2 Distinctives
Mission statement	Personal missions or credos of key leaders
Values statement	Subministry purpose statements
Vision statement	Team or committee purpose statements
Strategy statement	Strategic objectives and goals
Mission measure statement	Leadership glossary

The purpose of this chapter is not to review the basic definition of the level 1 distinctives. If you need a greater understanding of these, we recommend that you read Aubrey's book *Advanced Strategic Planning.* We also recommend bringing in a coach or consultant to help you with the process. Here, however, is an example of a level 1 document: a well-developed mission, values, and mission measure statement from Abundant Life Church in Clear Lake, Texas.

Mission:

To lead everyday people to become fully devoted followers of Jesus Christ.

Values:

People

Lost people matter to God and therefore matter to us.

Demonstrated by intentionally focusing our time and resources toward the needs and interests of people outside of the church (Luke 15:3–7; 5:31).

Relationships

Authentic relationships are the essence of church life.

Demonstrated by encouraging and expecting each person to develop honest, loving relationships (Matt. 18:15–17; Gal. 6:2; Eph. 4:15).

Devotion
Full devotion to Christ and his cause is normal for every believer. Demonstrated by continually pursuing God and courageously taking his next step for our lives (Mark 12:30–31; Luke 9:23; 6:46).

Excellence
Excellence honors God and inspires people. Demonstrated by giving our absolute best to Christ and his cause both publicly and privately (1 Cor. 10:31; Col. 3:17).

Leadership
Gifted leadership enables the church to function at its best. Demonstrated by creating a culture in which leaders are identified, developed, and supported in every ministry initiative (Rom. 12:8; 1 Peter 5:1–4).

Mission Measure:
(What does a fully devoted follower look like?)
   Growing spiritually
   Using spiritual gifts
   Involved in biblical community
   Dedicated to reaching others
   Exercising stewardship

At Abundant Life, the cultural distinctives of the church are stated in a one-sentence mission, in five values reduced to one word (and then expanded), and in five mission measures using the acronym GUIDE. There is also a five-component strategy icon that we will share later in the chapter.

An example of a level 2 distinctive is from Clear Creek Community Church in League City, Texas. For years I (Will) recruited, motivated, and trained small-group leaders at this church. One of the key components in these steps is outlining the kinds of activities that should happen in a small group. Over the years, we were amazed by how difficult it was to develop well-balanced groups. It seemed that most groups excelled either at study or service but never both. Then at one staff retreat, we crafted a little phrase that turned out to be a catchy jingle: "Scripture, prayer, service, care, always fill the empty chair." This little phrase stuck like a magnet in leaders' minds. Then we abbreviated it further by using the letters "SPSCF" as a teaser in different ways. I was shocked by the effectiveness of this little verbal handle. Within three weeks, after rolling out the SPSCF language, I had an unprecedented number of study group leaders interested in service projects. Why did this happen? Our value for studying Scripture, praying, serving, caring, and evangelism had not changed. They were always distinctives of the culture. What changed was how we talked about them. In other words, we gave the important aspects of our culture an effective label. As a result, leaders caught the vision and groups became more balanced.

Keep in mind that the first two brushstrokes are in an intentional order. Leaders must identify and label the ideas of the culture after they have been modeled. Obviously, if a leader names a value that is not true to the culture, the label will have no meaning (which is why there are many mission and values statements hanging on the walls of churches that are not in people's hearts). But if the label is provided while a value is being modeled, it will create a powerful synergy toward the assimilation of the value into the leader's life.

North Point Church, led by Andy Stanley, is an outstanding example of this truth. The core values are modeled so well for leaders that, when the church provides training on values, they call it "Why I Love This Place." They assume that people have already experienced the benefits and the atmosphere of the leadership culture. Then they label what has been experienced. The tone would go something like this: "Do you know why you enjoy the Sunday morning experience so much? It is because of our value for 'strategic service.' We have hundreds of people serving in diverse areas on Sunday morning, from the parking lot to children's ministry. Why don't you find a place for strategic service as well?"

As you identify distinctives, remember that the language you use is very important. Invest a lot of time in word crafting. Follow the principle of saying more by saying less. I have found that the extra time invested to do this always pays off. When churches do this right, it takes six to nine months to complete the process of identifying and writing distinctives.

CONNECTING THE DOTS BY GUIDING OTHERS

How many weekly ministry decisions are made within your current leadership community? Depending on the size of your leadership base, the number could be scores, hundreds, or even thousands. Now, how many of these decisions are made with a clear understanding of the church's identity and direction? However many it may currently be, the leader as cultural artist is on the perpetual journey of increasing this percentage. Pastors must discover how to guide others, in very practical ways, to the things that matter most in the church's leadership culture.

In a sense they are always trying to connect the dots of organizational activity into the big picture.

We have already focused on the leader's personal role in modeling the values. Now we turn to the leader's organizational role of guiding others. There are five specific ways that a leader can help connect the dots toward shaping leadership culture. These are asking questions, offering appreciation, choosing battles, seizing teachable moments, and responding to crises.

1. Asking Questions

Leaders connect the dots and guide others by asking the right questions. Many times it is too easy just to give answers when questions would work better. A well-crafted question will create many positive dynamics, demonstrating what is important to the leader and revealing areas of focus and priority. At the same time, a question can guide others toward the right answers. Depending on the kind of question, it may communicate the leader's genuine interest and his or her teachable or approachable spirit. The best part of using a question is that it reveals what is important to the leader while stimulating thinking and creating ownership in those answering the questions.

For example, let's say a pastor walks into a room and asks a volunteer leader the following question: "Frank, how many more parking lot attendants do you think we will need for the special event after church this Sunday?" Consider the dynamics with this question. First, because this is the first thing the pastor asks when he walks in the room, it reveals his focus. Second, it also highlights a priority for the experience of guests (the value of evangelism) during the special event. Third, it guides the volunteer leader toward the right kind of issue, in this case recruitment. And finally, because Frank was asked a question rather than told an answer, he will probably have greater confidence in his ability to do the task at hand and a higher sense of ownership at its completion.

2. Offering Appreciation

Leaders connect the dots and guide others by offering appreciation and rewards. While this topic is covered in chapter 9, we feel it is worth restating. Public appreciation, for example, sends a shockwave of awareness about what is important in the culture of the organization. I (Will) experienced this firsthand the other day. The owner of the company I work for handed out Starbucks gift cards for the timely completion of performance goals. I handed mine in late and was part of the minority who did not receive the token of appreciation. It is amazing how missing that small token of appreciation hit the core of my being! The use of rewards strongly clarifies the expectations and values within the culture.

It is critical to show appreciation within the context of the church. Many of the leaders are volunteering their time, so the appreciation of others is the closest thing they have to a payday. And the appreciation does not have to be a large financial investment. Grace Point Church in San Antonio has a special parking spot for each core value. Leaders or volunteers who exemplify a particular value are honored with an opportunity to park in the parking spot of the corresponding value.

3. Choosing Battles

Leaders connect the dots and guide others by demonstrating what battles are worth fighting. In the course of organizational life, some issues will present themselves that aren't worth too much emotional trauma or self-sacrifice. But other issues, particularly issues related to core values and vision, must be defended with vigor. When others see the issues that the point leader is willing to defend, this will send a clear signal as to what is important in the leadership culture.

A powerful illustration of choosing battles is a story that a pastor recently shared. The church had a large amount of debt (from a recent building campaign), and current giving had not increased over the prior year. The pastor decided to call 130 of his key leaders to a higher commitment of sacrificial giving. He gathered the leaders and shared the vision and values of the church. Then, before giving them an opportunity to give (on the spot), he announced that he was voluntarily reducing his salary for the next year. This was more than a strong model. The pastor was illustrating that the issue of conquering debt was one he was willing to defend. None of the leaders left that night without a fresh awareness of the value of stewardship.

4. Seizing Teachable Moments

Leaders connect the dots and guide others by seizing teachable moments. A teachable moment is a window of time when another leader is particularly open to a word of instruction. These moments may arrive through certain incidents, failures, challenges, successes, personal struggles, or many other causes. The key is for the leader to be attuned to the environment so that he or she can offer an appropriate word at the appropriate time.

Noel Tichy, in his book *The Leadership Engine,* describes what he calls the leader's "teachable point of view."[11] He argues that leadership development requires a disciplined commitment of upper-level leaders to develop and share stories that teach leadership lessons from previous work-life experience. He makes the point that "great leaders are great teachers not only because they know what they think, but also because they take the time to organize their thoughts in ways so that they can communicate them clearly."[12] In other words, he encourages leaders to develop leadership testimonies ahead of time so they can be delivered during a teachable moment. After working through his book, I (Will) identified eleven of my top leadership life-lessons. I am still in the process of writing out short testimonies based on these stories.

What does a teachable moment look like? Each one will be a little different, based on the uniqueness of each situation and the leader's personality. Recently at work I (Will) sent an e-mail to a team member who is just out of college. In one day we had had multiple problem-solving situations, and I had been pretty demanding with regard to learning from our mistakes. Sensing her deep frustration, I sent her an e-mail note of appreciation that included a teaching-moment thought. It had to do with learning how to deal with mistakes and disappointments on the job. It was just the right time for such a comment and it seemed to help my young colleague.

5. Responding to Crises

Sometimes the finest hour of creating a leadership culture occurs during unexpected, difficult times. The way in which a leader responds to a crisis will send definitive signals about the organization's values. During these seasons, the attention of the leadership community is riveted on the point leader. It is as if the leader is saying everything through a microphone. Therefore, leaders should be prepared to leverage the opportunity for creating culture.

When Tylenol navigated the devastating incident of product tampering, they responded with a recall that galvanized in the eyes of their customers how much the company values consumer health. As a result, they turned a nightmare into a values-defining moment.

Before the 9/11 tragedy of 2001, a local church had planned several months of programming. The week after the national tragedy, the programming team committed to reinventing the fall programming schedule to be responsive to the congregation's concerns. The work required a tireless effort from many leaders, but in the end the core value of relevance was strengthened among the leadership community and throughout the church.

TURNING UP THE HEAT BY INCREASING YOUR PASSION

As we work with churches across the country, we are continually confronted with a passion vacuum among church leaders. This is troubling, because we are convinced that creating culture requires a white-hot heart. Here is a typical conversation in a day of my (Will's) life as a consultant:

> Will: Pastor, on a scale of one to five, with five being crystal clear, how clear is your church's identity and direction?
>
> Pastor: About a four.
>
> Will: So I take it that you have a mission and values statement as a starting point?
>
> Pastor: Yes.
>
> Will: I would love to hear your mission and values. Could you share them with me now?
>
> Pastor: (awkward pause): Well, let's see. Our mission is to know Christ and make him known, starting in the Bay Area and extending to the ends of the earth.
>
> Will: How about your values?
>
> Pastor: Just one second (shuffling papers in a file drawer). Well, I don't have them right in front of me, but I think I can list them. There are ten in total. Let's see. They are worship, community, relevance, excellence (short pause), prayer, and evangelism (short pause). Well, I can't think of the rest, but there are several others.
>
> Will: Thanks for sharing those, Pastor.

When I have a conversation like this, I want to give the pastor the gift of a passion transfusion. How in the world can a local church develop a leadership culture when they talk about their mission with the same fervor that they have when they discuss the weather?

I want to be sensitive to the difficult contexts in which some ministers work, and I am not talking about passion as a plastic smile or some kind of false optimism. Rather I am talking about a sense of conviction, clarity, and expectation that draws others into the leadership current. I am thinking of a leader whose life becomes a fountainhead of contagious enthusiasm about what God is doing.

When Noel Tichy studied companies that excel at developing leaders, he discussed the concept of a leader's E^3: emotional energy and edge. He defines *emotional energy* as the ability to get energy out of everyone. He defines *edge* as the courage to see reality and act on it. I believe that both of these qualities are connected to the development of passion in the leader's life.[13]

As we peer into the heart of Jesus, we find an unbelievable passion from which cultural artists must learn. Think of his determination as he "resolutely set out for Jerusalem" in Luke 9:51. Jesus knew his mission and his destiny, and as a result, he lived with "edge." Think also of the intensity of Jesus' passion: "for the joy set before him [he] endured the cross" (Heb. 12:2). Surely Jesus lived and led with an extraordinary emotional energy.

So how do we cultivate passion in our lives and stoke the fire in our hearts? We believe it is possible through intentional work that we call the discipline of enthusiasm. Some feel that passion is inborn, but regardless, it is also something you can cultivate. The following may help you develop passion:

- Realize that all vision casting involves a transfer of enthusiasm.
- Think intentionally about the kind of atmosphere you create when you walk into a room. How can you raise the emotional energy?
- Spend time with other passionate leaders.
- Ask other passionate people about the source of their passion.
- Practice smiling when you feel good about something. Let your face express the way you feel inside. Remind yourself that there is a time to be focused on your thoughts and goals but there are also times to be focused on those around you, letting your facial expression show your enthusiasm.
- Maintain a perspective that problems and challenges are opportunities for growth both personally and organizationally.
- Be very clear about the identity and direction of your church, ministry, or leadership culture. Clarity and passion work hand in hand. If your personal mission, values, or spiritual gifts and abilities are out of alignment with the organization, your passion may be prevented from developing. In this case you may need to consider a change in ministry context.
- Pray for supernatural energy, especially when you are exhausted and still have to lead. And pray that God will help you develop passion for the thing he has called you to do.

The Culture Made Me Do It

An illustration of how a leadership culture reproduces behavior is an action step I (Will) took this week. Let's first look at what I did and then the culture that helped produce the action.

While in the shower on a Saturday morning I was thinking about my unchurched neighbor, whom I have wanted to invite to church.

His name is Mark and he is from Europe, working in the States for about a year. I remembered that his wife was out of town and that he was watching their one-year-old son. It just so happened that I was watching my own kids by myself the same weekend. While in the shower, I realized that this weekend would be a particularly good invitation opportunity, because I could invite him to lunch and his kid could hang out with my kids (after all, every dad needs a little relief when Mom is out of town). By the time I got out of the shower, I had a complete invitation plan in my head, on which I followed through later that day.

As a seminary-trained individual, I know that Scripture teaches that I am to be an ambassador for Christ. I have both attended and led training sessions on how to share the gospel. And I have the Holy Spirit to guide and lead my daily thoughts and decisions. But with all of that in place, I believe that my involvement in a leadership culture played a significant role in my spontaneous thought to invite my neighbor to lunch and then ultimately to church. Let me share just a few aspects of that leadership culture.

First, my church has a clearly stated value of people, including people who are far from God. Note how this value is stated formally in the church: "People—*Lost people matter to God and therefore matter to us,* demonstrated by intentionally focusing our time and resources toward the needs and interests of people outside of the church."

This value is not just hanging in a picture frame. The leaders teach and discuss and celebrate the core values, including the value of lost people. The pastor models this value personally in front of the leaders. He tells stories about the people in his life whom he is trying to win to Christ. Because I am conscious of this value, when I run into Mark, a spiritually lost individual, I am reminded of the tremendous value of his life to Jesus Christ.

Second, last week in the worship service, a testimony was offered that again highlighted the power of personal initiation and invitation with lost people. This testimony was an intentional programming element designed to support our affirmation that we value people.

Third, the welcoming system at my church is incredibly well run. Not only does the culture remind me of the importance of lost people, but it builds confidence that when I take my friend to church, it will be a very positive experience for him.

Fourth, one of the tools that the church has developed to nurture the leadership culture is what I call a strategy icon. It reminds leaders of the preferable pathway of involvement in the life of the church. The five circles by themselves appear as part of the church's logo on all of the print communications.

The open door symbol in the upper left-hand corner represents the Sunday morning worship service. It is the starting point and natural point of invitation to the church. The next three symbols along the path represent the other components of church life that we believe are necessary for spiritual growth—newcomers class (the alpha symbol), small-group involvement, and service. The shaking-hands symbol in the lower right represents a life dedicated to reaching others.

Even as I write this chapter and look at this symbol, I cannot help but think of Mark, who I pray will discover Jesus as his personal Savior. And that is my point in even showing you the icon. It is one small part of the overall culture, the complex intermingling that produces consistent patterns of thought and behavior. When I invited Mark to church the next day, my action was spawned and nourished by this culture.

As you build the house of leadership development, remember that the goal is not just brick and mortar; the goal is a home. A home is a place where values, thoughts, attitudes, and actions play a vital role in the development of leaders. The work that you invest will pay off significantly as the leadership culture builds momentum and its thinking and behavior are reproduced in your church. But watch out—a contagious leadership culture will turn your local church into a local movement!

Questions for Reflection and Discussion

1. What is the closest experience you have had with a well-developed leadership culture?
2. On a scale of 1 to 5 (with 5 being the most developed), how well developed is the current leadership culture in your church or ministry?
3. As a leader (cultural artist), which tools (brushes) do you tend to use well? Which ones do you not use very often?

4. As a leader (cultural artist), what key actions (brushstrokes) do you tend to do well? Which ones have you not developed as much?

5. Who is a current leader in your life who models the ability to create culture?

Part 4

Looking at Model Homes

The Product of Developing Leaders

14

The Story of a Small Church

Developing Leaders in Small Churches

In the introduction to this book, we emphasized the difference between a process and a product. If you carefully examine many successful church plants, you'll discover that they used a similar process in their development. However, the churches themselves, the products, are different. The key to successful church planting is to know and follow the process, not copy or mimic some product of the process—a growing church you have observed—such as Stonebriar Community Church, pastored by Chuck Swindoll. The reason you should not try to mimic this church is that there's only one Chuck Swindoll. Also, most likely, you're not planting a church in Frisco, Texas (near Dallas). Your church or product must be endemic to your community. You accomplish this by following the process.

The same holds true in designing and implementing a leadership-development process for your church. What we've presented in the preceding pages is a process, not a product. In these final chapters, we'll present two different products that resulted from taking two different churches through the same process.

Why these two chapters? We want to demonstrate to those who deeply desire to implement a leadership training process in their ministries that this process works in both small and large churches. The stories that follow of two very different churches show how the process can be applied in each unique context. This should prove both encouraging and instructive for ministry leaders.

Leadership Development at Faith Temple Baptist Church

Faith Temple Baptist Church is a traditional Baptist church located in Irving, Texas, a suburb northeast of Dallas. The church began in 1956 and attendance now averages around one hundred people.[1] The pastor is Lewis Cooper, who is also pursuing pastoral studies at Dallas Theological Seminary.

Pastor Lewis is leading his church out of a growth plateau. He believes that a leadership-development process is crucial to its revitalization. With a current aging leadership, there is a critical need for trained leaders. Faith Temple's leadership-development process, through which the pastor will lead his church step-by-step, follows.

Step 1: Determine Support

Determine if the empowered leadership will support the leadership-development process.

Pastor Lewis has initiated the leadership-development process at Faith Temple Baptist Church with the support of the board. Eventually there should be funds available to help facilitate the process. Five other leaders in the church will assist the pastor. One is responsible for worship, another for missions and evangelism, a third for ministry, a fourth for membership, and the last for maturity and Christian education. Pastor Lewis wants to complete the development of the process in four months, so every week he will spend some time on it.

Step 2: Recruit a Leader

Recruit someone to initiate and lead the development process.

Over time, Pastor Lewis plans to train another person to lead Faith Temple Baptist's leadership-development process. He prefers that this person meet the character qualifications found in 1 Timothy 3:1–13 and Titus 1:6–9. This person must value leadership training and have both a passion and a vision for it. This visionary individual should have the spiritual gift of leadership and other gifts, such as administration, discernment, and wisdom, and be a disciplined person who is a good communicator and is people oriented. Having a history of training leaders would be helpful but isn't a requirement.

This person's job description is modeled after the description in chapter 7 of this book.

Job Title: Pastor of Leadership Development

Job Profile: The Pastor of Leadership Development needs abilities or gifts in leadership, discernment, and administration. This person is expected to create and develop the process and then administer it. This person should have a passion for emerging and existing leaders. Currently Pastor Lewis is serving in this capacity, but he hopes to recruit someone to take his place.

Job Summary: The Pastor of Leadership Development is responsible for developing, implementing, and administering the church's leadership-development process (recruiting, assessing, selecting, placing, and training leaders).[2] The Pastor of Leadership Development is expected to

1. cast the vision for leadership development.
2. design an overall, intentional, systematic leadership-development process.
3. implement the process.
4. lead and operate this process.
5. raise up and train a lay team to help lead and operate this process.
6. alter the church culture so that leadership becomes and remains a core value.
7. keep abreast of what is taking place in leadership development in America and abroad.

Reports to: Senior Pastor

Works with: Pastor of Lay Mobilization

Step 3: Recruit a Team

Recruit and develop a lay-leadership team.

Pastor Lewis has recruited a qualified lay leadership-development team with a mission. The team consists of the five leaders mentioned above who have the following qualifications: They are members in good standing, agree with the church's statements (values, mission, vision, strategy, doctrine), are diverse in age, and have a passion for training leaders. These leaders are willing to take time from their busy schedules to serve the church in this role. Also, they're creative thinkers who are willing to challenge the status quo. Finally, the team's mission is to assess and develop current and potential leaders for the church's ministries. Their intention is to nurture the character and capabilities of these leaders and to clarify the direction necessary for influential leadership.

Step 4: Develop a Definition

Arrive at a consensus definition of leadership.

Pastor Lewis defines leadership as the ability to influence others based on one's character, capabilities, and the clarity of the ministry's direction. Those working with him agree with his definition and are using it as their working definition to discover, deploy, and develop the church's leadership.

Step 5: Identify Leadership Levels

Identify the various leadership levels in your ministry.

Pastor Lewis and the team are taking the broad approach to identifying the church's leaders. They have leveled or typed the leadership and prefer to use the term *team* instead of *level*. The following summarizes who the leaders are at Faith Temple Baptist Church.

Team 1: Unpaid, nonvocational leaders who volunteer to serve God and the church at the entry level of ministry.
Leaders: Sunday school teachers, ushers and greeters, nursery workers, AWANA leaders and listeners, and ministry teams (building and grounds, worship and drama, fellowship committee, and others).

Team 2: Unpaid, nonvocational leaders who volunteer to serve alongside the church staff (paraprofessionals).
Leaders: Deacons.

Team 3: Both paid and unpaid leaders who are potential staff. They are more likely to go on to vocational ministry.
Leaders: Pastor's leadership team, church secretaries, interns, residents.

Team 4: Paid, vocational ministry leaders.
Leaders: Senior pastor, associate pastors, pastor of worship, pastor of youth.

Step 6: Discover New Leaders

Discover new leaders for development.

Faith Temple Baptist Church's process of leadership development has three parts: discovery, deployment, and development. The ministry's potential leaders will touch the discovery and deployment bases. All leaders will pursue development as long as the ministry exists.

The person on the five-man lay leadership-development team who is responsible for ministry will lead the discovery phase for all four teams. Pastor Lewis will assist him with team 4, which consists of the paid, vocational ministry leaders. The discovery phase consists of three parts: recruitment, exploration, and assessment.

RECRUITMENT

The church's potential leaders are several kinds of people. Most will be members who haven't been involved in leadership. Others will be new members in addition to attenders who haven't been able to join because of extenuating circumstances. Also, the church will consider interns and residents from outside as well as within the church. Finally, the church desires to train young people who are in senior high school.

The church will recruit these prospective leaders in a number of ways: a churchwide assessment program, a ministry brochure on leadership training, word of mouth, a personal invitation or referral from the pastor or someone on the leadership-development team, and inquiry from a prospective leader.

EXPLORATION

In the exploration phase, the person responsible for ministry will make an appointment with the potential leaders. During this time the ministry leader will accomplish the following: introduce himself, try to get to know the potential leader if he doesn't already, cast the church's vision for training leaders, explain the leadership training process and the ministry's expectations of its leaders, discuss the qualifications for leaders, explain the benefits of being a leader, and explore the prospective leader's interest in becoming a leader.

In the future Pastor Lewis plans to place four of the leaders on the team over one of the church's four leadership teams. At that time the leader with oversight will be responsible for executing the discovery phase with the leaders on his team and will determine if the prospective leaders meet the qualifications necessary to lead at that level. These qualifications are:

1. good character
2. spiritual maturity
3. spiritual and natural leadership gifts
4. prior leadership experience outside the ministry
5. prior leadership experience within the ministry
6. good reputation
7. nonuser of tobacco
8. desire or passion to lead
9. temperament conducive to leadership
10. good recommendation
11. prior and present training
12. love for people
13. high school education

The teams will emphasize different qualifications. Team 1 asks that prospective leaders meet the first seven qualifications. The other three teams want their leaders to meet all thirteen qualifications.

ASSESSMENT

The final part of the discovery phase is assessment, in which leaders will seek to gain additional information about potential leaders and aid them in discovering their divine designs. Currently two men on the five-man leadership-development team—the one who is responsible for membership and the one who is over ministry—will work with the other leaders in assessment. As mentioned above, Pastor Lewis sees this as a temporary arrangement. He hopes that eventually four members of the leadership-development team will take responsibility for assessing each potential leader's gifting, passion, and temperament.

Step 7: Deploy New Leaders

Deploy the new leaders into their positions of leadership.

The deployment phase involves the placement in ministry of those who meet the above qualifications. Initially Pastor Lewis will place prospective leaders on the various teams. He desires, however, to turn much of this responsibility, except for team 4, over to two people on the leadership-development team—the one responsible for membership and the one over ministry. In addition, the Sunday school director, youth leader, and chairperson of the nursery committee will deploy people on team 1.

Step 8: Develop Leaders

Develop new and current leaders for their ministries in the church.

The church feels it's most important that it spend time training its leaders at team ministry levels. This training will develop leaders in three areas: character, knowledge, and skills.

The team 1 leaders consist of Sunday school workers, ushers and greeters, nursery workers, ministry teams (committees), and volunteer secretaries. Their first area for development is character, which Pastor Lewis and his leadership team determined means that a team 1 leader must be growing spiritually, a team player, Christlike, and a church member in good standing. A personal interview with team members will assess where they are in their character development. Team 1 leaders will develop themselves by having a daily quiet time, doing regular self-evaluation, and completing the Christian Life Development Class (CLD) 201: Bible Study Methods—a class offered by the church that covers personal Bible study, prayer life, tithing, and Sunday school ministry.

The second area for development is knowledge. Team 1 members must know the basics of the Bible and the fundamentals of the faith. They must know the specifics of how to serve people in their ministry areas, which will be developed area by area but will include the ability to articulate the church's philosophy of ministry and ministry strategy.

Sunday school workers will read a book on Sunday school principles, view a video instructing them on age-group characteristics, listen to an audio tape by Lucien Coleman on teaching the Bible, and read one book on teaching.

Ushers and greeters will read the "Manual for Ushers and Greeters." Nursery workers will read a book on ministering to infants. All will be required to take CLD 101: Discovering My Membership and CLD 301: Discovering My Ministry. The Sunday school teachers will take CLD 202: Survey of the Old Testament and CLD 203: Survey of the New Testament.

The third area of training is skills. Team 1 members must have good people skills, communication skills, and leadership skills. These will be developed through various books and articles on skill sets, a one-month apprenticeship, CLD 401: Discovering My Life's Mission, and workshops specific to each ministry.

There are four character requirements for team 2 leaders, the deacons: They must show notable spiritual growth, have a team player mentality, display Christlike behavior, and be church members in good standing. The deacon body and the pastor will be responsible for assessing these qualities. The process will develop these characteristics through encouraging a daily quiet time, regular self-evaluation, CLD 201, involvement in a small-group ministry, and studying Gordon McDonald's book *Ordering Your Private World*.

Team 2 members must know the Bible basics, the fundamentals of the faith, and their ministry role in supporting the church's mission. They will develop these skills in several ways. The deacons must know and be able to articulate the church's philosophy of ministry and ministry strategy. They'll read through and answer questions in the "Deacon Ministry Manual." They'll read various assigned articles in *Deacon* magazine, and they will view the video *Deacon, Servant of the Church*. Finally, they'll take CLD 101: Discovering My Membership, CLD 301: Discovering My Ministry, CLD 202: Survey of the Old Testament, and CLD 203: Survey of the New Testament.

Deacons must be skilled in three areas: people skills, communication skills, and leadership skills. They will develop these skills by reading a book on conflict resolution and reading John Maxwell's *Developing the Leader within You*. They'll also read management articles on the basics of a deacon ministry. In addition, the deacons will take CLD 401: Discovering My Life's Mission and various workshops on caring skills.

Leaders on teams 3 and 4—the pastor's leadership team, staff, the church administrator, and any interns and residents—will develop the same way. Their character qualities, assessment, and development are the same as for team 2, and they must know the same content as team 2, as well as material specific to their ministries in the church. They will take the same classes as team 2, plus CLD 201: Bible Study Methods. Concerning skills, they must have the same skills as team 2, plus specific ministry skills, and they will develop themselves the same way; however, they will take classes from the Center for Biblical Studies at Dallas (these are courses taught by seminary students to laypeople in the Dallas–Fort Worth Metroplex).

Step 9: Evaluate

Regularly evaluate your leadership-development process.

Pastor Lewis plans for leadership evaluation to take place at all team levels. All leaders on team 1 (Sunday school teachers, ushers, and others) will be evaluated twice a year by their ministry leaders. Pastor Lewis, in turn, will evaluate these ministry leaders. However, in time, he plans for a minister of ministries to take over this responsibility.

The deacon chairman will evaluate the deacons, on team 2, individually twice a year. Since the deacons are responsible for assisting the pastor in shepherding various families in the church and reporting on this at their monthly deacon meetings, some evaluation of their service will take place at this time.

Teams 3 and 4 consist mostly of people who are employees of the church (pastor, staff, and others). The personnel director will evaluate all paid staff twice a year. The pastor will evaluate the men on the leadership team biannually.

Pastor Lewis's evaluation is primarily of his leaders. He also will need to evaluate his developmental processes to receive maximum benefit from this step.

Step 10: Reward Regularly

Regularly reward those in the leadership-development process.

Pastor Lewis has designed a process to reward leaders according to their team level. There are four types of reward for all four teams: an annual churchwide appreciation banquet, at which all the leaders will be treated as honored guests; notes of encouragement and acknowledgment for their ministry from the pastor; appreciation notes from their ministry leaders; and monthly recognition, through the newsletter and bulletin as well as other places, of a leader as minister of the month.

An additional reward for team 2 members is an annual appreciation supper, hosted by the pastor, for all those involved at this team level.

Learning from Faith Temple Baptist's Experience

That's the leadership-development plan of Faith Temple Baptist Church in Irving, Texas. Their experience can teach small churches (and the majority are) that they too can cultivate their own leadership-development process, no matter the size of their church.

So what is holding you back from forming a process that will keep you in fresh supply of leaders who will form the spiritual backbone of your ministry?

15

The Story of a Large Church

Developing Leaders in Large Churches

Clear Creek Community Church is an independent, interdenominational church located in the Clear Lake Area of Houston, Texas. Pastor Bruce Wesley started the church with a handful of families in October 1993. For the first nine years, they met in a school until they moved into their first facility in May 2002. Eighteen months into their new building, the attendance is reaching three thousand on Sunday morning.

I (Will) served on the staff at Clear Creek for about four years before transitioning to coaching and consulting full-time. The following presents Clear Creek's leadership development process.

Leadership Development at Clear Creek Community Church

Step 1: Determine Support

Determine if the empowered leadership will support the leadership-development process.

Pastor Bruce started the church with a high value for leadership development. As the church grew from launch to eight hundred people, he led the leadership-development process himself, with the close assistance of his pastoral staff and the full support of the elder team.

Step 2: Recruit a Leader

Recruit someone to initiate and lead the development process.

As the church continued to grow, Pastor Bruce delegated the leader-ship- development process to me in my role as spiritual formation pastor, but he wanted executive team involvement as well. The executive team consisted of the senior pastor, the executive pastor, and the teaching pastor. At Clear Creek, all ministries are operated within a small-group structure, and I was providing general oversight of our small-group lead-ers, which included oversight of leadership development, so overseeing the leadership-development process was a natural fit for me.

Before bringing me on his staff, Pastor Bruce had assessed my tem-perament, as well as my skills in leadership and communication, so his delegation of the leadership-development role to me was calculated. Another key factor was the eighteen months during which I had dem-onstrated leadership on his staff.

Step 3: Recruit a Team

Recruit and develop a lay-leadership team.

Our strategy for recruiting a team involved using an entire layer of leaders, called coaches, as the functional but undefined lay-leadership team. They are the leaders of our small-group leaders. Any significant aspect of leadership development or change to our process was first discussed with this group.

Step 4: Develop a Definition

Arrive at a consensus definition of leadership.

We defined leadership around our mission. Leaders are those who model the process of leading unchurched people to become fully devoted followers of Christ. To evaluate this more specifically, we used the five Gs—grace, growth, groups, gifts, and good stewardship—as measures of full devotion. We emphasized the importance of leaders being models because they're people who have responsibility for other people as well as for church funds.

For several months the pastor and I met once a week as we moved toward formalizing the leadership-development process. As a result, we came up with the following presuppositions and considerations. We felt that we had to communicate them to maintain clarity with a growing church staff and leadership base.

PRESUPPOSITIONS

1. God gives the gift of leadership to individuals and expects all believers to exercise leadership through a disposition of love and grace toward others (Rom. 12:8).
2. A primary pastoral function is to enlist, equip, and empower leaders in the church (Exodus 18; Eph. 4:11–12).
3. The end of all leadership is to lead people to full devotion to Christ as reproducing disciple makers. The leadership gift is not required to make disciples in groups (Matt. 28:18–20; Eph. 4:13–15).
4. Disciple making within community is the biblical model. Therefore, leadership training will center around developing biblical community.
5. The capacity and scope of our ministry as a church will be directly proportionate to our ability to train leaders.
6. In our cultural setting, excellence, service, change, and flexibility will be required to have an effective training strategy.

CONSIDERATIONS

1. How do we keep our mission and values at the center of our training strategy?
2. How do we develop whole leaders with sharp minds, large hearts, and skillful hands while maintaining a balance between character and competence? (This was our way of interacting with the leader's developed capabilities, as discussed in chapter 9.)

Step 5: Identify Leadership Levels

Identify the various leadership levels in your ministry.

The leveling process was very simple at Clear Creek because of the church's small-group infrastructure. Since all ministries are structured as small groups, all ministries are small groups and all small groups are ministries. For example, those who work with children also participate in a small group together. And those who study the Book of John in a small group also participate in service projects together. The following are the different levels of leadership at Clear Creek Community Church.

Level 1—Apprentice Group Leaders. These are potential leaders who are slowly getting their feet wet in the role of apprentices in small groups. They are growing to understand what it means to model the church's mission in their lives. They have been approached and initiated into the process, most likely by an existing leader.

Level 2—Group Leaders. Group leaders are people who are modeling the church's mission in their lives and have taken the initiative to lead one of five kinds of small group: a service, study, social, seeker, or support group. They are becoming fully devoted followers of Christ by aligning their lives with the five Gs—grace, growth, groups, gifts, and good stewardship—as measures of full devotion.

Level 3—Apprentice Coaches. These are people who represent the qualifications of a group leader and are considering leading other group leaders. They are assigned to a coach to observe and learn the roles of the coach.

Level 4—Coaches. These leaders lead up to five other group leaders, usually clustered around affinity groups (men's groups, study groups) or ministry service areas (children's ministry, worship team). While they may be very good group leaders themselves, they are not necessarily the best group leaders, as coaching and group leading require some different skill sets.

Level 5—Ministry Staff and Pastoral Staff. Ministry and pastoral staff receive compensation from the church as vocational ministry leaders. In some cases the role is identical to that of the coaches. In many cases ministry and pastoral staff provide oversight to coaches.

Level 6—Elders. The elder team represents the highest level of authority in the church. While the level 5 leaders essentially run the church, they do so under the direction of the elders, who also maintain direct oversight of doctrinal issues and church discipline situations.

Step 6: Discover New Leaders

Discover new leaders for development.
The discovery of new leaders takes place at four levels:

1. Recruitment to entry-level leadership events through general announcements in church services and in church print communications
2. Brainstorming and personal invitation from church staff
3. Placement from the SHAPE ministry assessment and placement process
4. Encouragement of all group leaders to have an apprentice through personal assessment and invitation

Step 7: Deploy New Leaders

Deploy the new leaders into their positions of leadership.
The deployment process includes four steps:

1. Complete the SHAPE ministry assessment and placement process for leaders who have not previously attended.
2. Complete the Group Life Starter Kit workbook. I developed this workbook as a basic step to assess the seriousness of a potential leader's interest. The workbook helps educate and guide him or her with regard to our small-group structure and how the person might fit in. This includes writing a purpose statement for the group and making a list of people who could serve the group's leadership nucleus (apprentice and host).
3. Have a personal interview with a coach or staff person. No leader gets placed before this critical assessment step. At this time the group leader's covenant is discussed, and the leader is asked to commit not just to leading a group but to modeling the five Gs as a fully devoted Christ-follower.
4. Develop a recruitment strategy. The final step includes reminding the new leader that the primary burden for recruiting group members (since all ministry happens in groups) lies with the leader. Usually a coach or staff person will brainstorm with the potential leader to come up with ideas or names for recruitment and will submit a request to announce in church publications the beginning of a small-group ministry so that people can sign up for it.

Step 8: Develop Leaders

Develop new and current leaders for their ministries in the church.
Apprenticeship is the primary venue for leadership development. The two secondary venues are getaways and seminars. Getaways are held in the summer, fall, and spring. Then there are three recommended decentralized training venues, as recorded in the chart below. The process was developed on paper when the church had an attendance of about nine hundred. By the fifteen hundred mark, the process was tweaked to its final form. The process has continued to serve the church well as it reaches three thousand in attendance.

Leadership Development at Clear Creek Community Church

Primary Training Venue	Secondary Training Venues	Recommended Decentralized Training Venues
Apprenticing	Getaways	Conferences
	Seminars	One-on-ones
		Huddles

The following chart shows an expansion of the venues, with frequency, target group, and purpose of each.

Event Driven			
Venue	**Times per year**	**Target**	**Purpose**
Getaways/ retreat	3	All leaders (group leaders and coaches) and emerging leaders	Build leadership community around mission and values and train on basics for Group Life and Life-on-Life (one-on-one discipleship relationship in a small group)
Special worship service (seminar format)	4	Worship attenders and group members	Teach the essential role of small groups for the church and the believer, using the four components of the Group Life mission
Training seminars	2	Leaders who miss getaways	Train on basics for Group Life and Life-on-Life
Appreciation night (seminar format)	1	Current leaders	Celebrate God's work in the prior year
Willow Creek Conference	1	Current leaders	Cast the vision
Vision night (seminar format)	1	Worship attenders and group members	Cast the vision
Process Driven			
Venue	**Times per year**	**Target**	**Purpose**
Apprenticing	Ongoing	All leaders	Model the leadership role and process through mentoring
Huddles	Ongoing	All leaders	Equip and problem solve for specific kinds of groups
One-on-one	12 or as needed	All leaders	Model and train in a small-group environment with specific, short-term goal to launch leaders

Step 9: Evaluate

Regularly evaluate your leadership-development process.

Clear Creek is ruthless when it comes to evaluation. Every leader fills out a written evaluation at every leadership event. I compiled these, and we reviewed them as a staff. We would spend several hours after each leadership event discussing our own self-evaluation as well. After the evaluation, I was responsible for implementing any improvement recommendations.

Step 10: Reward Regularly

Regularly reward those in the leadership-development process.
We try hard to develop appreciation as a way of life. At Clear Creek, staff and coaches tell group leaders when they do things well (a verbal well done). The staff holds each other accountable to write occasional notes of encouragement on church stationery. When we plan special events and worship services, public appreciation opportunities are built in.

More formally, Clear Creek plans an appreciation night every year that is held just for group leaders and coaches. Also, the church has an annual membership banquet at which leaders are honored. Finally, the annual vision night is an opportunity for leaders to "get charged" about the common mission. These three events together become key "reward checkpoints" in the leader's calendar.

Learning from Clear Creek's Experience

That's the story of Clear Creek Community Church near Houston, Texas. We believe it's imperative that, like small churches, large churches develop a leadership-development process for their context to sustain healthy growth. Every church needs to develop leaders at every level of the ministry.

Appendix A

Leadership Development Audit
Why a Ministry May Not Be Developing Leaders

The following is a list of reasons ministries aren't developing leaders. Do any describe your ministry situation? Use it as an audit of your attitude or that of your ministry toward training leaders. Place an actual or mental check in front of any items that characterize your situation.

___1. The church thinks that it's developing leaders, but it isn't. It's missed the distinction between developing mature disciples and leadership. Mature disciples are foundational to leadership but not equivalent to it. All leaders must be mature disciples, but not all healthy disciples will necessarily become leaders. Many will be followers.

___2. The church hasn't had the time. It's called the tyranny of the urgent. The ministry is growing rapidly, and its leaders can cover only what they believe are the ministry basics: preaching, marrying, and burying. Due to its rapid growth and lack of staff, they can't keep up.

___3. The church is simply trying to keep the doors open. It's been around a long time. It's seen many people come and go. However, more have gone lately than come, and it finds itself in steep decline if not slipping into a coma. If the staff takes valuable time out to develop leaders—assuming any are still on the scene—the church may die.

___4. The church isn't willing to make the changes that are necessary to develop its leaders. There could be several reasons. It doesn't want to challenge the establishment—it might have to pay too high a price. Some people are in positions of power and want it to stay that way. Training new leaders would pose a threat to them. The ministry is simply afraid of change, not knowing what change may bring.

___5. The church is a niche ministry, specializing in a particular ministry area. The focus is on some aspect of the Great Commission rather than the commission itself. It may be preaching, teaching, counseling, family, evangelism, or some other ministry area.

___6. The church chooses not to attempt to lead or develop leaders. The leader prefers less demanding responsibilities and desires to avoid the hardships that accompany such roles and programs. This is because leading a ministry in the early twenty-first century is tough. Consequently the leader is afraid to rock the ministry boat.

___7. The church realizes the importance of training leaders. However, it prefers to leave it to outside organizations, such as schools, seminaries, and various leadership seminars and conferences. It prefers to trust somebody else to do it.

___8. The ministry attracts good leaders because it's prosperous and growing. However, it is naive about leadership development. It assumes that what it's doing is somehow producing, not merely attracting, good leadership. So it pursues its present course, assuming that leadership—as in the past—will take care of itself.

___9. The pastor—who may have attended seminary—is a stronger teacher than leader. Consequently he doesn't have a desire or passion to develop leaders. He may develop other Bible teachers but not other biblical leaders.

___10. The church simply doesn't know how to develop Christ-centered leadership. It sees the need and wants to equip such leaders, but its pastor or leaders don't know how.

Appendix B

Church Leadership Questionnaire

Answer the following questions to the best of your ability. While some may seem a little personal, they will help us to know you better, to qualify you for leadership, and to direct and enhance your future ministry here at the church.

1. Are you a Christian? What does one have to do to become a Christian?

2. Read the qualifications for leadership in 1 Timothy 3:1–13 and Titus 1:6–9. As far as you understand these qualifications and realizing that no one is perfect, do you feel that you meet them as a potential leader? Are there any that are questionable?

3. Do you consider yourself teachable? How do you know? Has anyone ever told you that you aren't teachable?

4. Have you committed your life to Christ? If so, what does this mean to you?

5. Would you describe yourself as a mature Christian? Please explain.

6. Have you read the church's statements (core values, mission, vision, strategy, doctrine)? Do you agree with them? Any there any statements with which you disagree?

7. Would you say that you have a good reputation in the communities in which you work and live?

8. Have you ever had legal problems or been arrested? If so, please explain.

9. Have you ever been divorced? If yes, what were the circumstances? How many times have you been divorced? Have you remarried?

10. Do you drink alcoholic beverages? If yes, have you ever had a problem with alcohol? If so, please explain.

11. Do you smoke? If yes, how often? Do you chew tobacco? If yes, how often?

12. Do you now or have you ever taken drugs other than those prescribed by a doctor or purchased over the counter? If yes, please explain.

13. Have you ever had or are you now having a problem with pornography? If yes, please explain.

Appendix C

Sample Leadership Configuration
Valleydale Baptist Church • Birmingham, Alabama

Team Valleydale Structure

Every Member a Minister

		R E C R U I T S	Expectations	
Team Member Category 4	**Member of a Team** • A Discovering Leader • Influencer		• Regular Attender • Ability and willingness to learn and follow • Reliable/Faithful • Cooperative/Flexible	
Team Leader Category 3	**Leader of One Team or Member of a Specialized Team** • A Developing Leader • Team Influencer	E Q U I P S	• Member • Ownership/Passion • Shepherding • Leadership Covenant • Read PDC Book • 101 [201, 301, 402]* • Ability to lead followers • Searching for SHAPE	**Increasing**
Team Coordinator Category 2	**Leader of More than One Team or Specialized Area** • A Determined Leader • Area-wide Influencer	E Q U I P S	• Member • Ownership/Passion • Shepherding • Leadership Covenant • Read PDC Book • 101 [201, 301, 401]* • Ability to lead leaders • Serving from SHAPE	**Leadership** **Responsibility**
Pastor/ Director Category 1	**Leader of an Entire Purpose or Age Group Ministry** • Demonstrated Leader • Church-wide Influencer	E Q U I P S	• Member • Ownership/Passion • Shepherding • Leadership Covenant • Read PDC Book • 101, 201, 301, 401 • Ability to lead leaders-of-leaders • Serving from SHAPE	

Appendix D

Task Skills Inventory

The following are some critical task skill sets for leaders. Rate your ability in each by placing a check in the appropriate box.

Skills	strong	above average	below average	weak	don't know
Preaching					
Teaching					
Researching					
Values discovery					
Communicating					
Mission development					
Mission casting					
Vision development					
Vision casting					
Strategizing					
Reflecting					
Time management					
Stress management					
Use of technology					
Prioritizing					
Writing					
General planning					
Strategic planning					
Making presentations					
Monitoring					
Praying					
Creating/creativity					
Implementing					
Organizing					
Budgeting					
Advertising					

Appendix E

Relational Skills Inventory

The following are some critical people skill sets for leaders. Rate your ability in each by placing a check in the appropriate box.

Skills	strong	above average	below average	weak	don't know
Listening					
Networking					
Conflict resolution					
Decision making					
Risk taking					
Problem solving					
Confronting					
Encouraging					
Trust building					
Inspiring/motivating					
Team building					
Consensus building					
Recruiting					
Hiring and firing					
Conducting meetings					
Recognizing and rewarding others					
Asking appropriate questions					
Disagreeing					
Confronting					
Counseling					
Mentoring					
Community building					
Challenging					
Trusting					
Empowering					
Evaluating					
Managing/administering					

Skills	strong	above average	below average	weak	don't know
Leading					
Delegating					
Disciplining					
Evangelizing					
Correcting					

Training Venues Comparison Chart

Legend:
- ● High ◉ Medium ○ Low
- **Process Oriented**
- Event Oriented

	Leader Competencies				Training Types				Characteristics											
	Knowledge	Skills	Character	Emotion	Content-driven	Learner-driven	Mentor-driven	Experience-driven	Relational	Interactive	Inspirational	Modeling	Broad content	Focused content	Beginner friendly	Time intensive	Long-term	Flexible scheduling	Preparation logistics	Cost
Classroom	●	○	○	○	●	○	◉	○	○	○	○	○	●	◉	◉	○	◉	○	○	○
Small Group	◉	○	◉	◉	◉	○	◉	○	●	◉	○	◉	◉	◉	○	○	◉	◉	◉	○
Turbo Group	◉	◉	◉	○	●	○	◉	◉	◉	◉	○	◉	○	●	○	◉	◉	◉	◉	○
Apprenticing	●	●	●	●	○	○	●	●	◉	◉	○	●	◉	●	◉	●	●	◉	◉	○
One-on-One	●	●	●	●	○	◉	●	○	●	●	◉	◉	◉	◉	◉	●	●	●	◉	○
Coaching	○	◉	●	◉	○	◉	●	○	●	●	◉	◉	○	●	◉	○	●	●	○	●
Consulting	●	◉	○	○	●	◉	○	○	○	◉	○	○	●	◉	◉	◉	◉	◉	○	●
Self-Led	◉	◉	◉	◉	○	●	○	◉	○	○	○	◉	●	◉	○	◉	◉	●	○	◉
Huddle	◉	●	○	○	○	◉	◉	◉	○	◉	○	◉	○	●	○	○	◉	◉	○	○
Seminar	●	○	○	○	●	○	○	○	○	○	○	○	●	◉	●	●	○	○	○	◉
Conference	●	◉	◉	○	●	○	○	○	◉	◉	◉	○	●	◉	◉	●	○	○	◉	●
Getaway	●	◉	◉	○	◉	◉	◉	○	◉	◉	◉	○	◉	●	◉	●	○	○	◉	●
Retreat	●	◉	◉	◉	◉	◉	◉	○	●	◉	◉	○	◉	◉	◉	●	○	○	◉	●
Workshop	●	●	○	○	◉	◉	◉	◉	○	●	○	◉	●	◉	●	●	○	○	◉	◉
Rally	◉	○	○	◉	○	○	○	◉	◉	◉	●	○	◉	○	◉	●	○	○	◉	◉
Benchmarking	◉	◉	○	○	○	●	○	◉	○	◉	◉	◉	○	◉	◉	○	○	◉	●	○

Notes

Introduction

1. Marshall Loeb, "Where Leaders Come From," *Fortune*, 19 September 1994, 24.

2. "USA Today Snapshots," *USA Today*, 26 June 2002, 1B.

3. Alan W. Weber and William C. Taylor, "Let's Promote the CEO" (letter from the editors), *Fast Company*, August 2001, 12.

4. James F. Bolt, "Developing Three-Dimensional Leaders," *Leader of the Future: New Essays by World-Class Leaders and Thinkers*, eds. Francis Hesselbein et al. (San Francisco: Jossey-Bass, 1996), 163.

5. George Barna, *Leaders on Leadership* (Ventura, Calif.: Regal, 1997), 18.

6. Bolt, "Developing Three-Dimensional Leaders," 163.

7. Exodus 12:37 states that there were six hundred thousand men during the exodus event. One million is a very conservative estimate considering the addition of women and children.

Chapter 1: Leaders, Who Needs Them?

1. Aubrey Malphurs, *Being Leaders: The Nature of Authentic Christian Leadership* (Grand Rapids: Baker, 2003). *Building Leaders* is a companion volume to *Being Leaders*.

2. I explore the definition of a leader in depth in *Being Leaders*.

3. For the reader's understanding, James M. Kouzes and Barry Z. Posner present both views in *The Leadership Challenge* (San Francisco: Jossey-Bass, 1987), 290–93.

4. Passages that show Jesus spending intentional time with these three disciples include Luke 8:51; 9:28; and Mark 14:33.

5. Bill Hybels, *Courageous Leadership* (Grand Rapids, Mich.: Zondervan, 2002), 122.

Chapter 2: Some Common Delays

1. The original idea of this distinction of how time is spent came from Steven Covey's book *The Seven Habits of Highly Effective People* (New York: Simon & Schuster, 1989), 54. He states that time is spent either in production or in production capacity improvement.

Chapter 3: The Challenge of Empowerment

1. Jim Collins, *Good to Great* (New York: HarperCollins, 2001), 35.

2. Reggie McNeal, *A Work of Heart* (San Francisco: Jossey-Bass, 2000), 134.

3. Stacy T. Rinehart, *Upside Down: The Paradox of Servant Leadership* (Colorado Springs: NavPress, 1998), 54.

4. Kenneth O. Gangel, *Feeding and Leading* (Wheaton, Ill.: Victor, 1989), 50.

5. Bill Bright, *Witnessing without Fear* (San Bernardino, Calif.: Here's Life Publishers, 1987), 67.

6. Eugene Peterson makes this observation in his book *Under the Unpredictable Plant* (Grand Rapids, Mich.: Eerdmans, 1992), 71.

7. The seed thought for these questions came from Rinehart, *Upside Down*, 157.

8. J. Oswald Sanders, *Spiritual Leadership* (Chicago: Moody, 1994), 168.

9. Rinehart, *Upside Down*, 48.

10. Carl George, *Prepare your Church for the Future* (Grand Rapids, Mich.: Revell, 1992), 112.

11. Kouzes and Posner, *The Leadership Challenge*, 290–95.

12. Ibid., 175.

13. Robert E. Coleman, *The Master Plan of Evangelism* (Grand Rapids, Mich.: Revell, 1963), 38–39.

14. I adapted this list of questions from a breakout training session led by Sheryl Fleisher at Small Groups Conference, Willow Creek Community Church, South Barrington, Illinois, spring 2000.

Chapter 4: How Jesus Developed Leaders

1. This is a hermeneutical issue. If you wish to pursue this further, see Aubrey Malphurs, *Doing Church* (Grand Rapids, Mich.: Kregel, 1999).

2. John F. Walvoord and Roy B. Zuck, eds., *The Bible Knowledge Commentary*, New Testament edition (Wheaton, Ill.: Victor, 1983), 108.

Chapter 5: How Jesus Used Metaphors to Develop Leaders

1. Warren Wiersbe, *Developing a Christian Imagination* (Wheaton, Ill.: Victor, 1995), 21.

2. David W. Bennett, *Metaphors for Ministry* (Grand Rapids, Mich.: Baker, 1993), 11.

3. David Bennett develops this division in more detail in his book *Metaphors for Ministry*. We have adapted it for the purpose of summary and to take it to the next step for making application to leadership development in the church.

4. For more detail on these, we recommend Bennett, *Metaphors for Ministry*.

5. Ibid., 59.

6. We have adapted our observations from a section in Bennett, *Metaphors for Ministry*, called "Major Themes," 61–66.

7. The two most common ways of listing the purposes of the church are (1) the three Es: evangelism, exaltation, and edification, and (2) the list from *The Purpose Driven Church* by Rick Warren: worship, evangelism, discipleship, ministry, and mission.

8. Thom Rainer, *Effective Evangelistic Churches* (Nashville: Broadman & Holman, 1996), 14–16.

Chapter 6: How Early Churches Developed Leaders

1. Roy B. Zuck, ed., *Vital Church Issues* (Grand Rapids, Mich.: Kregel, 1998), 107 (see chapter 12, "Can Fallen Leaders Be Restored to Leadership?" by Jay E. Smith).

Chapter 7: Who Will Read the Blueprints?

1. Peter F. Drucker, *Managing the Non-profit Organization* (New York: HarperCollins, 1990), 145.

2. Jim Collins, *Good to Great* (New York: HarperCollins, 2001), 41.

3. Empowered sources also exist outside the congregation and may strongly influence the empowered sources within the congregation. These may be a bishop, synod, or other person who has the authority to direct the leadership within a ministry. They also affect church polity.

4. Colleen Townsley Hagar, "An Interview with Ken Blanchard," *Next*, April-June 1999, 4, 12.

5. Leith Anderson, *Leadership That Works* (Minneapolis: Bethany House, 1999), 51.

6. J. Robert Clinton, *The Making of a Leader* (Colorado Springs: NavPress, 1988), 14.

7. Lewis Cooper is the pastor of Faith Temple Baptist Church in Irving, Texas. He is one of Aubrey's students.

8. Kouzes and Posner, *The Leadership Challenge*, 26. Actually, this is Vance Packard's definition, with which they agree.

9. Sanders, *Spiritual Leadership*, 31.

10. Steve Stroope is the pastor of Lake Pointe Baptist Church in Rockwall, Texas. He is Aubrey's pastor.

11. Gary Wills, *Certain Trumpets: The Call of Leaders* (New York: Simon & Schuster, 1994), 17.

12. Edgar J. Elliston and J. Timothy Kauffman, *Developing Leaders for Urban Ministries* (New York: Peter Lang, 1993), 10–16.

Chapter 8: Putting the Process in Motion

1. Aubrey Malphurs, *Maximizing Your Effectiveness* (Grand Rapids, Mich.: Baker, 1995); *Network* is available through Willow Creek Association, P.O. Box 3188, Barrington, IL 60011-3188; 847-765-0070; (fax) 847-765-5046; www.willowcreek.com; SHAPE is available through Saddleback Valley Community Church, 1 Saddleback Parkway, Lake Forest, CA 92630; 949-586-2000; www. saddleback.org/ministry/.

Chapter 9: How to Grow Leaders

1. These elements are very close to the three major classical learning theory systems: the affective (emotions), cognitive (knowledge), and behavioral (experience) domains. Character would fall into the affective domain with emotions. We would place emotions and values under character, believing that Scripture emphasizes the latter. See William R. Yount, *Called to Teach* (Nashville: Broadman & Holman, 1999), 28.

2. Kouzes and Posner, *The Leadership Challenge*, 284.

3. Ibid.

4. Ibid., 285.

Chapter 11 The Finishing Touches

1. We recommend that you read chapter 11 on evaluation in Aubrey's book *Advanced Strategic Planning* (Grand Rapids, Mich.: Baker, 1999).

Chapter 12: Home Improvement

1. Leroy Eims, *The Lost Art of Disciple Making* (Grand Rapids, Mich.: Zondervan, 1978), 60.
2. Bill Hybels, *Courageous Leadership* (Grand Rapids, Mich.: Zondervan, 2002), 127.
3. Carl George, *Prepare Your Church for the Future* (Grand Rapids, Mich.: Baker, 1991).

Chapter 13: Turning a House into a Home

1. George Barna, *A Fish Out of Water* (Nashville: Integrity, 2002), 119.
2. Timothy E. O'Connell, *Making Disciples* (New York: Crossroad, 1998), 76.
3. Michael Slaughter, *The Unlearning Church* (Loveland, Colo.: Group Publishing, 2002), 99.
4. Bill Jensen, *Simplicity* (Cambridge, Mass.: Perseus, 2000), 90.
5. Erwin Raphael McManus, *The Unstoppable Force* (Loveland, Colo.: Group Publishing, 2001), 113.
6. Slaughter in *The Unlearning Church* discusses the difference between information and experience, 65.
7. Kouzes and Posner, *The Leadership Challenge*, 195.
8. John P. Kotter and James L. Heskett, *Corporate Culture and Performance* (New York: Free Press, 1992), 4.
9. Kouzes and Posner, *The Leadership Challenge*, 198.
10. Slaughter, *The Unlearning Church*, 98.
11. Noel M. Tichy, *The Leadership Engine* (New York: HarperCollins, 1997), 50.
12. Ibid., 51.
13. Ibid.

Chapter 14: The Story of a Small Church

1. Gary McIntosh, in his book *One Size Doesn't Fit All* (Grand Rapids, Mich.: Revell, 1999), 18, says that small churches have 15–200 people, whereas large churches have 401 or more.
2. Note that this ministry description is primarily for someone who is a designer and implementer of programs. Once the program is in line, this type of person may move on to some other area and develop it. Thus the ministry description might change to a more administrative role.

Index

abdicating, by established leaders, 43–44
Adam, 150
Advanced Strategic Planning (Malphurs), 37, 226
American church, and lack of leadership, 9
Andrew, 64–66, 68, 69, 70
Apollos, 98, 100
apostle, 79. *See also specific apostles*
apprenticing training venues, 164–65, 181
Aquila, 98
Aristotle, 75
Arthur Andersen, 148
assessment of leaders, 137–40, 244
atom, scientific model of, 46
authority of leaders, 41–44, 51–54, 85–87

balanced leadership development, 80–85
Barna, George, 9, 212, 214
Barnabas, 96, 100, 101
Bartholomew, 66

Battle of Chapultepec story, 217, 218
being, and leadership competencies, 147–48
Being Leaders (Malphurs), 15, 20, 22, 42
benchmarking training venues, 179–80
benefits of leadership, 137
Bennett, David, *Metaphors for Ministry*, 76
biblical illustrations, 68–69, 72, 96, 129, 222–23. *See also specific biblical characters*
Bolt, James, 9, 10
Bright, Bill, 47
business leadership development issues, 8–9

capability, concept of, 22
cause-dominated leadership development, 81–82
cause-oriented metaphors, 76, 78–80
Chapultepec story, Battle of, 217, 218

churches:
  American church, and lack of
    leadership, 9
  Clear Creek Community
    Church, 249–55
  contemporary, 12, 15, 26–27,
    34–37, 98
  culture of leadership, and
    influence of, 216
  early, 95–102
  Faith Temple Baptist Church,
    9, 10, 240–47
  Lake Pointe Church, 9–10,
    109–10
  large, 249–55, 270n1(chap.14)
  ministry outside, 90–92
  and model for training of
    leaders, 13
  and polity, 98
  Saddleback Community
    Church, 139, 173
  small, 239–47, 270n1(chap.14)
  Willow Creek Community
    Church, 139
churches, early 95–102
classroom training venues,
  160–61
Clear Creek Community Church,
  249–55
coaching leaders, 15, 167–68
Coleman, Robert, 55
Collins, Jim, 45
community, and leadership, 76,
  77–78, 80, 82–83, 202–5
conference training venues,
  173–74
connecting the dots, 223, 228–31
connecting with others, and empowerment, 54–58, 59
consulting training venues, 15,
  168–69
contemporary churches, 12, 15,
  26–27, 34–37, 98

contemporary metaphors, 84–85,
  218–19
content-driven training, 152–54
context, concept of, 22
control, and established leaders,
  32–33, 45–49, 59
Cooper, Lewis, 9
Corporate Culture and Performance (Kotter), 223
covenant, leadership, 139–40
Covey, Steven, The Seven Habits
  of Highly Effective People,
  267n1(chap.2)
credibility, concept of, 21
culture of leadership, 211–36
  and biblical illustrations,
    222–23
  church influence on, 216
  and connecting the dots, 223,
    228–31
  definition of, 212–16
  and handles for people, 223,
    225–28
  and shared experience, 219–21
  and space, 221–22
  and story, 217–18
  and symbol, 218–19
  and turning up the heat, 223,
    231–33

David (king), 149
Deacon (magazine), 246
Deacon, Servant of the Church
  (video), 246
deep-end metaphor, 203–4, 205
deployment of leaders, 71–72,
  100–101, 244, 252–53
Developing the Leader within You
  (Maxwell), 246
development steps, for leaders,
  156–81
  apprenticing training venue,
    164–65, 181

benchmarking training venue, 179–80

classroom training venue, 160–61

coaching leaders, 167–68

conference training venue, 173–74

consulting training venue, 15, 168–69

event-oriented venues, 159, 171–80

getaway training venue, 174–75, 181

huddle training venue, 171

launching step, 141–43

one-on-one training venue, 166

process-oriented venues, 159–70

rally training venue, 178–79

retreat training venue, 176

self-led training venue, 169–70

seminar training venue, 172–73, 181

small group training venue, 161–62, 181

turbo group training venue, 163–64, 181

workshop training venue, 177

directing, by established leaders, 42–43, 44

disabling, by established leaders, 44–45

discipleship, 33–34, 66–67, 76, 190–91

discovery of leaders, 128–40, 143, 243, 252

doing, and leadership competencies, 149

Drucker, Peter, 105, 125

ego, starving the, 51–54, 58, 59

Eims, Leroy, *The Lost Art of Disciple Making*, 190

elders, 15, 97–98

emerging leaders, 41, 203–5

empowerment, 40–58
    and abdicating by established leaders, 43–44
    alternatives to, 42–45
    applied, 40, 45–58
    and authority of established leaders, 41, 42, 43, 44, 51–54
    and boundaries, specified, 42
    challenges of, 39, 58–59
    and connecting with others, 54–58, 59
    and control by established leaders, 45–49, 59
    definition of, 40–42
    and directing by established leaders, 42–43, 44
    disabling, by established leaders, 44–45
    and ego, starving the, 51–54
    and expandable-power pie, principle of, 53–54
    and faith through embracing uncertainty, 46–48, 58, 59
    and humility, 52–53, 54, 59
    idea of, introducing, 39–40
    and love through connecting with others, 56, 59
    Moses, and challenges of, 58
    and patience, 50–51, 59
    and responsibility of established leaders, 42, 43, 44
    and slow-down dynamic, 49–51, 58, 59
    unintentional transfer and, 41

Enron, 148

environment, and leadership culture, 221–22

established leaders:
    abdicating by, 43–44
    authority of, 41, 42, 43, 44, 51–54

continued development of,
    203–4, 205
control and, 32–33, 45–49, 59
developing leadership by, 32–
    33, 45–49, 59
    directing by, 42–43, 44
    disabling by, 44–45
    responsibility of, 42, 43, 44
evaluating leaders, 84, 183–86,
    188, 246–47, 254–55
evangelism, 47, 67, 88–94, 222–
    23, 268n7(chap.5)
Eve, 150
event-oriented venues, 159,
    171–80
    benchmarking, 179–80
    conference, 173–74
    getaway, 174–75, 181
    huddle, 171
    rally, 178–79
    retreat, 176
    seminar, 15, 172–73, 181
    workshop, 177
Executive Development Associ-
    ates, 9
expandable-power pie, principle
    of, 53–54
expansion of ministry, 25–26
expediency, and slow-down dy-
    namic, 49–51, 58, 59
experience, shared, 219–21
experience-driven training,
    155–56
exploration process, 134–37,
    243–44

faith:
    Jesus, and building, 47–48
    leaders, and role of, 70
    through embracing
        uncertainty, 46–48, 58, 59
Faith Temple Baptist Church, 9,
    10, 240–47

Fast Company, 9
feeling, and leadership compe-
    tencies, 150–51
A Fish Out of Water (Barna), 212
followers, impact on, 22–23
foot-washing, 21, 55
Fortune, 8

George, Carl, 197
getaway training venues, 174–75,
    181
godly leadership, 11, 28
Great Commission, 33

handles for people, 223, 225–28
Hatfield, Elaine, 214
heart-building exercises, 46, 48–
    49, 50–51, 56–58, 59
Hendricks, Howard, 147, 160, 167
Holy Spirit, and leadership, 97,
    100
humility, 52–53, 54, 58, 59, 79
Hybels, Bill:
    and culture of leadership, 218
    and evangelism, 222–23
    and qualifications of leaders,
        193–94
    and recruitment of leaders,
        130
    and training, 26, 179

IBM corporate culture, 212
Indian Guides program, 213
influence, concept of, 22, 87–94,
    216
isolation, and connecting with
    others, 54–58, 59

James, 65–66, 68–70, 79
Jensen, Bill, Simplicity, 218
Jesus. See also metaphors
    on authority, 85–86
    and connecting with others, 55

and culture, establishing, 214
and discipleship, 34, 66–67
and faith building, 47–48
and foot-washing, 21, 55
and humility, 52
and leadership development
    process, 63–73
and model of leadership
    development, 24
and prayer before deployment
    of leaders, 101
and servant, concept of, 20–21
and shared experience, 219
and sheep-shepherd analogy,
    25
Jethro, 10, 11
Joe, Grow-grow, 27
John:
    feeling, and leadership
        competencies, 150
    and fisherman metaphors, 79
    as man of faith, 70
    and phases of leadership
        development, 64, 65, 66
    and recruitment step, 68
    and selection of leaders, 69
John Mark, 96
Judas, 66, 70

Keller, Helen, 47
King, Martin Luther, Jr., 23
knowing, and leadership compe-
    tencies, 148–49
knowledge development of
    leaders, 245
Kotter, John, Corporate Culture
    and Performance, 223
Kouzes, James, 54, 154, 156, 224

Lake Pointe Church, 9–10, 109–
    10
launching step, 141–43
lay leaders, 15, 97–98

leaders. See also under empower-
    ment; established leaders
    and benefits of leadership, 137
    Christian, 20
    definition of, 20, 84, 242,
        250–51
    and penetrating influence of,
        87–94
    qualifications of, 97–98, 99–
        100, 193–94
    quality of, 25
The Leadership Challenge (Kouzes
    and Posner), 156
leadership culture. See culture of
    leadership
leadership development, 11, 19–
    20, 23–28, 33–34, 63–73. See
    also development steps, for
    leaders; leadership develop-
    ment process; maintaining
    leadership development
    process
The Leadership Engine (Tichy),
    230
leadership vs. discipleship, 33–34
Leading the Leader (Malphurs),
    15
learner-driven training, 152
legacy of leader's ministry, 28
levels of leadership, 147–51, 242,
    251–52, 269n1(chap.9)
Ligonier Ministries, 223
living out loud, 223–25
Loeb, Marshall, 8
The Lost Art of Disciple Making
    (Eims), 190
love, and connecting with others,
    56, 59
lumberjack story, and slow-down
    dynamic, 49

maintaining leadership develop-
    ment process, 189–209

and centralized training of
    leaders, 195–202, 253–54
and decentralized training of
    leaders, 195–202, 253–54
and making disciples, 190–91
M-myth, 191–95
nonleader problems, 191–95
and qualifications of leaders,
    193–94
and sand-dollar syndrome, 197
and task-dominated ministry,
    205–9
Malphurs, Aubrey:
    Advanced Strategic Planning,
        37, 226
    Being Leaders, 15, 20, 22
    Maximizing Your Effectiveness,
        139
The Malphurs Group, 167
Matthew, 65, 66, 69, 70
Maximizing Your Effectiveness
    (Malphurs), 139
Maxwell, John, 55, 130, 203, 246
McDonald, Gordon, *Ordering
    Your Private World*, 246
McManus, Erwin, *The Unstop-
    pable Force*, 219
McNeal, Reggie, 46
meaning of leadership, 19–20
mentor-driven training, 154–55
metaphors, 75–94
    apostle, 76, 85
    authority, 85–87
    and balanced leadership
        development, 80–85
    branch (of a vine), 76, 79, 81,
        85, 87
    brother (sister), 76, 77, 80
    cause-oriented, 76, 78–80
    community-oriented, 76,
        77–78
    contemporary, 84–85
    fisherman, 76, 78, 79, 80

harvester, 76, 78, 79, 80, 85
and images of things, 79–80
and light, 76, 79, 80, 81, 87
messenger, 78, 79, 80
and penetrating influence of
    leaders, 87–94
people, 78–79
salt, 76, 79–80, 81, 87
servant, 76, 78–79, 80
sheep, 76, 78, 80, 87
shepherd, 76, 78, 79, 80, 85, 87
soil, 76, 79, 81, 87
son/child, 76, 77, 80
the Twelve, 76, 78, 80
vine, branch of, 76, 79, 81, 85,
    87
wedding imagery, 76, 78, 80
wheat, 76, 79, 80, 81
Metaphors for Ministry (Bennett),
    76
Microsoft corporate culture, 212
ministry, 25–26, 28, 90–92. *See
    also* task-dominated minis-
    try
missional catalysts, 88–94
    assimilation process,
        engaging, 92–93
    clear focus, 88–89
    evangelism, model for, 89–90,
        92–93
    ministry outside churches,
        90–92
    time for missional pursuits,
        93–94
    welcoming systems,
        intentional, 92
M-myth, 191–95
models:
    atom, scientific model of, 46
    and balance of relationships
        and tasks, 84
    church model for training of
        leaders, 13

evangelism, model for, 89–90,
    92–93
Jesus, and leadership
    development, 24
and large churches, 249–55,
    270n1(chap.14)
modeling of balance of
    relationships and tasks, 84
and small churches, 239–47,
    270n1(chap.14)
Moses, 10–11, 58, 148–49, 267n7

Nathanael, 64, 66
Network (Willow Creek Commu-
    nity Church), 139
nonleader problems, 191–95

one-on-one training venues, 166
Ordering Your Private World
    (McDonald), 246

Pastoral Epistles, 33
pastors, 15, 32–33
patience, and slow-down dy-
    namic, 49–51, 58, 59
Paul (apostle):
    and culture, establishing, 215
    and deployment of leaders,
        100, 101
    on humility, 53
    and qualifications of leaders,
        97–98
    and selection of leaders, 97–98
    and task-dominated ministry,
        27, 206
    and Timothy, leadership
        development of, 23, 26, 28,
        96, 98–99
    and training of leaders, 98–99,
        100, 146
Paul, Pragmatic, 27
Perot, Ross, 23
personal development coach, 15

Peter, 66, 68, 70, 79, 97–98
Pharisees, 88
phases of leadership develop-
    ment, 64–67
Philip, 64, 66, 68, 70
point person, approach to leader-
    ship development, 15
polity, church, 98
Posner, Barry, 54, 154, 156, 224
power, 53–54, 59, 67, 98. See also
    empowerment
prayer, 69–70, 101
Priscilla, 98
problems with developing leader-
    ship, 11, 31–38
process-oriented venues, 160–70
    apprenticing, 164–65, 181
    classroom, 160–61
    coaching, 167–68
    consulting, 15, 168–69
    one-on-one, 166
    self-led, 169–70
    small group, 161–62, 181
    turbo group, 163–64, 181
The Purpose Driven Church
    (Warren), 268n7(chap.5)

qualifications of leaders, 97–98,
    99–100, 193–94, 242

Rainer, Thom, 90
rally training venues, 178–79
ratio of leaders to people, 11
recruitment of leaders, 128–34
    and biblical illustrations, 68–
        69, 72, 96, 129
    and early church, 95–96, 101
    and large churches, 250
    and small churches, 240–43,
        270n2(chap.14)
retreat training venues, 176
rewarding leaders, 183–84, 186–
    88, 247
Rinehart, Stacy, 46

Saddleback Community Church, 139, 173
sand-dollar syndrome, 197
Sanders, Oswald, *Spiritual Leadership*, 51
Scripture, 68–69, 72, 96, 129, 222–23. *See also specific biblical characters*
selection of leaders, 69–70, 72, 96–98, 101
self-led training venues, 169–70
seminar training venues, 15, 172–73, 181
servant, concept of, 20–21
service, personal, 79
The Seven Habits of Highly Effective People (Covey), 267n1(chap.2)
Shackleford, Karl, 9
shallow-end metaphor, 203–5
SHAPE (Saddleback Community Church), 139
shared experience, 219–21
sheep metaphors, 76, 78, 80, 87
sheep-shepherd analogy, 25
shoe factory metaphor, 190–91
Silas, 96
Simon Peter, 64, 66, 69
Simon the Zealot, 66
Simplicity (Jensen), 218
skills development, in small churches, 245, 246
Slaughter, Michael, 216, 224
slow-down dynamic, 49–51, 58, 59
Smith, Bill, leadership story, 7–8
social leadership development issues, 9
space, and leadership culture, 221–22
Spiritual Leadership (Sanders), 51
sports league illustration, 32, 33, 34, 35

Sproul, R. C., 222–23
Stanley, Andy, 228
story, and creating leadership culture, 217–18
Stroope, Steve, 9
symbol, and leadership culture, 84–85, 218–19

task-dominated ministry, 26–27, 35–36, 81–85, 205–9, 267n1(chap.2)
team building, complementary, 84
team recruitment, 241–42
Thaddeus, 66
Thatcher, Margaret, 23
Thomas, 66
Tichy, Noel, 230, 232
Timothy, 23, 26, 28, 96, 98–99
Tom, Taskmaster, 27
training of leaders. *See also* training venues
  centralized, 195–202, 253–54
  and Church, early, 98–100, 101
  church model, 13
  content of, 84
  decentralized, 195–202, 253–54
  Jesus and, 70–71, 72
  problems with leaders and, 31–33
  process, 145–57
  structure for, 84
  training types, 156–57
training venues, 159–81
  apprenticing, 164–65, 181
  benchmarking, 179–80
  centralized, 195, 196, 197–98, 199–202
  classroom, 160–61
  coaching, 167–68
  conference, 173–74
  consulting, 15, 168–69

decentralized, 195–97, 198–202, 253–54
getaway, 174–75, 181
huddle, 171
and large churches, 253–54
one-on-one, 166
self-led, 169–70
small group, 161–62, 181
turbo group, 163–64, 181
traits of leaders, 97–98, 99–100, 193–94, 242
truth pictures, of Jesus, 75
turbo group training venues, 163–64, 181
turning up the heat, 223, 231–33
the Twelve:
  deployment of, 66, 71–72
  development of, 24, 66
  leadership selection by, 97, 100

metaphors and, 76, 77, 80
names of, 66
selection of, 69, 97
training of, 71

The Unstoppable Force (McManus), 219

value of people, recognition of, 26–27

Warren, Rick, *The Purpose Driven Church*, 268n7(chap.5)
Wiersbe, Warren, 75–76
Willow Creek Association, 223
Willow Creek Community Church, 139
"window and mirror" pattern, 45
workshop training venues, 176

Aubrey Malphurs is a visionary with a deep desire to influence a new generation of leaders through his classroom, pulpit, consulting, and writing ministries. He is involved in a number of other ministries ranging from church planting and growth to leadership development. He has pastored three churches and is the author of numerous books and articles on leadership and church ministry. Currently he is a professor at Dallas Theological Seminary, president of The Malphurs Group, and a trainer and consultant to churches, denominations, and ministry organizations throughout North America and Europe.

Will Mancini is a church consultant, working with scores of churches each year in the areas of vision, strategy, and leadership development. He received his Th.M. in pastoral leadership from Dallas Theological Seminary. To contact Will, go to www.willmancini.com.